The War of 1812
Conflict for a Continent

This book is a narrative history of the many dimensions of the War of
1812 – social, diplomatic, military, and political – that places the war's
origins and conduct in a transatlantic perspective. The events of 1812–
1815 were shaped by the larger crisis of the Napoleonic Wars in Europe.
In synthesizing and reinterpreting scholarship on the war, Professor
J. C. A. Stagg focuses on the war as a continental event, highlighting its
centrality to Canadian nationalism and state development. The book
introduces the war to students and general readers, concluding that it
resulted in many ways from an emerging nation-state trying to contend
with the effects of rival European nationalisms, both in Europe itself
and in the Atlantic world.

J. C. A. Stagg is Professor of History at the University of Virginia. He
is the author of two books on James Madison, as well as many articles
on the political, military, and diplomatic history of the early American
republic. He has edited or coedited seventeen volumes of *The Papers
of James Madison*. He currently serves on the editorial board of *The
War of 1812 Magazine* and the board of the James Madison Memorial
Fellowship Foundation.

CAMBRIDGE ESSENTIAL HISTORIES

Series Editor

Donald Critchlow, Arizona State University

Cambridge Essential Histories is devoted to introducing critical events, periods, or individuals in history to students. Volumes in this series emphasize narrative as a means of familiarizing students with historical analysis. In this series leading scholars focus on topics in European, American, Asian, Latin American, Middle Eastern, African, and World History through thesis-driven, concise volumes designed for survey and upper-division undergraduate history courses. The books contain an introduction that acquaints readers with the historical event and reveals the book's thesis, narrative chapters that cover the chronology of the event or problem, and a concluding summary that provides the historical interpretation and analysis.

Titles in the Series

Edward D. Berkowitz, *Mass Appeal: The Formative Age of the Movies, Radio, and TV*

Ian Dowbiggin, *The Quest for Mental Health: A Tale of Science, Medicine, Scandal, Sorrow, and Mass Society*

John Earl Haynes and Harvey Klehr, *Early Cold War Spies: The Espionage Trials that Shaped American Politics*

James H. Hutson, *Church and State in America: The First Two Centuries*

Maury Klein, *The Genesis of Industrial America, 1870–1920*

John Lauritz Larson, *The Market Revolution in America: Liberty, Ambition, and the Eclipse of the Common Good*

Wilson D. Miscamble, C.S.C., *The Most Controversial Decision: Truman, the Atomic Bombs, and the Defeat of Japan*

Charles H. Parker, *Global Interactions in the Early Modern Age, 1400–1800*

For my colleagues on *The Papers of James Madison*

Unsung Heroes in an Unjust War

The War of 1812

Conflict for a Continent

J. C. A. STAGG
University of Virginia

CAMBRIDGE
UNIVERSITY PRESS

CAMBRIDGE UNIVERSITY PRESS
Cambridge, New York, Melbourne, Madrid, Cape Town,
Singapore, São Paulo, Delhi, Tokyo, Mexico City

Cambridge University Press
32 Avenue of the Americas, New York, NY 10013-2473, USA

www.cambridge.org
Information on this title: www.cambridge.org/9780521726863

First published 2012

Printed in the United States of America

A catalog record for this publication is available from the British Library.

Library of Congress Cataloging in Publication data

Stagg, J. C. A. (John Charles Anderson), 1945–
The War of 1812 : *Conflict for a Continent* / J. C. A. Stagg.
    p.   cm. – (Cambridge essential histories)
Includes bibliographical references and index.
ISBN 978-0-521-89820-1 (hardback) – ISBN 978-0-521-72686-3 (paperback)
1. United States – History – War of 1812.   I. Title.
E354.S83   2011
973.5′2 – dc23   2011025093

ISBN 978-0-521-89820-1 Hardback
ISBN 978-0-521-72686-3 Paperback

Contents

List of Maps

Acknowledgments

Contrary to what some might imagine, I have not devoted my life to studying the War of 1812. There have been other, and very different, endeavors that have engaged my attention over the years. Nevertheless, I am grateful to Lewis Bateman and Donald Critchlow for giving me the opportunity to write this book. That opportunity was also opportune in the sense that we are about to commemorate the bicentennial of the War of 1812, although I suspect that occasion was not uppermost in the minds of the editorial staff of Cambridge University Press when it decided to commission a book on what has long been regarded as the most unsatisfying and least well understood of all the wars of the United States. It will, therefore, be interesting to see how the descendants of the parties to the war observe that bicentennial. Americans north of the forty-ninth parallel have already commenced their celebrations of what they regard as a decisive moment in the development of a Canadian nation. Americans south of the forty-ninth parallel are rather less certain about what to remember from a war that has been aptly described as "a nightmare from the nation's childhood." And it remains to be seen whether the British will decide to remember or to forget yet again the events of 1812–1815. For the Indian peoples on both sides of the Canadian-American boundary, the bicentennial will give rise to conflicting emotions. The First Nations of Canada made a decisive contribution to the preservation of their lands for the British Empire. In the United States it was generally assumed that the Indians had simply sided with the British, but that is not true. Many of them contributed to the defense of a republic whose citizens quickly forgot all that they had done.

The invitation to write this book also presented me with a challenge that I had not previously thought of taking on – to see whether I could compose to a brief that stipulated a word limit (of about seventy thousand words) and to do so in a style that would be accessible to readers in both the university world and the general public. I think I have managed with respect to the word limit. Whether I have succeeded with the other requirement will be for others to judge. But for facilitating the opportunity to meet both challenges, I am grateful to the College of Arts and Sciences at the University of Virginia for a sabbatical that permitted me to finish a manuscript and also for some research funds that allowed Rick Britton to furnish the book with his elegant maps. Many of the problems that we encounter today in understanding the War of 1812 arise from the fact that the political geography of North America has changed greatly since 1815. Too many of the locations and place-names that were central to the conflict either have been changed or have disappeared from the map altogether. Unlike the decisive events and sites of the American Revolution and the Civil War, they no longer form part of a collective historical memory that we can continue to draw on as readily identifiable moments from the nation's past. If this book goes even a small way toward remedying that situation, it will have achieved some of its purpose. Here a special word of thanks is due to Eric Crahan, Brigitte Coulton, Katherine Faydash, and Abigail Zorbaugh for all their efforts in seeing this book through every stage of its production, from conception to final publication.

As the dedication is intended to make clear, I owe an enormous debt to my colleagues on *The Papers of James Madison*. Over the years they have tolerated and accommodated some of my peculiar agendas even as they go about making a much more important contribution than this book – or any other scholarly monograph for that matter – will ever make, namely the compilation of a comprehensive and reliable edition of the papers of the American president who was at the center of the War of 1812. Too many scholars believe that there is nothing more to be learned about the War of 1812 – or even that there is anything to learn at all. Such views are not merely wrong; they are also foolish. The errors and limitations of such thinking can be only hinted at in a work as short as this, but over time *The Papers of James Madison*, in conjunction with all the other modern editions of the papers of the founding fathers, will lead future generations of historians to provide us with vastly improved interpretations of critical developments in the formative years of the American republic, including the War of 1812. The importance of these modern scholarly editions has not always been appreciated as fully and properly as it should be and it is to be greatly regretted that the historical profession has not acquitted itself better on this score than it has done so far.

On a more personal note, I am grateful to many other historians who have worked on the early American republic and the War of 1812, in both the United States and Canada, and I look forward to their contributions in the years to come. Friends have also assisted with this project, especially by giving my drafts the benefit of their critical faculties – in every sense of the word *critical* – and it is a pleasure to acknowledge in this matter the generosity of Fred Greenstein, Joe Kett, and Ken Lockridge. Ken's contribution was all the more noteworthy for its being accomplished as he was in the throes of relocating to Sweden, and Sweden's gain will be America's loss. Some have helped by not reading the manuscript at all, and others have played a part by simply being friends, especially Brian and Karen Parshall and Philip and Therese Rousseau (fellow refugees from the Antipodes). In the preparation of the index, I am greatly indebted, as I have been on many occasions in the past, to Sue Perdue. And to Holly Shulman my gratitude, as always, can hardly be expressed adequately in words. I can only hope that my actions do not deviate too greatly from what those words should otherwise say.

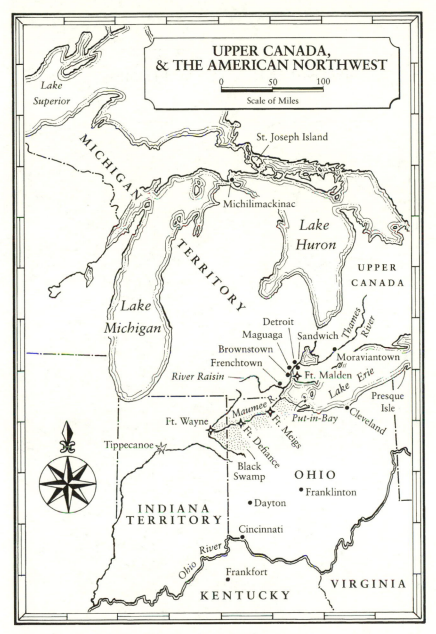

MAP 1. Upper Canada and the American Northwest

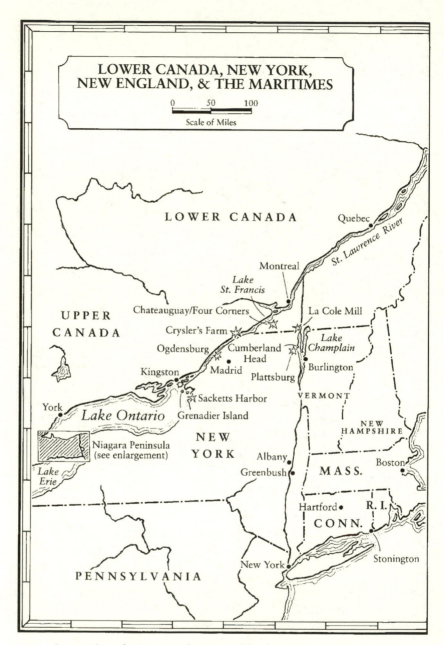

MAP 2. Lower Canada, New York, New England, and the Maritimes

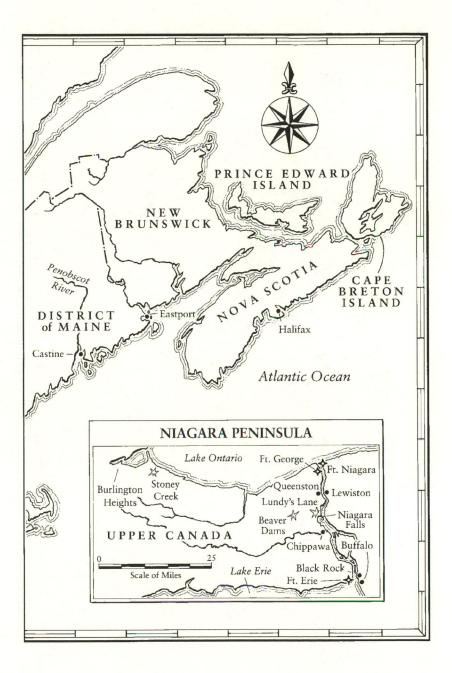

PRINCE EDWARD
ISLAND

NEW
BRUNSWICK

Penobscot River

DISTRICT
of MAINE

— Eastport

NOVA SCOTIA

CAPE
BRETON
ISLAND

Halifax

Castine —

Atlantic Ocean

NIAGARA PENINSULA

Lake Ontario   Ft. George

Ft. Niagara

Burlington
Heights   Stoney
Creek

Queenston   Lewiston

Lundy's Lane

Beaver
Dams   Niagara
Falls

UPPER CANADA

Chippawa   Buffalo

0   25

Black Rock

Scale of Miles   *Lake Erie*   Ft. Erie —

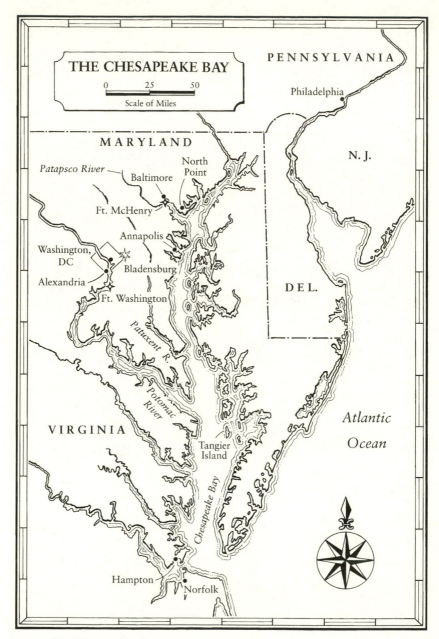

THE CHESAPEAKE BAY

0   25   50
Scale of Miles

PENNSYLVANIA

Philadelphia

MARYLAND

N. J.

Patapsco River — Baltimore   North Point

Ft. McHenry

Annapolis

Washington, DC   Bladensburg

Alexandria

Ft. Washington

DEL.

Patuxent R.

Potomac River

VIRGINIA

Atlantic Ocean

Tangier Island

Chesapeake Bay

Hampton

Norfolk

MAP 3. The Chesapeake Bay

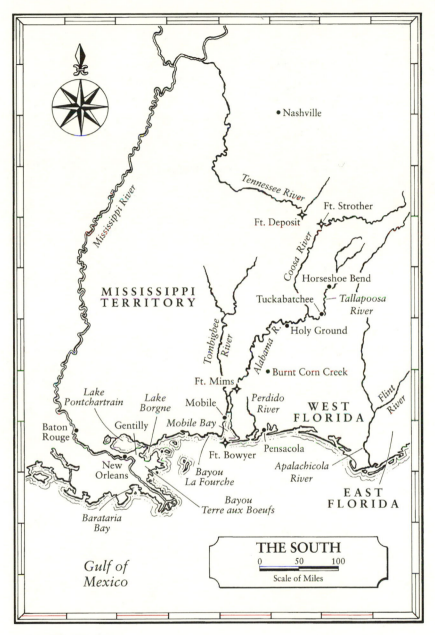

MAP 4. The South

Introduction

I

Americans approaching the bicentennial of the War of 1812 will find it difficult to place the conflict in a coherent narrative of their nation's past. Certainly, they are familiar with some of its more dramatic moments, including the burning of Washington, D.C., by the British in August 1814 and their subsequent repulse from Baltimore, a victory that inspired Francis Scott Key to compose the verses that were designated as the national anthem in 1931. They can also recall Andrew Jackson's defeat of the British at New Orleans in January 1815, and to a lesser extent the earlier failure of the Shawnee leader Tecumseh to unite the Indians of the Old Northwest in a confederation to halt the seemingly inexorable advance of the American frontier. Beyond that, memories begin to dim. Occasionally, naval buffs celebrate the triumphs that were to guarantee the position of the U.S. Navy in the nation's defense establishments, but thereafter oblivion descends. Only specialists in the field of ethnohistory now pay much attention to the struggle of the Creek Indians, paralleling that of Tecumseh, to preserve their territorial integrity in the Southwest and along the Gulf coast. And almost nothing is remembered of the ten attempts made by the United States between 1812 and 1814 to invade the Canadian provinces of Great Britain – nearly all of which ended as miserable and often bloody failures. Indeed, while standing in the British post of Fort George on the Niagara Peninsula in the summer of 1989, I recall hearing an American tourist protest very loudly that she had no idea that Canada had ever been attacked by the United States.

It was not always so. For Americans who came to maturity in the period between 1815 and 1860, the War of 1812 was a decisive event in their understanding of the nation's development. Americans began publishing books on the war within a year of its conclusion – the first titles appear as early as 1816 – and the use of the term *War of 1812* as a title also dates from that year. Equally common were references to "the late war with Great Britain," a description that encouraged Americans to think of it as a sequel to the earlier war with that nation, the American Revolution itself. Consequently, it became natural, if not inevitable, for them to regard the events of 1812–1815 as a "second war for independence." The war that began in 1812 was a struggle that was forced on the United States to consolidate the achievements of the Revolution against the efforts of Great Britain to nullify them after 1783, particularly by its violations of the neutrality of the republic during the era of the Napoleonic Wars. This way of thinking eventually received its fullest expression in *The Pictorial Field-Book of the War of 1812*, a massive tome that was comprehensively researched through written accounts and oral interviews and published in 1868 by the New York journalist Benson J. Lossing.[1]

Lossing began by asserting that the Revolution had failed to realize all the hopes of Americans, who in 1783 had become "free but not independent." Why they were not "independent" he explained in terms of their failure to form a strong nation and "power to be respected," particularly by the former mother country, whose ministers in the years leading to 1812 exploited American weakness as part of a larger scheme to destroy "the whole fabric of government in the United States" and return its people "to their allegiance as colonists of Great Britain." More than one thousand pages later, after relating all the campaigns of the war on land and on sea and describing the story of the peace negotiations that culminated in the Treaty of Ghent, Lossing concluded that the war had finally established "the positive and permanent independence of the United States." Great Britain had been taught the lesson that the republic would no longer "tolerate an insult or suffer its sovereignty to be questioned." The American people were at last "truly free" to start afresh "on a grand career of prosperity, with marvelous resources, developed and undeveloped – known and unknown."[2]

---

[1] For a brief discussion of how the war in 1812 became the War of 1812, see Donald R. Hickey, *Don't Give Up the Ship! Myths of the War of 1812* (Urbana, IL, 2006), 363–68.

[2] Lossing, *The Pictorial Field-Book of the War of 1812* (New York, 1868), 19, 1067, 1069.

Accounts of this sort were more than mere narratives. They were also an important component of an emerging sense of American identity. In that context, the events of the War of 1812 could be drawn on as a fund that furnished an endless supply of anecdotes, icons, and images for the fabrication of the exuberantly nationalistic popular culture of antebellum America. The war was celebrated not merely in books but also in stage plays and in poems, most of which are now mercifully forgotten. Who today has the stamina to struggle though Richard Emmons's four volumes – first published in 1827 and many times thereafter – of *The Fredoniad; or, Independence Preserved: An Epick Poem on the Late War of 1812*, the opening installment of which begins in hell and passes through heaven, Detroit, and Washington, D.C., before concluding at the river Raisin, south of Detroit, ten cantos later? Or to view Emmons's epic *Tecumseh; or, The Battle of the Thames, a National Drama in Five Acts*, his 1836 re-creation of how Richard M. Johnson supposedly killed the Shawnee leader, who sank to the stage declaiming, "The Red man's course is run; I die – the last of all my race"?[3]

Artists, printmakers, potters, and sculptors of the antebellum era re-created scenes from the engagements of the war and recast the images of the heroes who had fought and died in them. Here the survival rate has been somewhat better. We can still admire Rembrandt Peale's painting of a noble William Henry Harrison; or Gilbert Stuart's close-up portraits of Thomas Macdonough, Stephen Decatur, and James Lawrence; or John Vanderlyn's classic depictions of Andrew Jackson; or E. C. Watmough's stirring *Repulsion of the British at Fort Erie, 15th August 1814*; and likewise Ferdinand Pettrich's deeply moving marble, *The Dying Tecumseh*. And politicians of all stripes burnished their claims to office by linking them to their service in the war. Without the War of 1812, it is unlikely that Andrew Jackson and William Henry Harrison could ever have won the White House, and between 1824 and 1852 many other candidates for the offices of president and vice president similarly drew on their war records to justify their election. Rituals of this sort penetrated into every aspect of American public life. The Battle of the Thames, for example, produced not merely one president and one vice president of the United States but also, in Kentucky alone, three governors, three lieutenant governors, four U.S. senators, and a score of congressmen.

Even so, cultures and memories change over time, and the prominent role of the War of 1812 in antebellum American memory did not survive

---

[3] The action occurred in act 5, scene 6, of the play.

the Civil War intact. That conflict, tragic on a scale of vastness previously inconceivable to Americans, altered the very meaning of war itself in the making and remaking of the republic. The consolidation of independence became a theme of lesser importance, to be trumped by the forging of a "new birth of freedom" that preserved the Union for posterity. To be sure, some memories of 1812 lingered, and performances of Francis Scott Key's "Star-Spangled Banner" ensured that the verse and its music – despite the origins of the latter in an English drinking song – would become inextricably linked with ceremonies that required the raising of the national flag. But the diminishing significance of the military events of the War of 1812, coinciding as it did with the emergence of the United States as a world and imperial power at the end of the nineteenth century, seemed to require that the war be fitted into a new narrative about the rise of a powerful nation. It was in this climate that Henry Adams, Alfred Thayer Mahan, and Theodore Roosevelt produced what have long been regarded as the finest accounts of events between 1812 and 1815. Roosevelt and Mahan, publishing in 1882 and 1905, respectively, concentrated on the naval aspects of the conflict, in part because they believed its land operations had been so inept as to be unworthy of study. More important was their concern with promoting the claim that the newly independent nation should not have neglected sea power as the best means for protecting its interests. And the lesson they really wished to reinforce was that the United States could not maintain any sort of standing as a power without the support of a serious navy.[4]

Adams was less certain than Mahan and Roosevelt that the new nation should have invested very much in naval power, but he agreed that it needed a stronger state. In Adams's view the difficulties of the war should have taught Americans some hard lessons about the impracticability of their republican notions of limited government, whereas the conflict as a whole, considered as an episode in the growth of the nation, provided an exemplary demonstration of the finite capacities of statesmen to control the impersonal and material forces that governed outcomes in human affairs. Thus, in the nine volumes of his classic *History of the United States during the Administrations of Thomas Jefferson and James Madison* that appeared between 1890 and 1896, Adams depicted the War of 1812 as a conflict that had commenced without its participants having a clear understanding of why it had done so while its conduct illustrated

---

[4] Theodore Roosevelt, *The Naval War of 1812* (New York, 1882); Alfred T. Mahan, *Sea Power in Its Relations to the War of 1812* (2 vols.; Boston, 1905).

both an abundance of human folly and the unintended, and often irrelevant, consequences of such folly. By imparting these perspectives with the ironical wit and polished literary style that graced his volumes, Adams created a sense of confusion and incoherence about the War of 1812 and its significance that remains with us to this day. Ever since Adams, Americans have wondered what the war had been all about and whether it had even mattered in the larger scheme of things anyway.

After World War I professional historians made a sustained effort to answer those questions by reinterpreting the war in light of the then-prevailing Progressive theories of American national development, most notably those associated with Charles A. Beard and Frederick Jackson Turner. Here the most important contributions were made in the 1920s by Louis M. Hacker and Julius W. Pratt, both of whom explained the origins and course of the war not so much in terms of the conflict with Great Britain over maritime rights as by relating it to the dynamics of interest-group conflict and regionalism within the expanding American republic. Of particular significance was the fact that the loudest advocates of war in 1812 resided along the southern and western frontiers of the nation, where settlers seemed to be less interested in maritime problems than they were in controlling restless Indian peoples and in obtaining additional expanses of fresh land, either from Great Britain in Canada or from Britain's Spanish ally in Florida. The War of 1812 thus became, in Pratt's formulation, a conflict with "two sets" of causes, only one of which involved disputes over maritime rights. The other, and possibly more significant, precipitants of conflict were the expansionist desires of Americans themselves, and Pratt's analysis of their arguments for war suggested that their most bellicose spokesmen, the so-called War Hawks of 1812, might be seen as anticipating the goals of Manifest Destiny, the popular ideology of the 1840s predicting that the boundaries of the republic would become coterminous with the geographical limits of the North American continent.[5]

This "expansionist" interpretation of the war can still be found in textbooks currently in use in the nation's high schools. It has also compounded popular confusion about the war by perpetuating an arid dispute over what should be deemed its "real" or most important causes. Were

[5] Louis M. Hacker, "Western Land Hunger and the War of 1812: A Conjecture," *Mississippi Valley Historical Review* 10 (1923–1924): 365–95; Julius W. Pratt, *Expansionists of 1812* (New York, 1925); and Pratt, "Western War Aims in the War of 1812," *Mississippi Valley Historical Review* 12 (1925–1926): 36–50.

these causes international or domestic in origin? That debate became both interminable and insoluble. Consequently, a new generation of scholars by the 1960s, in the age of so-called consensus history associated with the early years of the Cold War, repudiated the views of Hacker and Pratt. The emphasis on interest groups and regional conflict was replaced by efforts to identify the ideals and values that united Americans in their decision to wage war in 1812. Initially, in the studies of Norman Risjord, these values were described as an outraged sense of "national honor" provoked by the conduct of Great Britain toward the United States on the high seas, but in the work of Roger Brown, concerns about "national honor" became part of a larger commitment to "republicanism" itself – both in the institution of the ruling Jeffersonian Republican Party and in the belief that republicanism as a national creed would be in jeopardy unless Americans made another effort to vindicate the independence that had supposedly been won in 1783.[6]

Arguments about the role of republicanism, both as an explanatory device for understanding the decision for war and as the essential source of an American commitment to nationhood, had a relatively short shelf life. By the 1980s, as early American historians began to explore the emergence of a capitalist economy and society in the United States, the primacy of republican ideas and values was replaced by a reassertion of the importance of the Lockean themes of individualism and liberalism that historians had long understood to be the basis of the Declaration of Independence itself. In this context the importance of liberalism as an ideology was its capacity to sanctify the self-interested aspects of personal acquisitiveness that provided the material bases for the autonomy of the individual citizen. The collective strivings of the citizenry, at the same time, laid the foundations for the expanding capitalist economy of the nineteenth century. On the face of it, those developments might not have much relevance for an understanding of the War of 1812 – least of all as a military conflict – but few societies emerge from the ordeal of war in precisely the same condition as when they had entered into it. It was, therefore, reasonable for historians of American culture to pose the question of whether the impact of the war had been sufficient to have affected the larger forces that were coming to define the collective

---

[6] Norman K. Risjord, "1812: Conservatives, War Hawks, and the Nation's Honor," *William and Mary Quarterly*, 3d ser., 18 (1961): 196–210; Risjord, *The Old Republicans: Southern Conservatism in the Age of Jefferson* (New York, 1965); and Roger H. Brown, *The Republic in Peril: 1812* (New York, 1964).

attitudes and behaviors of antebellum Americans. And as had been the case in the past, the events of the War of 1812 seemed malleable enough to furnish insights into such broader questions about American culture and society.

How could they do so? Early-nineteenth-century America consisted of communities and citizens struggling with the consequences of rapid and destabilizing economic change, including the spread of such undesirable conduct as unfettered ambition, an increase in factionalism of all sorts, and a general loss of social cohesion. To many of the Republican leaders who called for war with Great Britain, it seemed possible that the contest, by requiring a stronger sense of national unity and more self-less notions about personal identity, might provide a means for arresting these developments. But far from vanquishing the excesses of individualism and selfishness from American life, the War of 1812 – and specifically the effects of the policies required for its prosecution, including extensive military mobilization, increased governmental expenditure, the expansion of banking and credit, and the growth of domestic manufacturing – only served to reinforce them. As a result, after the war, many of the hallmarks of a "culture of capitalism" – a heightened sense of individuality, the increasing importance of the consumption of material goods, and extensive geographical and social mobility – became more firmly entrenched than ever, all at the expense of older notions of communal republican virtue. In these ways the conflict could be seen as a decisive moment in the emergence of the United States as a modern capitalist society.[7]

It was probably no coincidence that such an interpretation of the War of 1812 emerged at the same time that the modern Republican Party seemed destined to consolidate its domination of contemporary American politics. Recent American history has also been characterized by major transformations in the nation's economic and social structures, as well as in its systems of communication. These changes have been accompanied by increasingly bitter domestic conflicts over politics and culture, to such an extent that historians have sensed that there are parallels between our own sharply polarized world and that of the era of the first American party system when Federalists and Republicans could find

---

[7] Steven Watts, *The Republic Reborn: War and the Making of Liberal America, 1790–1820* (Baltimore, 1987). A more recent statement of this view is Walter Hixson, *The Myth of American Diplomacy: National Identity and U.S. Foreign Policy* (New Haven, CT, 2008), 48–54.

no common ground as they quarreled over the meaning of the French Revolution and the Napoleonic Wars. Considerations arising from this state of affairs clearly influenced the first major interpretation of the War of 1812 to appear after the turn of the century, *America on the Brink: How the Political Struggle over the War of 1812 Almost Destroyed the Young Republic*, published by Richard Buel Jr. in 2005. In contrast with the views that had traced the war to unifying concerns with national honor and republicanism, Buel linked it to the ideological extremism of its opponents, the Federalist Party. By 1812, that party had been reduced to little more than a narrowly based New England rump of its former self, and one that was incapable of accepting either its minority status in national politics or the Francophile tendencies of American policy as shaped by Thomas Jefferson and James Madison. As a result, the Federalists compensated for their weakness by linking their concerns to those of the British in the years leading up to 1815, even going so far as to contemplate secession from the Union as a way to escape from Republican rule. Driven by fears that the Federalists might prevail, the Republicans waged war against Great Britain to vanquish the specter of a Federalist resurgence. To the extent that the war killed off the Federalist Party, it might be deemed to have been a success, but Buel judged the risks posed to the survival of the nation as too high to have justified them. The War of 1812 has thus become a tale for our times – a warning against the dangers of extremism and ideologically driven politics.

II

All such American views of the War of 1812, be they those of Lossing or Buel, are centered on the conflict as a formative element in the history of the American nation-state. It should not be forgotten, though, that the events of this war, like those of the Revolution before it, gave rise not to one new nation but to two, or rather that these wars not only created and preserved the United States but also helped consolidate a fragmented set of British North American communities that would eventually become the Dominion of Canada. For that reason alone studies of the American War of 1812 should take cognizance of many of the most important Canadian dimensions of the conflict. Nineteenth-century Canadian writers – or at least those of an Anglophile and Anglophone disposition – developed regional rather than nationalistic interpretations of the war in which they had escaped conquest by the United States. They also wrote more slowly and on a smaller scale than their American

counterparts – necessarily so, as there was no Canadian nation to celebrate before 1867, and the various provinces of the new confederation
had radically different experiences and memories of the events of 1812–
1815. Much of this early Canadian literature originated in Upper Canada
(Ontario) for the obvious reason that it was that province that had borne
the brunt of the American invasions. And the significance that Upper
Canadians attached to their deliverance from a republican future was to
emphasize the importance of loyalty to the British Crown as the basis for
their resistance to the Americans and, subsequently, as the foundation for
an emerging sense of Canadian identity and patriotism.

This putative link between loyalty and incipient nationalism had been
discovered in the war itself, most notably in a sermon delivered in November 1812 by the Reverend John Strachan of York (now Toronto) in which
he made the prediction that future historians of Upper Canada would tell
how the militia of the province, virtually unassisted by regular troops,
took up arms and vigorously repelled the American invader. After 1815
this version of events was recycled on any number of occasions that celebrated the survival of the Canadian colonies, such as the dedication of
the second monument to Sir Isaac Brock on the Niagara Peninsula in
1859 and the visit of the Prince of Wales to North America in 1860.
It was further embellished by accounts of the trials and tribulations of
heroic Canadian women such as Laura Secord, who was cast as a kinder,
gentler version of Paul Revere by virtue of the claim that in June 1813
she had walked nearly twenty miles in the hot sun from Queenston to
Beaver Dams with a milk pail in hand and accompanied by a cow, to alert
British forces to the movements of an advancing American army. Over
time, too, this loyalty of the Upper Canadians was construed to mean the
loyalty, specifically, of those British Americans who had fled the United
States at the conclusion of the Revolutionary War in 1783. Loyalty thus
became the exclusive property of the United Empire Loyalist Associations
of Canada, and it dominated the Canadian writings on the War of 1812
that appeared between the centennial celebrations of the Loyalist exodus
in 1884 and the conclusion of World War I.[8]

After 1918 the patriotic fervor (or anti-Americanism) associated with
what would become known as the Ontario militia myth diminished

---

[8] See the discussions by Norman Knowles, *Inventing the Loyalists: The Ontario Loyalist
Tradition and the Creation of Useable Pasts* (Toronto, 1997) and David Mills, *The Idea
of Loyalty in Upper Canada, 1784–1850* (Montreal, 1998). The classic statement of the
Loyalist viewpoint can be found in Egerton Ryerson, *The Loyalists of America and Their
Times: From 1620 to 1816* (2 vols.; Toronto, 1880).

somewhat. The horrors of World War I reduced both enthusiasm for the British Empire and distrust of the United States, but the myth was not finally overturned until the 1950s, when the Canadian military historians George Stanley and Charles Stacey pointed out that it was simply incorrect to claim that the militia of Upper Canada had either saved or created the nation. That honor, more properly, belonged to the regular soldiers and generals of the British army, to say nothing of the contributions of the Royal Navy whose control of the seas protected the Maritime Provinces and allowed the British ministry in London to maintain a flow of supplies and men to the regions of the upper St. Lawrence River and the Great Lakes that sufficed to thwart the American invasions. Stacey also reminded Canadians that there had been little that was heroic or ennobling about the war in Upper Canada. The areas that had experienced the heaviest fighting were devastated by the conflict, which left in its wake bitter memories and disputes that persisted for many years. For their loyalty to the British Crown, Upper Canadians paid a very high price.[9] All subsequent studies of the War of 1812 by Canadian military historians have more than confirmed and amplified the findings of Stanley and Stacey on these matters.

This reappraisal of the relative significance of regular and militia forces, however, hardly reduced the importance of the War of 1812 to Canadians. To this day, these "other" North Americans still regard the events of 1812–1815 as a pivotal point in their national development; to them the war ranks third in importance in their history, after confederation itself in 1867 and the completion of the Canadian Pacific Railroad in 1885. But the demolition of the Ontario militia myth also liberated Canadian historians to undertake wider-ranging inquiries into both the military and the social histories of all regions in Canada during the war. Of critical importance here has been their growing awareness that Upper Canada by 1812, far from being the stronghold of a deeply rooted anti-American Loyalist sentiment, was, in fact, in the process of being transformed into a predominantly "American" province by ties of economic interdependence and a steady stream of emigrants from the United States who had come northward to take advantage of the generous terms on which the British Crown made land available to settlers. Many Americans assumed, and all British officials feared, that these so-called late Loyalists were not loyal

[9] See George F. G. Stanley, *Canada's Soldiers, 1604–1954: The Military History of an Unmilitary People* (Toronto, 1954), 178–79; and Charles P. Stacey, "The War of 1812 in Canadian History," *Ontario History* 50 (1958): 153–59.

at all and that they would serve as a fifth column during the American invasions. This was a prospect that inspired the British army to make far more vigorous efforts to defend Canada than its American counterpart ever made for its conquest.

The responses of ordinary Canadians to the war, however, suggests that their attitudes and conduct were often ambiguous and ambivalent and that they should not, in all fairness, be described as either pro-British or anti-American. Even in Upper Canada, where opinions were most sharply divided and the burdens of the war most acutely felt, they were – with a few notable exceptions – an amalgam of both pro-American and pro-British tendencies that, in the fullness of time, would eventually contribute to the formation of a more distinctively Canadian American identity.[10] In the Maritimes, the War of 1812 was far less problematic. Protected by the Royal Navy in Halifax, the provinces' inhabitants were free either to engage in privateering or to enjoy a prosperous trade borne of wartime conditions, especially by trading, or rather smuggling, with their supposed enemies in New England. But by trading with the enemy, the Maritimes, far from undermining the British defense of Canada, actually assisted it.[11] Somewhat similar conditions prevailed in Lower Canada (Quebec). Its predominantly Francophone population had been augmented by flows of American emigrants settling in the Eastern Townships adjacent to Montreal, but as had been the case in the Maritimes, Lower Canada was scarcely threatened by a serious American invasion at any point between 1812 and 1815. And although its Canadien peoples were by no means completely reconciled to being ruled by the British after the conquests of 1759–1760, they had little interest in the disputes that were dividing the British and the Americans. Nor were they even remotely attracted by the prospect of living under a republican form of government,

---

[10] For the fullest statement of these arguments, see Jane Errington, *The Lion, the Eagle, and Upper Canada: A Developing Colonial Ideology* (Montreal, 1987); and George Sheppard, *Plunder, Profit, and Paroles: A Social History of the War of 1812 in Upper Canada* (Montreal, 1994). British anxieties about the loyalty of Upper Canadians culminated in the Ancaster Assizes of 1814, after which eight "traitors" – who might be better described as looters and horse thieves – were hanged. The most notable traitor was Joseph Willcocks, who was neither an American nor a Canadian but an Irish-born member of the provincial assembly who, in 1813, formed a company of Canadian Volunteers that fought with the Americans until Willcocks's death during the siege of Fort Erie in September 1814.

[11] For a brief discussion, see D. A. Sutherland, "1810–1820: War and Peace," in *The Atlantic Region to Confederation: A History* (Phillip A. Buckner and John G. Reid, eds.; Toronto, 1994), 234–60.

should an American victory in the war have brought about that result. Consequently, Lower Canadians were left largely unhindered – to ignore the war, to serve in some of its battles, or to trade with the enemy as they saw fit.[12]

III

In these ways, successive generations of American and Canadian historians developed two parallel streams of historiography about the place of the War of 1812 in their national narratives, with little thought being given to the possibility that the streams might, or should, intersect. In the case of Great Britain, the other main party to the war, the situation is rather different, and its historians have contributed much less to our understanding of the conflict. The relative paucity of British literature on the subject is often thought to have been explained by the Anglo-Canadian writer William Kingsford, who remarked in 1895 that "the events of the War of 1812 have not been forgotten in England for they have never been known there."[13] This is a nice witticism, but it is somewhat misleading. British newspapers reported regularly on the war and did so in ways that took the edge off the celebration of more glorious British accomplishments against Napoleonic France, especially when it came to the matter of explaining American naval victories over British frigates. And the English lawyer William James, who had been detained as an enemy alien in Philadelphia in 1812, was just as quick as any American to go into print about the war by producing four volumes on its military and naval events by 1818. James, moreover, wrote to rebut what he regarded as the ridiculously inflated claims that Americans were already making about winning the war – indeed, at one point he wrote that his goal was to teach Americans to "venerate truth" – and such was the extent of his influence in the nineteenth century that it drove Theodore Roosevelt, more than sixty years later, to present

---

[12] The classic account is Fernand Ouellet, *Lower Canada 1791–1840: Social Change and Nationalism* (Patricia Claxton, trans.; Toronto, 1980). Studies of Canadien participation in the war have largely centered on accounts of the Battle of Chateauguay in September 1813, whereas Canadien misgivings about the conflict were most dramatically expressed in the Lachine riot of July 1812. That riot is now understood not as a protest against the war so much as it was the manifestation of more localized concerns about how British authorities were implementing the militia laws. See Sean Mills, "French Canadians and the Beginning of the War of 1812: Revisiting the Lachine Riot," *Histoire Sociale/Social History* 35 (2005): 37–57.

[13] See William Kingsford, *History of Canada* (10 vols.; Toronto, 1887–1898), 8:579–80.

much of the evidence in his own naval history as a refutation of James's work.[14]

Yet not all nineteenth-century British writers were as hostile as James. In 1817 the prominent dissenting radical Edward Baines produced a history that was surprisingly sympathetic to the United States; it even earned a guarded measure of praise as a "respectable performance" from no less an authority than James Madison.[15] Memoirs produced by veterans of the war, invariably officers, many of whom had served in both Europe and North America, also enjoyed considerable popularity. By far the best-known example of this genre is the epistolary account of the campaigns of the British army against Washington and New Orleans in 1814–1815 by George Robert Gleig, a young ensign who had served with the Duke of Wellington in Spain before being transferred across the Atlantic. Despite his not liking Americans very much for their "low cunning," Gleig wrote in an engaging style that reflected a tolerant personality, and his account was reprinted many times in both Great Britain and the United States.[16] There is, nevertheless, a grain of truth in the claim that for Britons the American events of 1812–1815 have never formed a conspicuous part of their historical memory, and this situation has not changed so greatly over the past two hundred years. To be sure, most British scholars can now concede that the United States had valid grievances against Great Britain in 1812, even if they sometimes suspect that Americans were overly sensitive about them and failed to make a fair allowance for the measures the British regarded as essential to defeat Napoleon. But they also take a certain quiet satisfaction in the knowledge that it is difficult, if not impossible, for Americans to claim that they indisputably won the War of 1812.[17]

More important than any British writings on the war have been the efforts of various interdisciplinary schools of American and Canadian

[14] See William James, *Naval Occurrences of the War of 1812* (2 vols.; London, 1817); and James, *A Full and Correct Account of the Military Occurrences in the Late War between Great Britain and the United States* (2 vols.; London, 1818). His remark that Americans needed to "venerate truth" appeared on page xxxi of the first volume of his *Military Occurrences*.

[15] *Baine's History of the Late War, between the United States and Great Britain* was published in an American edition in 1820. For Madison's assessment, see his letter of 26 December 1820 to Ebenezer Harlow Cummins, James Madison Papers, Library of Congress.

[16] See "A Subaltern" [George Robert Gleig], *A Narrative of the Campaigns of the British Army at Washington and New Orleans* (London, 1821).

[17] A recent example of this way of thinking is Jon Latimer, *1812: War with America* (Cambridge, MA, 2007), which might be described as a more restrained statement of some of the views of William James.

studies to create broader perspectives that can accommodate the reality that Canada and the United States, despite their differences, have often shared a common destiny. Their two histories have been profoundly shaped by the obvious fact of geographical proximity as well as by powerful forces exerted by the Atlantic Ocean and the physical features of the North American continent. The first such accounts of what might be called an Atlantic North America appeared in the years between the two world wars of the twentieth century, and their findings have been reinforced and extended by more recent work in the field of historical geography. Their distinctive contribution has been to demonstrate how the early development of Canada and the United States was shaped by a series of triangular relationships that embraced not only the two North American nations but also Great Britain (and even its West Indian colonies as well). Patterns of settlement and trade that had been established before 1776 continued thereafter, despite the collapse of the first British Empire and the political division of the North American continent in 1783. And at no period was their influence more strongly felt than during the years between 1803 and 1815 – when the control of both the Atlantic trade routes and the resources of the North American continent were sharply contested by Americans, Britons, and Canadians as they responded to the circumstances of the Napoleonic Wars.[18] Those rivalries, of course, had always been a staple item in the historiography of the War of 1812, but recently in the hands of Alan Taylor, they have been reinterpreted as a resumption of the conflicts that occurred during and immediately after the American Revolution itself. From this vantage point, the War of 1812 has ceased to be a conflict between two nation-states and has become, instead, a civil war among the fragments of the first British Empire whose constituent groups were not yet reconciled to the settlement that had been made in 1783.[19]

---

[18] For three classic statements from this perspective, see Alfred L. Burt, *The United States, Great Britain, and British North America from the Revolution to the Establishment of Peace after the War of 1812* (New Haven, CT, 1941); Marcus Lee Hansen and John Bartlett Brebner, *The Mingling of the Canadian and American Peoples* (New Haven, CT, 1940); and John Bartlett Brebner, *North Atlantic Triangle: The Interplay of Canada, the United States, and Great Britain* (New Haven, CT, 1945). For their ongoing influence, see the first two volumes of Donald W. Meinig's multivolume work *The Shaping of America: A Geographical Perspective on 500 Years of History* (New Haven, CT, 1986 and 1993).

[19] See Alan Taylor, *The Divided Ground: Indians, Settlers, and the Northern Borderland of the American Revolution* (New York, 2006); and Taylor, *The Civil War of 1812: American Citizens, British Subjects, Irish Rebels, and Indian Allies* (New York, 2010).

This argument may push some interesting insights too far, but Taylor's larger perspective draws its strength from the fields of "transnational" and "borderlands" history that emerged in the closing years of the twentieth century, in part in response to the forces of "globalization" that promise or threaten to transform a world order that has assumed that the sovereign nation-state was its basic organizational unit. Practitioners in these fields have placed greater emphasis on developments and experiences that cross, or transcend, state lines than they do on events that originate within the borders of individual nation-states. In the case of the North American continent, this perspective has also served to cast into sharp relief the plight of the Indian nations whose understanding of their interests seldom coincided with the boundaries and the new communities that European imperial powers were attempting to create on the Atlantic coast and in the continental hinterland. This struggle between indigenous and Euro-American peoples came to a climax in the years between 1756 and 1783, after which the new rivalry between Great Britain and an ever-expanding United States greatly reduced the ability of the Indians to manipulate a continental balance of power as a means to preserve their autonomy.[20] The efforts of the northwestern and southwestern Indians in the early nineteenth century to form confederations to resist the expansion of American settlement represented a desperate attempt to break free from these constricting pressures. Had they succeeded, both Tecumseh and his southwestern counterparts, the Creek prophets, might have looked forward to a revitalization, or perpetuation, of their traditional ways of life, but it was not to be. Instead, their failures marked the final phase of a much longer contest for the control of the regions of the upper St. Lawrence River, the Great Lakes, and the Gulf coast that had earlier been set in motion in the middle of the eighteenth century.

IV

From this survey of the memories and historiographies of the War of 1812, it should follow that any new account of the conflict must take into consideration a wide range of perspectives and themes. The war was a critical episode in the emergence of North America's nation-states, in

[20] The essential statement here is Richard White, *The Middle Ground: Indians, Empires, and Republics in the Great Lakes Region, 1650–1815* (New York, 1991), but see also François Furstenberg, "The Significance of the Trans-Appalachian Frontier in Atlantic History," *American Historical Review* 113 (2008): 647–77.

their internal development, and in the history of their indigenous peoples, as well as in many of their shared experiences. It was also a conflict that meant very different things to its participants, depending on their location and the nature of their involvement in its events, all of which played out on a vast geographical and historical canvas that extended from Eastern Europe to the Pacific Ocean and from the Great Lakes to the Gulf of Mexico and that continued to influence developments in North America well into the late nineteenth century. Ideally, therefore, the historian of the War of 1812 must acknowledge and synthesize the political histories of three, if not more, nation-states, the entire diplomatic, military, and naval history of the age of Napoleon, and the ethnographies of the indigenous peoples of the North American continent.

Despite the difficulties of this enterprise, however – or because of them – any historian of the War of 1812 must also impose a certain degree of coherence on the complex events that shaped the lives of Americans, Britons, and Canadians in the first two decades of the nineteenth century. And for the purpose of explaining specific wars between empires and nations, the nation-state itself must remain a factor of major analytical importance, even in larger conceptions of regional or transnational histories. Fortunately, it is not necessary to discard the subject of the nation-state to understand its behavior in more than one dimension, especially when all states must endeavor to operate as both independent and interdependent agents in a larger international context. For this reason, it still makes the most sense to organize a new history of the War of 1812 around the story of the United States while at the same time setting that story in as many contexts as possible. The United States started the war with its declaration against Great Britain in June 1812, and it has produced by far the greater bulk of the relevant historiography. It issued its declaration to break the impasse it had reached with the former mother country over the meaning of neutrality in the Napoleonic era, and its purpose in attacking Canada was to compel Great Britain to sign a treaty that would guarantee as a matter of international law future respect for American rights and interests. Once that treaty had been signed, the United States could end its status as a belligerent in the European wars and return to its preferred position as an independent, neutral nation. In that sense, the War of 1812 was fought not so much for "free trade and sailors' rights" or for territory and empire, as many historians have supposed, but more for a scrap of paper that by the end of 1814 had failed to materialize.

What follows is an explanation for why the United States never got the treaty it wanted. It is the story of how a new and weak republic tried to impose its will on circumstances that were largely beyond its control. It is also the story of how an old empire was able to preserve its position in North America and an account of the fate of those Indian peoples who were caught in between the new republic and the old empire. As far as the United States is concerned, it is a story of how the new institutions of government that had been created after 1787 – particularly the U.S. Army – proved less than adequate for the purposes of waging a successful war. In its own distinctive way, the "second war for independence" recapitulated for Americans some of the more difficult aspects of its predecessor, the first American war for independence. On that occasion, in 1775–1776, the new United States had also tried, briefly and unsuccessfully, to seize Canada, and its armies thereafter usually experienced defeat more often than victory on the battlefield. Yet even as the military events of the American Revolution were being played out, it was the international context that proved to be of decisive importance in determining the end of the conflict and the nature of its peace settlement.[21] Similarly, in the case of the War of 1812, it was the changing nature of international politics at the end of the Napoleonic era that permitted American diplomacy to transform what had been a very mixed war effort into something that could be considered a triumph. Finally, it is also a brief account of the longer-term significance of the War of 1812 for the two nations of North America that were most affected by it.

[21] This point is made most persuasively in Jonathan Dull, *A Diplomatic History of the American Revolution* (New Haven, CT, 1985).

I

War

I

Sometime in late May 1812, James Madison began drafting a "war message" that he would send to Congress on 1 June. As he did so, his mind ranged over the troubled history of Anglo-American relations following the establishment of American independence in 1783. Indeed, Madison even went so far as to allege in his draft that Great Britain had been unjustifiably hostile toward the United States from the very first moments after the end of the Revolutionary War. As proof he adduced the many difficulties the new republic had encountered in establishing diplomatic and trade relations with the former mother country. Matters had only become worse, Madison continued, after Great Britain became a party to the wars of the French Revolution between 1793 and 1801. Those conflicts had been characterized by serious British violations of American neutral rights, as Madison understood those rights according to the eighteenth-century law of nations, and Great Britain had resorted to such unjust conduct again in 1803, on the occasion of the resumption of its war with France, now under the rule of the most formidable general of modern times, Napoleon Bonaparte.

At that point, after writing no more than a single page, Madison discarded his draft. Why he did so is not entirely clear. Possibly, it occurred to him that his political opponents – concentrated mainly in the Federalist Party but also including Republicans from the New England and Middle Atlantic states – could have reminded him that there was a time when Anglo-American relations had not been so contentious, particularly in the years after the Jay Treaty of 1794 had gone into effect. That interval of relative harmony had been of considerable benefit to the United States. But such recollections were probably not helpful to a president who was trying to construct a catalog of British aggressions against America that might persuade Congress to declare war. Madison accordingly abandoned his memories of the first two decades of Anglo-American relations after 1783 and commenced a new draft, opening with the remark that it was not necessary to go "back beyond the renewal in 1803 of the war in which Great Britain is engaged" for the legislators to understand in what ways that nation had pursued "a series of acts, hostile to the United States, as an Independent and neutral nation."

What followed was a list of grievances, laid out in roughly chronological order rather than in a ranking that reflected a considered assessment of their relative seriousness as violations of American rights. In 1803, when the Anglo-French war resumed, the United States and Great Britain had been engaged in negotiations that might have ended the British practice of impressing seamen, especially Americans, from neutral vessels on the high seas as a way of conscripting crews for the Royal Navy. The British ministry had seemed willing to compromise, but it had not, Madison noted, followed through with an agreement. That problem was compounded, he added, by the casual contempt with which British naval vessels violated American territorial waters, even to the point of entering American harbors and "wantonly" spilling "American blood" there. Here the president was alluding to an incident in April 1806 when HMS *Leander* had sailed into New York Harbor and delivered a broadside that killed an American seaman named John Pierce, but the imagery Madison invoked would also have reminded his audience of a similar and more serious episode in June 1807, when HMS *Leopard* had attacked the USS *Chesapeake* off the Virginia coast, disabling it, killing several members of its crew, and seizing four more for service in the Royal Navy.

Moving on to what had become the most serious dispute in Anglo-American relations, Madison next condemned Great Britain's doctrines and practices of blockading the ports of France and its allies to deny them the resources they might have received through neutral trade. Madison did not doubt that belligerents had a right to blockade, but he insisted it be exercised according to his reading of the law of nations, namely that blockades should be openly proclaimed and administered through "the presence of an adequate force." Great Britain, he complained, did not observe these requirements, and after 1806 it had resorted to a "sweeping system of Blockades, under the name of orders in Council" that permitted British naval vessels to seize and confiscate neutral shipping and cargoes virtually at will and almost anywhere on the high seas. Even worse, the British had declared that they would not abandon these practices

until the United States had compelled France to accept British goods as
neutral property in French ports, a demand that Madison denounced
as "contradicting [Britain's] own practices toward all nations, in peace
as well as in war." For the president this demand was also proof that
the British government was not so much concerned with denying France
access to resources as it was attempting to destroy legitimate trade by
neutral nations to promote illegitimate trade between belligerents. As
Madison put it more bluntly, Great Britain wanted to conduct "a war
against the lawful commerce of a friend that she may the better carry on
a commerce with an enemy; a commerce polluted by the forgeries and
perjuries, which are, for the most part, the only passports by which it can
succeed."

Madison reminded Congress that the United States had not passively
acquiesced in these restrictions on its maritime and neutral rights. It had
responded with trade regulations of its own, most notably the Non-
Importation Law of 1806, the Embargo of 1807–1809, and the Non-
Intercourse Laws of 1809 and 1811, in an attempt to coerce Great Britain
into treating American trade more generously. Successive administrations
in Washington had also offered to negotiate these matters, only to see
ministries in London either rebuff the initiatives or, if they did not rebuff
them, deal with Washington in bad faith – as Madison believed had been
the case in 1809 when London had repudiated an agreement reached in
Washington that would have lifted the Non-Intercourse Law in return
for the removal of the Orders in Council. And as further proof of British
perfidy on that occasion, Madison pointed to evidence he had uncovered
to the effect that Great Britain had employed a secret agent in the United
States in 1809 for the purpose of "a subversion of our Government, and
a dismemberment of our happy union."

Finally, the president drew attention to the recent outbreak of hostilities on the northwestern frontiers of the republic between the local
Indian nations and the westward-moving American settlers, hostilities
that Madison assumed had been instigated by "British traders and gar-
risons" operating from Canada. More specifically, this was an allusion
to the Battle of Tippecanoe, fought on 7 November 1811 between an
army led by the territorial governor of Indiana, William Henry Harrison, and the warriors of a loose confederation of Indian nations, based
at Prophetstown in Indiana, under the leadership of the Shawnee brothers Tenskwatawa (the Prophet) and Tecumseh. Harrison claimed that he
had won the engagement, but Madison nevertheless deplored the commencement of this conflict for its recourse to a form of "warfare which is

known to spare neither age nor sex, and to be distinguished by features peculiarly shocking to humanity." The president also mentioned that he had evidence to prove that British influence was responsible for those "features" that were so "shocking to humanity."

Madison then came to the climactic moment of his message. He summarized again the British actions that had harmed the United States, actions he believed could be undertaken only by a belligerent power and not by one that was supposed to be at peace with a neutral, and he repeated how the American response of "moderation and conciliation" had been of no avail. "We hold, in fine," he concluded, "on the side of Great Britain a state of war against the United States; and on the side of the United States, a state of peace towards Great Britain." Surprisingly perhaps Madison did not follow this rhetorical flourish with a request for Congress to declare war. The reason he did not do so was his respect for section 8 in article 1 of the Federal Constitution, which confined the right to declare war to Congress. It was for this same reason that Madison had also rejected the suggestion made by Treasury comptroller Richard Rush that he and his cabinet colleagues appear before Congress to deliver the "war message" in person. But to prod the legislators toward the decision he sought, the president asked whether they could "continue passive under these progressive usurpations, and these accumulating wrongs." Should they not, he suggested, "oppose force to force in defence of their national rights" and "commit a just cause into the hands of the Almighty disposer of events" in order to bring about "an honorable re-establishment of peace and friendship" with Great Britain? Madison chose to flatter the legislators by presuming they would be incapable of reaching any decision that would not be "worthy [of] the enlightened and patriotic Councils of a virtuous, a free, and a powerful Nation."

Madison might well have stopped at that point. He had made a tightly argued and seemingly compelling case for war with Great Britain, one that summarized the issues at stake, and he had done so in ways that conformed to his long-held views about the proper constitutional roles of the executive and the legislature as these related to war and peace. Yet he was not quite finished. In many respects, his mind instinctively resisted thinking in the clear-cut terms of right and wrong that he had employed in his message, and he knew full well that its contents had, in many ways, oversimplified the problem he was presenting to Congress. He therefore attached one more paragraph to the message, noting that France had often been as guilty of the same infractions of American neutral rights as Great Britain. In the context of Madison's contemplating a war with the leading naval power in Europe, this was an extraordinary admission. In the minds of many in his audience it seriously weakened the case he had just made against Great Britain. Even so the president pressed on, promising he would pursue the disputes with France after the arrival of additional information from Europe.[1] And the implication of the final sentence of his message was that the United States might then have to go to war with France. But how had Madison, and the United States, arrived at a situation in which the president was considering war against the two most powerful nations in the world – whose governments were also at war with each other?

II

As Madison had mentioned, the source of his difficulties was the Anglo-French war of 1803. That conflict was hardly unique. It was merely the seventh occasion on which France and Great Britain had gone to war since 1689, in a series of conflicts that historians now refer to as either "the Second Hundred Years' War" or the wars of "the long eighteenth century," the duration of which was determined by the accession of William and Mary to the throne of England in 1688 and the final defeat of Napoleon at Waterloo in 1815. For British ministries the problem was always how to construct diplomatic coalitions and to utilize naval strength in ways that would prevent France from consolidating its pretensions to be the hegemonic power on the European continent. Direct military interventions by the British army on the continent itself were occasional rather than regular features of British policy. Usually Great Britain preferred to subsidize European nations to combat the armies of France and its allies. For the rulers of France, the issue was how to maintain its military supremacy on land, and that requirement usually mandated heavy commitments of manpower, especially in the Low Countries, in northern Italy, and in central Europe. Yet at the same time France also had to compete with Great Britain as a colonial and maritime power, if for no other reason than to sever the imperial roots of its enemy's fiscal and naval resources.

In the wars of the first half of "the long eighteenth century" – the Nine Years' War (1689–1697), the War of the Spanish Succession (1702–1713), the War of the Austrian Succession (1740–1748), and the Seven

---

[1] For the draft and text of the "war message," see *The Papers of James Madison: Presidential Series* (6 vols. to date, Robert A. Rutland et al., eds.; Charlottesville, VA, 1984–), 4:431–39.

Years' War (1756–1763) – Great Britain had been more successful at balancing those requirements than was France, so much so that by 1763 the British had succeeded not merely in destroying French imperial power in both North America and India but also in virtually vanquishing France's claim to be regarded as the leading nation of Europe. In the second half of the eighteenth century, Great Britain began asserting claims to preeminence that had previously been the prerogative of France as that nation suffered a dramatic loss of influence and prestige, especially in central and Eastern Europe. The desire to avenge these humiliations led France to ally with the rebellious American colonies in 1778, in the hope that the destruction of British imperial power in North America and the Caribbean would enable France to reverse its European decline. By 1783 French strategy had succeeded to the extent that Great Britain lost its most valuable colonies on the North American mainland, a development that reduced the British American Empire largely to its sugar colonies in the West Indies and a handful of undeveloped and thinly populated settlements in what had formerly been French Canada (or Quebec) before 1763.

Yet France failed to reap any great benefit from the disruption of the first British Empire. The Bourbon monarchy of Louis XVI was unable to repay or manage the debts it had incurred during the war for American independence. Nor did it invest much in the expansion of French military and naval power that would have advanced its recovery as a leading colonial and maritime power. Great Britain, however, under the leadership of the younger William Pitt, undertook the necessary measures to reform its finances and to strengthen the Royal Navy for the next round of war with France. That conflict came soon enough, as a result of the French Revolution of 1789. In 1792 the European powers of Austria and Prussia, worried about the spread of revolutionary tendencies, invaded France, in part to reinstate the rule of Louis XVI, who had been captured in a badly mismanaged attempt to escape from his kingdom in order to head the counterrevolution and restore the ancien régime. The armies of France stopped the invasions, and the French National Assembly, in 1793, executed the king, declared France to be a republic, and broadened the European war by extending it to Great Britain, Holland, and Spain. To respond to continental ambitions of such magnitude, the French republic resorted to new forms of warfare, most notably the celebrated levee en masse, which permitted it to mobilize its superiority in manpower over its enemies in ways that had not been possible in earlier wars.

For the remainder of the 1790s, as the revolution became increasingly violent and disruptive in France, the enormously enlarged armies of the republic defeated most of their European enemies – but not Great Britain. In the course of doing so France more than recovered the status it had lost in 1763 as Europe's preeminent power. It also extended its eastern frontiers into what had previously been the German territories of the Holy Roman Empire, and it greatly reduced the political influence of Austria in both central Europe and northern Italy. But it made no comparable gains in its efforts to increase its colonial and maritime strength. Indeed, France lost effective control over its largest and most prosperous Caribbean colony, Saint-Domingue, following the uprising of its slave population in 1791, and the attempts made after 1798 to extend French power into the eastern Mediterranean Sea and from there into Egypt and possibly into British India were frustrated by the Royal Navy. Yet these reverses only inspired France to contemplate alternative imperial and maritime strategies – this time in the Caribbean and North America. As Napoleon transformed his military triumphs in Europe into the basis for his becoming the unopposed ruler of France, he and his foreign minister, Charles-Maurice de Talleyrand-Périgord, plotted the restoration of French control over Saint-Domingue as well as the recovery of France's former colony of Louisiana, which had been transferred to Spain in 1762. To accomplish this, however, it was necessary to end the wars in Europe, and Napoleon and Talleyrand agreed to this at the end of 1801. Great Britain, though undefeated, had been exhausted by the strain of nearly nine years of war. Its ministry consented to peace, even if it was with the awareness that it was more likely to be a truce than a permanent settlement of its long-standing rivalry with France.

III

The European wars created countless difficulties for the new American nation. Given the premise that the United States did not wish to become a party to them, the most serious problem was how it might define and vindicate a policy of neutrality, a task that was complicated by the fact that the 1778 treaties of alliance and commerce with France were still in effect. In 1793 the French republic did not expect the United States to participate directly in the European conflict, but it did assume that its ally would conduct its commercial policies in ways that would counter efforts by the Royal Navy to restrict trade with France. It also presumed that the United States would not prevent French diplomats and secret agents, as well as French naval vessels and privateers, from using American territory as a base for subversive activities against British and Spanish colonies in the New World. Great Britain made it clear, however, that it would not tolerate any such definition of American neutrality, and beginning late in 1793, it demonstrated the reach of its naval power by seizing more than three hundred American merchantmen in the Caribbean, where they had flocked in the expectation of picking up neutral cargoes from the colonies of France and Spain. British admiralty courts in the West Indies confiscated the vessels and their cargoes under the "rule of 1756" – a maxim that held that Britain's enemies could not escape its navy simply by entrusting their colonial commerce to a neutral when that neutral had not shared the commerce in times of peace. As for the crews of the American merchantmen, Royal Navy officers treated them harshly, often by impressing them into British service.

The immediate result was a "war crisis" in the American capital of Philadelphia over the winter of 1793–1794, which the administration of George Washington defused only by sending Chief Justice John Jay to London in a desperate effort to settle the issues in dispute. Jay gained the barest minimum of concessions required to remove the grounds for an outbreak of war with Great Britain, but at a cost. The United States had to abandon the foundation of its commercial policy as a neutral nation – the notion that free ships made free goods – and it accepted instead a definition of contraband of war that gave British naval vessels greater latitude to seize cargoes that could contribute directly to the military capacities of Britain's enemies. Great Britain also insisted that the United States forgo the right to resort to discriminatory practices against British commerce – a policy that had been much favored by Secretary of State Thomas Jefferson and Representative James Madison in their efforts after 1789 to extract better terms for Anglo-American trade. The effects of these provisions were to apply for a period of ten years after the ratification of the treaty or for two years beyond the termination of the current wars in Europe, depending on which development occurred first.

Many Americans felt that Jay had purchased peace at too high a price. That sentiment fused the various elements of a previously inchoate opposition to the Washington administration into the more formidable force of the Republican Party whose adherents, for the following two decades, always responded passionately to the suspicion that efforts to promote reconciliation with Great Britain undermined American independence. Only policies more sympathetic to France, they believed, could truly sustain that independence. The French government no more liked Jay's treaty than did the Republicans, and after 1796 it adopted the position that whatever violations of their neutral rights that Americans tolerated from Great Britain, France was entitled to retort them on the United States. That attitude, in fact, governed much French policy toward the United States for the subsequent decade and beyond, and it was one reason why Madison, in 1812, had to confront the prospect of war with France as well as with Great Britain. The immediate consequence, however, was the deterioration of Franco-American harmony into the discord of the Quasi-War between 1798 and 1800. Although formal hostilities were never declared, the two republics engaged in an extensive naval and privateering war, during which the administration of John Adams greatly expanded the American armed forces, founded the U.S. Navy, and attempted to suppress its Republican opponents by passing the Alien and Sedition Acts of 1798. Some of Adams's more enthusiastic Federalist supporters wished for full-scale war with France, but in 1800 Adams broke with them by ending the Quasi-War with the Convention of Mortefortaine, an agreement that Napoleon accepted to advance French imperial ambitions in the Caribbean and Louisiana.

These problems of neutrality notwithstanding, the European wars after 1793 also brought many benefits to Americans. Once the United States had agreed to trade according to British notions of neutral rights, American commerce increased very substantially under the Jay Treaty and extensive commercial growth and prosperity did much to stabilize the nation's economy and finances. The Jay Treaty also ended, for the moment, the potential for a dangerous alliance between the Indian nations in the American Northwest and British forces based in both Canada and in a series of forts below the Great Lakes and along the St. Lawrence River. The British had held on to the forts in violation of the 1783 peace treaty, but they abandoned them in 1796. Great Britain was also prepared to open its West Indian ports to Americans – after having closed them in 1783 – but the U.S. Senate rejected the article Jay had negotiated on this issue as being too restrictive. On the French side of the balance sheet, the war crisis after 1798 provided the United States with far stronger military and naval forces by 1800 than it might otherwise have had, and most important of all, it terminated the French alliance as an impediment to American neutrality. By 1801, therefore, at the dawn of a new century and with a Republican administration in power – led by Jefferson as president and with Madison as secretary of state – the situation of the United States had improved. And when France and Great Britain agreed to make peace at the end of 1801 and provided that peace lasted long enough to allow some of the more unpopular provisions of the Jay Treaty to expire, it finally seemed possible that the United States would be able to consolidate as the independent and neutral nation that its founders had originally envisioned.

IV

Such hopes were illusory. The European peace lasted barely eighteen months, although not before France bequeathed to the United States the Louisiana Purchase, which Napoleon, after failing in his plans to regain control of Saint-Domingue, delivered to the republic in April 1803 for the sum of $15 million as an advance on the financing of his next round of war with Great Britain. That transaction also had the effect of reviving Francophile tendencies in the Republican Party, admittedly much reduced as a consequence of the Quasi-War, while reinforcing at the same time its instinctive Anglophobia. Nevertheless, for a period of nearly two years after the resumption of war in Europe, Anglo-American relations remained relatively tranquil. In part this was because Great Britain, throughout 1804, was more preoccupied with preparing for a possible French invasion than it was with policing neutral trade, and the ministry in London continued to act as if the Jay Treaty were still in effect. On the American side, the Jefferson administration had little desire to renew quarrels with London, and it even hoped for British support in a separate dispute with Spain – now restored to its traditional alliance with France – where the United States was pressing Madrid to transfer the province of West Florida to American control under the terms of the Louisiana Purchase treaty.

After October 1805 the relative tranquility came to an end when the British admiral Horatio Nelson destroyed the combined French and Spanish fleets at Trafalgar, and Napoleon, who had crowned himself emperor in 1804, shattered an anti-French coalition by defeating Austria and Russia at the battles of Ulm and Austerlitz, respectively. Thereafter, for almost the next decade, France and its allies – including various satellite kingdoms in Italy, Holland, and Spain that Napoleon parceled out to his relatives as he redrew the map of Europe – reigned supreme on the continent while Great Britain remained unchallenged on the high seas. Because neither of the two leading belligerents could directly engage the other for the purpose of waging a decisive battle, they each resorted to forms of indirect conflict in a prolonged war of attrition that was intended to expose and exploit their differing strengths and weaknesses whenever their

interests clashed at any point on the globe. And it was in this context
that the United States became peculiarly vulnerable as a neutral, in ways
that went far beyond any of the difficulties it had experienced between
1793 and 1801.

Many of these new problems for the United States originated in the
capacities and the needs of the Royal Navy. After 1803 Great Britain
maintained a fleet of more than nine hundred vessels on active duty,
which, in turn, necessitated the recruitment and provisioning of crews
that totaled somewhere between 130,000 and 140,000 men. Yet Great
Britain could not supply that many seamen by voluntary enlistment from
its own population, so to man the fleet, it resorted, with increasing rigor,
to the time-honored form of conscription known as impressment. Consequently, after 1805, Royal Navy officers became less discriminating
in their recruiting practices. Foreigners were enlisted and naturalized as
British subjects, and neutral vessels on the high seas were stopped and
their crews checked for the presence of British mariners – on the assumption that the king was entitled to call on his subjects at any time and in any
place, and those subjects could not plead their being naturalized by other
nations as a bar to such demands. Perhaps inevitably, as the Royal Navy
stopped more and more American vessels, its officers began to impress
Americans as well, regardless of whether they were native born or naturalized. After all, the Royal Navy was needy, and its officers could always
say it was impossible to distinguish between Americans and Britons on
the basis of their accents. How many Americans were forced into British
service in this way is difficult to determine. By 1812 the State Department
reckoned that 6,257 had been impressed in the five years after 1807, but
it may well have been the case that nearer to 10,000 Americans had been
so seized between 1803 and 1812.

The matériel demands of the Royal Navy were equally exacting. Extensive supplies of various sorts of seasoned timber, as well as flax, canvas,
and pitch, were essential to keep vessels afloat, and, as was the case with
its seamen, the navy could not meet all of its requirements within the
British Isles. As the leading historian of the subject has noted, the Royal
Navy was "the largest industrial unit of its day in the western world,
and by far the most expensive and demanding of all the administrative
responsibilities of the [British] state."[2] Its costs to the British taxpayer

[2] The history of the Royal Navy for this period is best consulted in N. A. M. Rodger,
The Command of the Ocean: A Naval History of Britain, 1649–1815 (London, 2004),
358–584.

exceeded £15 million per year throughout the war against Napoleonic France. That situation forced Great Britain into extending its access to timber and raw materials in many parts of the world, but particularly in the Baltic, the Mediterranean, and North America. Asia was not exempt from this quest either, and by 1809 the British had even tried to use timber from kauri trees in New Zealand. Such activities necessarily drew Great Britain into rivalries with other nations that had interests in these regions, and as we shall see, the search for timber and other resources as the lifeblood of the Royal Navy would exacerbate Britain's relations with several nations in eastern Europe – and by 1812 with the United States as well over the export of timber from the forests of North America.

But it was the uses Great Britain made of its navy that were most problematic for neutrals. The duties of the Royal Navy far exceeded those of engaging in combat. Among other matters, its task was to promote and to protect the expansion of British trade (both export and import), such trade being essential for revenue purposes and for the prosperity of an economy that was in the first stages of an industrial revolution. Expanded trade also enlarged the pool of trained seamen who might later serve in the fleet. More important, the Royal Navy not only had to defend Britain's territories and control the sea routes that connected Europe to the rest of the world (especially North America and the Caribbean) but also had to police neutral trade according to British notions of belligerent rights to ensure that its enemies could not use neutral nations to nullify the effects of British sea power. Here was an abundant source for conflicts with the United States. Great Britain had never accepted the American (and French) view that free ships should make free goods, and it adhered to more flexible definitions of contraband of war that permitted it to seize cargoes, either of direct military value or even of potential military value, according to its needs. And after 1805, it began to meet those needs by an extremely vigorous enforcement of the "rule of 1756," especially against Americans engaged in the shipment of West Indian colonial produce to the United States and Europe. Moreover, to minimize the chances that any such produce might reach a market on the continent, Great Britain, starting in May 1806, proclaimed increasingly extensive blockades of the ports of Europe, including a blockade – known as Fox's blockade after the British foreign secretary Charles James Fox – that extended across almost the entire northern coastline of the continent.

After Trafalgar Napoleon was powerless to contend with Great Britain on the oceans, but as he gained more control over central and Eastern

Europe in 1806 and 1807, he took what countermeasures he could. Following the defeat of Prussia at the Battle of Jena in November 1806, the French emperor inaugurated his Continental System with the Berlin Decree, a blockade in reverse that prohibited all trade by any nation with Great Britain and subjected all goods and merchandise of British origin to confiscation. That system was extended to Russia and the Baltic region the following year as a consequence of the French victory at the Battle of Friedland, after which Alexander I of Russia – whose dislike of British maritime policies matched that of Jefferson and Madison – allied with France against Great Britain in the Treaty of Tilsit. The British government responded with two sets of Orders in Council – a form of executive mandate – that expanded its blockades. The first, in January 1807, allowed the Royal Navy to control the coastal trade around Europe, whereas the second, in November of that year, imposed a ban on any vessels trading with Europe unless they passed first through a British port, unloaded their cargoes, and paid a duty of 25 percent. Napoleon retaliated in December 1807 with his Milan Decree, which confiscated every ship that could be found to have obeyed these orders. Thereafter, for the following five years, the two belligerents vied with each other to see how much neutral (i.e., American) shipping they could seize. Their success was impressive, and it seemed as if France and its allies could almost match the British, vessel for vessel. Over the longer term between 1803 and 1812, however, Great Britain remained the most serious aggressor, seizing more than nine hundred American vessels in all. France took more than five hundred, and an undetermined number, possibly in the hundreds, were seized by European allies of France, such as Denmark and Spain.[3] The primary purpose of the seizures was for each belligerent to damage the trade and economy of its adversaries, but that goal could hardly be divorced from another – to compel the United States to shape its neutrality to conform to the policies of one or the other of the major belligerents.

V

Despite the impact of these belligerent measures, the United States was slow to react. The sheer difficulty of negotiating solutions with nations

---

[3] See *American State Papers: Documents, Legislative and Executive of the Congress of the United States* (Walter Lowrie et al., eds.; Washington, D.C., 1832–1861); *Foreign Relations*, 3:583–85.

that were determined to prevail at all costs was one reason Jefferson and Madison hesitated to make too vigorous a response that might risk war, although this is not to say that they failed to make diplomatic protests against the rising tide of impressments and ship seizures. Another factor that made for a cautious approach was administration fiscal policy, which, in order to retire the national debt by 1817, had required substantial reductions in military and naval expenditures after 1801. Greater levels of preparedness, to say nothing of war itself, were too much of a threat to Jefferson's long-term goal of a debt-free republic for him to contemplate them with equanimity. And if peace should return to Europe in the near future – and Jefferson hoped it would – such measures would be unnecessary anyway. Still, the severity of the belligerents' assault on American neutrality was bound to generate calls for action, a sentiment reflected in Congress over the winter and spring of 1805–1806 in the form of resolutions to ban British imports. The idea behind these resolutions derived from good Republican Party doctrine – the belief that the United States could manipulate trade for diplomatic purposes – but in 1806 Republicans were far from united about how to put it into effect. The result was the Non-Importation Act of April 1806, a relatively mild protest that excluded none of the most important items, such as textiles and metal goods, that made up the bulk of American imports from Great Britain. That measure was promptly further weakened by its suspension for a period of nine months to allow for a diplomatic solution to emerge.

The call for diplomacy, however, came from the Senate rather than the administration and Jefferson acceded to it with reluctance. Nevertheless, he and Madison decided to give negotiations a chance, in part because Foreign Secretary Fox was not unsympathetic to the United States, and they chose a Baltimore lawyer, William Pinkney, to join James Monroe, the resident American minister in London. The instructions Madison wrote for Monroe and Pinkney allowed for the settlement of almost every issue in contention with Great Britain, but only two matters were essential for an agreement: an end to impressment and a modification of the rule of 1756 to allow American merchantmen greater freedom to ship cargoes from French and Spanish colonies in the Caribbean in a manner similar to that tolerated by the British in the days when the United States had accepted the Jay Treaty. Unfortunately for the Americans, while the negotiations were proceeding, Fox died and Napoleon promulgated his Berlin Decree. Both developments limited Britain's willingness to make concessions. The best Monroe and Pinkney could do was to conclude a treaty, in December 1806, that omitted to end impressment (albeit with a note attached to its text that promised to practice it with restraint) but that did allow for Americans to ship West Indian produce to Europe provided it had been neutralized by a prior importation into the United States. As for any other issues, the diplomats dealt with them by largely reenacting the commercial provisions of the Jay Treaty, to which the British added a further qualification reserving the right to retaliate against the United States if it failed to resist the Berlin Decree. When Jefferson read the treaty in the spring of 1807, he refused to send it to the Senate, citing its failure to end impressment as his justification.

Historians have frequently criticized Jefferson for rejecting the Monroe-Pinkney treaty, on the grounds that by doing so he and Madison missed an opportunity to avoid the train of events that culminated in war in 1812. But the president had not yet concluded that negotiations were entirely at an end, and he devoted much of the spring of 1807 to consulting with political and commercial leaders about how the treaty might be improved. What brought that process to an abrupt halt was the attack by HMS *Leopard* on the USS *Chesapeake* on 22 June 1807. The episode amounted to a serious escalation of the dispute over impressment. Although Americans had always regarded British claims about the "right" to impress on the high seas as a violation of neutral rights and a flagrant derogation of American sovereignty (inasmuch as Britain's refusal to accept American naturalization practices debased its standing as a sovereign nation), no British ministry or naval officer had ever asserted a right to impress from vessels of a foreign navy. Jefferson therefore saw an opportunity to link the unresolved problem of impressment generally to the abuse of the practice in the *Chesapeake* case, hoping to compel Great Britain to make the settlement of the former dispute the precondition for a resolution of the latter. He also began making preparations for war, assuming that the *Chesapeake* affair was the first step in a British policy to extend the European war to the United States in order to abolish the rights of neutrals on the oceans altogether. This strategy had, in fact, already been advocated by several prominent British pamphleteers, most notably James Stephen in his celebrated *War in Disguise or the Frauds of Neutral Flags*, as the best way to maximize British naval power after Trafalgar.

At this juncture, the preservation of peace – and the success of Jefferson's diplomacy – depended on the response of the British ministry, now dominated by such Tory leaders as George Canning and Spencer Perceval, who were far less sympathetic to the United States than the late Charles James Fox had been. It is perhaps unlikely that these Tory leaders would have regarded their freedom of action as being restricted by the Monroe-Pinkney treaty even if it had gone into effect, but the ministry, nevertheless, immediately disavowed the attack on the *Chesapeake*. It did not, however, accept that there was any connection between the case of the *Chesapeake* and the dispute over impressment generally. That decision reduced the risk of an immediate outbreak of war, but by the time the news reached Washington in the fall of 1807, it was accompanied by developments of a much more alarming nature. Not only did the Royal Navy announce that it would step up its rate of impressment, but also British newspapers began to report rumors of even more stringent antineutral policies that were eventually to go into effect with the November 1807 Orders in Council.

Had Jefferson waited for official notification of the orders and for evidence of their enforcement by the Royal Navy, the case for war with Great Britain would have been both overwhelming and unavoidable. But Jefferson did not wait on these events. Instead, he anticipated them by persuading Congress, in the final week of December 1807, to adopt an embargo to prevent American vessels from leaving port. That policy would reduce the number of American merchantmen exposed to seizure under the British orders, and it also promised, particularly in the view of Madison, to apply increased pressure to the British imperial economy as a way of forcing Great Britain – and to a lesser extent France as well – to reverse their antineutral measures. These decisions marked the beginning of Jefferson's Embargo, which was not so much a single stroke of policy as it was a series of continuously fluctuating measures that evolved according to the circumstances of the moment. After starting with a ban on the departure of vessels, it progressed to the prohibition of moving all goods across the frontiers the United States shared with British Canada and Spanish Florida, and these policies, in turn, were supplemented with increasingly draconian measures of enforcement.

All these efforts failed. By the end of 1808 public support was waning, the Treasury was running short of revenue from lost trade, and there was little evidence that the Embargo was having much effect on the European belligerents. Indeed, in the case of Great Britain, that nation was to receive an entirely fortuitous addition to its colonial trade as a result of the commencement of the revolutions of the Spanish-American colonies against the prospect of French domination after Napoleon had invaded Spain in the spring of 1808. Moreover, as Jefferson and Napoleon attempted to seal off the North American and European continents, British merchants and naval officers proved to be unusually resourceful in finding

ways of carrying on trade by smuggling. Their success in doing so transformed such obscure points on the globe, such as Grand Manan Island
and Passamaquoddy (off the coast of Maine), Amelia Island (in Spanish East Florida), and Heligoland (to the west of the Jutland Peninsula),
into major entrepôts for the exchange of British manufactured goods and
American colonial produce. After fifteen months of such experiences,
Republicans in Congress were ready to call it quits. Three days before
Jefferson retired to Monticello, they repealed the Embargo and replaced
it with the Non-Intercourse Law of March 1809, a measure that allowed
Americans to resume trade with the world, provided that they did not do
so with France and Great Britain.

VI

That was the situation inherited by Madison as the fourth president. His
position was hardly an easy one, and its difficulties were compounded
by the fact that he was not the unanimous Republican choice to follow
Jefferson. Monroe had opposed him in the 1808 election – to protest the
rejection of the 1806 treaty – as did Jefferson's second vice president,
George Clinton of New York, who found a small but significant number
of supporters among the newspaper editors and Republican senators in
the states between New Hampshire and Virginia who had become impa-
tient with the overreliance on commercial restrictions as the preferred
way to defend American neutrality. These disaffected or "malcontent"
Republicans favored more aggressive responses to belligerent depredations on American commerce, although they seldom made it clear what
other policies – better preparedness or outright war – would have satisfied
them. They also blamed the Swiss-born Treasury secretary Albert Gallatin
for exercising too much influence over foreign policy, and some of their
number, notably Senators Samuel Smith of Maryland and William Branch
Giles of Virginia, had already blocked Madison's attempt to name Gallatin as his successor in the State Department by forcing him to appoint
Robert Smith – Samuel's brother – to the position instead.

At first, that setback might not have mattered too much. Within a
few weeks of taking office, Madison and Robert Smith, working with the
British minister in Washington, David Erskine, negotiated a settlement
of the dispute over the Orders in Council. In return for the ministry in
London repealing the orders, the administration in Washington would
lift the Non-Intercourse Law as it applied to Great Britain while leaving
it in force against France. Madison's popularity soared, briefly. Erskine,

in his eagerness to make an agreement, had withheld some key British conditions for the removal of the orders – conditions that no American administration could have accepted – and when the British foreign secretary, George Canning, learned what had happened, he repudiated the agreement and recalled his minister. He replaced him with Francis James Jackson, a coarse and unsubtle diplomat who had become infamous for his role in Britain's violation of the neutrality of Denmark in 1807 when the Royal Navy destroyed the Danish fleet to prevent it from falling under French control as Napoleon plotted to extend the alliances he had formed at Tilsit. Jackson's appointment indicated that the United States could expect no concessions on neutral rights.

The president was entangled in several awkward dilemmas. When he received the news of Canning's repudiation of Erskine, he had already retired for the summer to his Montpelier plantation. Congress was no longer in session, and the entire American merchant fleet had put to sea in pursuit of commercial opportunities. A return to the Embargo was impossible, and a declaration of war seemed neither desirable nor practicable. Too much mercantile property would have been vulnerable to wholesale seizures by the Royal Navy, and the U.S. Army was in no condition to engage in any sort of combat. Its largest single detachment of some two thousand men, based near New Orleans, had been incapacitated by disease and illnesses resulting from the decision of its commanding officer, Brigadier General James Wilkinson, to encamp it on an unhealthy, swampy site beneath a levee on the Mississippi River. And Madison was not even sure whether he could restore the Non-Intercourse Law against Great Britain on his own initiative, but if he did not, he would run the risk of provoking Napoleon into taking more extreme antineutral measures to punish the United States for failing to resist the British more strenuously. After some reflection Madison returned to Washington in August 1809, where he restored nonintercourse against Great Britain by proclamation.

Even so, that decision left major problems unaddressed. Americans might not be able to trade with France and Great Britain, yet the United States had no means of preventing its merchants from trading through third parties – most notably Spain and its possessions – in ways that would enable the two major European belligerents to receive American cargoes. Moreover, government revenues, which had been greatly swollen by neutral trade in the years before 1807, were falling, and Gallatin, who had remained at the Treasury, made it plain that he needed more revenue from trade if he were to avoid the alternatives – borrowing and taxation. His solution was to resort to an American navigation act, known as

Macon's Bill No. 1, which would have allowed trade with the European belligerents but only in American vessels. Its intent was to revive both trade and revenue while at the same time giving France and Great Britain an incentive to modify their antineutral policies if they wished to have their vessels admitted into American ports. The bill passed the House of Representatives in January 1810, but it failed in the Senate – where it was criticized for being both too weak to be effective, yet strong enough to provoke the belligerents into additional measures of retaliation.

Madison tried to supplement trade policy with diplomacy and preparedness. The former failed, as Minister Jackson repeatedly insisted that the president had been personally responsible for the flaws in the Erskine agreement. Madison then declared him persona non grata to avoid dealing with his insults. The latter also failed, as neither branch of Congress would support Madison's request, made in January 1810, that it fill the ranks of the army, organize volunteer forces, refit the navy, and hold militia detachments in readiness for federal service. After that Congress gave up altogether in its attempts to deal with the European belligerents. In May 1810 it passed Macon's Bill No. 2, which freed American trade from all restraints and allowed the president to resort to nonintercourse again only if one of the major belligerents abandoned its antineutral policies first and the other failed to follow suit within three months. Madison signed the bill, but he was disgusted by its "feeble" aspects and he declared (privately) that Congress was in a permanently "unhinged state."[4]

But "feeble" though it may have been, Madison detected possibilities in Macon's Bill No. 2. The main consequence of freeing American trade from restrictions, the president realized, would be to allow Great Britain to monopolize most of it – as that nation stored neutral cargoes in warehouses before slowly releasing them (under a license system) for reexport to Europe.[5] As these policies would also glut the British market with neutral goods, they would lead to a decline in the prices goods fetched, an effect that Congress and American producers (if not merchants) might eventually find to be intolerable. Furthermore, that same situation might prompt Napoleon into considering the repeal of his Berlin and Milan decrees, if he wished to prevent Great Britain from receiving and controlling so much American trade. The latter prediction proved correct, though

---

[4] James Madison to Thomas Jefferson, 23 April 1810, *Madison Papers: Presidential Series*, 2:321.
[5] Americans could purchase these licenses from the British government – at a steep price. Such fiscal expedients served only to reinforce Madison's belief about the hypocrisy underlying British policies toward neutrals.

in ways that Madison could not have foreseen. As he read the provisions of Macon's Bill No. 2, Napoleon, in August 1810, directed his foreign minister, the Duc de Cadore, to deliver to John Armstrong, the American minister in Paris who was about to leave for home, a note promising to repeal his antineutral decrees by 1 November 1810 on the condition that the United States had taken steps to make the British respect the American flag. The note was a cunningly worded hypothetical conditional – one that required Madison to act first while leaving Napoleon some latitude thereafter to judge the adequacy of the president's response.

Madison was not blind to the problematic aspects of Napoleon's move, and he was not, as many historians have believed, simply duped into making a response. After reading the Cadore letter, he decided, on 2 November 1810, to accept it as a declaration, in principle, of the repeal of the Berlin and Milan decrees, and he put Great Britain on notice by proclaiming his intention to restore nonintercourse within three months if the Orders in Council were not removed. By these means Madison believed he could test the sincerity of Great Britain's claim that it had resorted to the 1807 orders only in retaliation against France's prior aggression against neutral rights in the 1806 Berlin decree. The implication of that argument was that if France changed its policies, Great Britain would follow suit. Madison did not assume that the ministry in London would abandon its efforts to control the flow of goods to Europe by repealing its orders altogether, but he thought it possible that it might adopt more narrowly defined and properly enforced blockades against France. Such a development would have amounted to a considerable improvement for the United States, and the president even anticipated that Great Britain could modify its policies, as he wrote to Armstrong, in ways that would "irritate France against our non-resistance [to future British blockades] without irritating us to the resisting point [of war against Great Britain]."[6] In short, Madison wished to use the Cadore letter to settle once and for all the dispute over the legality of Great Britain's blockades.

This proved a miscalculation that would set the stage for war. The exact status of the French decrees remained unclear for the next seventeen months while Napoleon, whose long-term goal was to push the United States into war with Great Britain, continued to seize American vessels, citing so-called municipal regulations in justification. The duplicity of this policy was so obvious that it destroyed any prospects that the Cadore letter might persuade Great Britain to lift its orders – as Pinkney,

---

[6] Madison to John Armstrong, 29 October 1810, ibid., 2:598.

who had remained as American minister in London, was to learn. After several unsuccessful attempts to convince the ministry that Napoleon had changed his ways, Pinkney quit his post to return home in February 1811, informing the State Department as he did so that Great Britain would never negotiate honestly with the United States. This diplomatic failure also had domestic political repercussions. Secretary of State Smith, with whom Madison had never enjoyed a comfortable personal or political relationship, began to voice open criticisms of the president's misjudgment, even to the British chargé d'affaires in Washington, and rumors began circulating that the "malcontent" Republicans would be joined by Armstrong, after his return from France, in an effort to replace Madison at the head of the party's ticket in the election of 1812.

Madison responded variously to these developments. In April 1811 he dismissed Smith, replacing him with Monroe. In doing so, the president reached out to some of his opponents from 1808, but another reason for the decision was the hope that the prince regent of Great Britain – who had assumed the powers of the monarchy in the spring of 1811 following the decline of George III into permanent insanity – would replace his father's Tory ministers with Whig leaders who were both known to Monroe and believed to be friendly to the United States. That hope was short lived. The regent could not find ministers who pleased him personally while also being able to command a majority in Parliament, and so George III's cabinet, with Spencer Perceval at its head, survived. Admittedly, the prince did appoint a new minister to Washington, Augustus John Foster, to replace the discredited Jackson, but Madison had long detested the "quackeries & corruptions" of Perceval and he could not believe that Foster would receive instructions to offer concessions to America.[7] He could only wait and see what news Foster would bring and allow Monroe – who believed that he could negotiate with Great Britain – a fair opportunity to exercise his diplomatic skills.

Foster reached Washington in early July 1811. His arrival coincided, and not by accident, with Robert Smith's attempt to vindicate himself by publishing his *Address to the People of the United States*, in which he criticized Madison for pursuing weak and pusillanimous policies toward the European belligerents. As a consequence, Madison and Monroe's negotiations with Foster were accompanied by a steady drumbeat of complaints – to which most of the other "malcontent" Republican leaders

---

[7] For Madison's contempt for Spencer Perceval, see his 6 November 1809 letter to Jefferson, *ibid.*, 2:55.

and newspaper editors contributed – to the effect that the administration would sell out American neutrality for another version of the Jay Treaty. At first, Monroe attempted to persuade Foster that the Berlin and Milan decrees were indeed repealed, but he met with no better success than Pinkney had in London. But far worse were the conditions that Foster did stipulate for the lifting of the Orders in Council. Not only would Napoleon have to repeal his decrees unambiguously, but also the ministry in London would not be convinced of his sincerity until he had agreed either to receive British goods as neutral property in American vessels or to restore neutral rights in Europe to the status quo that had prevailed in the year 1806 – that is, before Napoleon had extended his control over much of the continent of Europe. In effect, Great Britain had announced that it would retain its Orders in Council for as long as it took to end Napoleon's domination over Europe.

Because Napoleon was only forty-two years old in 1811 and had yet to sustain any major defeats on the continent, the day for the removal of the Orders in Council became remote in the extreme. Madison quickly concluded as much, complaining to one of his correspondents that Great Britain had taken "yet another ground" in justifying its orders "on which it is impossible to meet her."[8] His response was to summon, on 24 July 1811, the Twelfth Congress into an early session in the first week of November – a decision that amounted to an intention to prepare for war. Not only would Great Britain now adhere to its orders for the duration of the European war – which would effectively nullify American neutrality for the duration – but Madison also realized that an American response limited to trade restrictions would no longer be adequate. The problems of smuggling, both in Europe and across the borders with Canada and Spanish Florida, had only multiplied in the months following the failure of the Embargo. In Europe, Napoleon had relaxed some of his efforts to keep all British goods out of the continent and opted, like the British, for a state-sanctioned system of smuggling (under licenses) that allowed his regime to receive and control the distribution of the revenues that such a scheme would produce. At the same time the emperor also worried – without much sense of his own consistency – that Russia would break away from the Continental System and admit a flood of British goods into the markets of central and Eastern Europe. That prospect, coupled with anxieties about the future intentions of Alexander I toward Poland, was to drive Napoleon to invade Russia in 1812, in the hope that the

[8] Madison to Henry Dearborn, ca. 23 July 1811, ibid., 3:390.

defeat of his former ally would put an end to all resistance to his efforts to dominate Europe.

Madison had already been alerted to the possibility of war between France and Russia. He understood that a Russian defeat could seriously weaken British commercial and naval power in Europe, but he also had to take account of the effects of smuggling closer to home in North America. These were not limited to the growing exchange of British goods and American products in the Canadian Maritime Provinces or across the Great Lakes and the St. Lawrence River. More troubling was the rapid growth of Canada itself, especially after 1807 following Napoleon's closure of the Baltic region to British trade through the Treaty of Tilsit. In response, the Royal Navy drew more and more on Canada for ship timber and naval stores, to such an extent that it is no exaggeration to say that Canadian timber sustained the British fleet for the duration of the war against France. That some of this timber and other goods shipped from Canada also came from the United States – as Americans engaged in smuggling to escape the effects of nonintercourse – was of no consolation to Madison. All such trade stimulated the imperial economy and in ways that would reduce British dependence on resources from the United States. For that reason an expanding Canada emerged as a significant factor in Anglo-American relations, and the one step that was not open to the president as he considered his options after July 1811 – in the context of the rising domestic criticism of his diplomacy – was for him to report to Congress in November that the negotiations with Foster had failed and then to take no further action. Of necessity Madison's response had to be more forceful – and that meant preparing for war with Great Britain and more particularly for a war to seize Canada.

VII

The day after the Twelfth Congress assembled, Madison, on 5 November 1811, released his annual message. Its contents summarized recent developments, criticized Great Britain for putting its orders into "more rigorous execution," and concluded with a list of preparedness measures: filling the ranks of the army; creating an "auxiliary force"; organizing volunteers and the state militias; preparing the navy; stockpiling munitions and war matériel; and providing appropriate funding, including "new loans."[9] As

---

[9] For the text of the message, see ibid., 4:1–6.

had become the custom with annual messages, Congress referred its various sections to select and standing committees whose members, in the House of Representatives, were appointed by the speaker, Henry Clay of Kentucky. (In the Senate, which was a much smaller and more informally organized body, such committees were usually elected.) In the House, those passages in Madison's message that dealt with foreign relations were sent to a select committee chaired by Peter B. Porter of New York. Porter and his committee then corresponded and met with Monroe to seek clarification about the administration's intentions. They learned, perhaps to their surprise, that the president was in earnest about going to war if British policies remained unchanged. The committee agreed to report the necessary legislation, on the understanding that there would be a definite decision on war or peace by the end of the session.

On 29 November Porter delivered a report from his committee. It stated the case for war in the strongest possible terms, with Porter defining the alternatives for Congress as submission or resistance to Great Britain, and it culminated in six resolutions granting the administration the substance of the preparations it had sought – an additional army of ten thousand men to serve for three years, a volunteer force of fifty thousand men, the organization of the militias for federal service, and the repair of all naval vessels. It also included a measure Madison had not sought – the authority to allow merchantmen to arm for self-defense on the high seas. In the ensuing debates Porter was followed by his committee colleagues, including John C. Calhoun of South Carolina, Joseph Desha of Kentucky, Felix Grundy of Tennessee, and John Adams Harper of New Hampshire, who reinforced the case for war with angry and bellicose rhetoric. These committeemen were the so-called "War Hawks" of the Twelfth Congress, but they were not a legislative faction, nor were they the makers of American policy. Rather, they served as a channel through which administration measures were transmitted to, and justified before, their fellow legislators.

With respect to the most important measure of preparation, the expansion of the army, the House agreed to fill the existing ranks and to create an auxiliary force of ten thousand, but the Senate, prompted by the "malcontent" Giles, replaced it with a very different bill to recruit twenty-five thousand men for five years. The administration regarded this as an impossible task, but all attempts to modify the Senate bill failed and the House eventually agreed to its terms on 9 January 1812. It was a similar story with the fifty thousand volunteers. The House passed the measure in late February – after a lengthy debate about whether the president could employ the force outside the United States – but another Senate "mal-content," Nicholas Gilman of New Hampshire, crippled it by entrusting its organization to the state governments rather to the War Department. Measures to fund these preparations fared little better. Treasury Secretary Gallatin, in January 1812, called for a comprehensive program of double duties, loans, and direct and indirect taxes, only to see the House accept the duties and the loans while balking at the taxes. It was to take until the first week of March 1812 before the House would swallow the taxes, but they were to go into effect only after the commencement of war "against a European nation." As the Federalist senator from Delaware, James A. Bayard, remarked, it was an open question whether "the war [would] float the taxes or the taxes sink the war."[10]

By March 1812, five months after the start of the session, Congress had passed the most important preparedness measures, but it had done so in ways that the administration regarded as impracticable. The reason for this state of affairs was that there was considerably more opposition to Madison's policies in Congress than met the eye. The problem did not lie in the House, which, leaving the issue of taxes aside, usually passed the measures requested of it by adequate majorities. Nor were the Federalists the sole source of the difficulties, as their numbers, in both branches, were too small in themselves to determine outcomes – unless they could cast their votes with dissident or "malcontent" Republicans. But that was exactly the situation that prevailed in the Senate, and it explained why the administration was unhappy about the progress of preparedness. As Madison himself remarked to Jefferson, Congress, "with a view to enable the Executive to step at once into Canada," had "provided after two months delay for a regular force requiring 12 to raise it, and after 3 months for a volunteer force, on terms not likely to raise it at all for that object." "The mixture of good & bad, avowed & disguised motives accounting for these things is curious eno[ough]," he added, "but not to be explained in the compass of a letter."[11]

Nevertheless, the administration still wanted to press on to war, but to do so would require a far greater degree of unity within the Republican ranks in Congress. It was to create such unity that Madison, on 9 March 1812, released the letters of John Henry. These documents revealed that Henry had been a British agent, employed by the Governor in Chief of

---

[10] James A. Bayard to Caesar A. Rodney, 9 March 1812, "James Ashton Bayard Letters, 1802–1814," *Bulletin of the New York Public Library* 4 (1900): 236.

[11] Madison to Jefferson, 7 February 1812, *Madison Papers: Presidential Series*, 4:168–69.

Lower Canada over the winter of 1808–1809, to assess the prospects for the secession of New England from the Union during the Embargo crisis. Not satisfied with the payment he had received, Henry offered his letters to the United States and obtained for them the considerable sum of $50,000. The outcry against both the British and the president's critics was initially all that might have been hoped for, and by mid-March Speaker Clay had met with Monroe to map out a strategy leading to war – namely a thirty-day embargo to keep American merchantmen at home before a declaration of hostilities and another preparedness bill that would allow the president to organize a ten-thousand-man volunteer force for immediate service. For its part, the administration did not wish to appear to be imposing a policy of war on the legislature, but Clay, on his side, indicated that Congress wanted to receive a clear signal that Madison was ready to assume the functions of commander in chief.

At that point the momentum toward war collapsed – for three reasons. The first was that congressional investigations of Henry's letters showed that, although he had reported much dissatisfaction in New England over the Embargo, he had not uncovered any evidence of treason and that Madison had paid a great deal of money for essentially worthless information. The second was that the exposure of these details coincided with the efforts of an executive agent, George Mathews, to overthrow the government of Spanish East Florida. Madison had sent Mathews to Florida – in the summer of 1810 – to take precautions against a British occupation of the province and to receive it for the United States, should its local leaders declare independence from Spain. But Mathews had no authority to organize a revolution for those purposes. The result was that Madison stood condemned for committing precisely the offense he was imputing to Great Britain for its employment of Henry. The third was the news that French frigates had recently burned at sea American merchantmen bound for Spain, an outrage that called into question – yet again – whether Napoleon's Berlin and Milan decrees were really repealed at all. If not, how could the United States go to war with Great Britain alone and not with France as well?

For his misconduct in East Florida, Mathews was immediately dis-avowed, but it would take longer for the administration to recover from the other setbacks. As it waited for the situation to improve, Monroe sought an extension of the thirty-day embargo he had recently requested of Clay to sixty days, and he also asked for a modification of the Giles army bill to allow the War Department to recruit a smaller force of fifteen thousand regulars for the term of eighteen months. Congress postponed consideration of the latter request until July while enacting the embargo on 4 April – but only after another "malcontent" senator, Michael Leib of Pennsylvania, had prolonged its duration to ninety days, in part to delay even further any progress toward war. Congress then compounded the delay by debating proposals for a recess and to repeal non-intercourse against Great Britain. The passage of either measure would have indicated that the legislature was not serious about war, but it proved difficult to vote them down, as nearly forty members of the House had already taken leaves of absence from Washington to return to their constituencies. Consequently, the House had to pass a resolution, on 13 May 1812, to recall all members to the capital by 1 June. In the interim, the only significant business transacted was the nomination of Madison for a second term by the congressional caucus on 18 May. The president received the unanimous endorsement of those Republicans present, but the degree of unanimity implied by that result concealed the much harsher reality that nearly one-third of the party's members boycotted the event to avoid either supporting or opposing the nominee.

The fate of the war policy now depended on the return of the dispatch vessel, the USS *Hornet*, from Europe with reports about the status of the antineutral measures of the belligerents. That news, reflecting developments up until mid-April 1812, arrived in Washington on 23 May. It failed to clarify matters. From Paris, the American minister, Joel Barlow, reported that he was discussing a new treaty of commerce but he could provide no information about the way in which France was implementing its decrees or whether it might restore American vessels that had been wrongly seized. In London, matters seemed no better. Certainly, the American chargé d'affaires, Jonathan Russell, mentioned that there was a significant protest under way against the Orders in Council, mainly in Britain's industrial districts, where manufacturers were attributing a recent and sharp downturn in the economy to American trade restrictions. But manufacturers were substantially underrepresented at Westminster, and it was to take a subsequent political crisis, arising from the assassination of Prime Minister Perceval on 11 May, before Parliament could be persuaded to end the Orders in Council on 23 June. In April, though, Russell could hold out no hope for their imminent repeal. Nor did Foster, who had received new instructions via the *Hornet*, have the authority to offer concessions that might have averted war. The most the ministry would consider was to allow Americans a greater share in its license trade to Europe, but Madison, who never believed that neutrals should pay the British to exercise a right to which they were already entitled under international law, regarded this as no concession at all.

The stalemate in Europe produced a moment of paralysis in Washington. And it was in this context that the notion that war could be justified only if it were declared against both France and Great Britain gained some traction. Madison agreed that the situation of the nation had become "more than ever puzzling," and he struggled with the idea of a "triangular war." He doubted the sincerity of its proponents, mainly Federalists and "malcontent" Republicans, and he fully appreciated both the absurdity of the matter and the "thousand difficulties" that such a policy would present.[12] It would mean, in effect, that the United States would be going to war with the entire continent of Europe and jokes were already circulating in the capital about how the French and British ministers would have to meet to coordinate policy against their common American enemy. Worse, the idea of war against France also risked dividing those Republicans who were already united on the question of war against Great Britain. Nevertheless, political realities in Congress required the president to take the idea seriously or, at the least, to pay some lip service to its potency, as the final paragraph in his "war message" of 1 June would reveal.

At that juncture the president received a visit from a congressional delegation of Republicans headed by Speaker Clay. What they discussed is unclear – although it is highly unlikely, as some historians have believed, that Clay threatened to deny Madison his reelection if he did not go to war – and it is more probable that the meeting was concerned with matters that the speaker had discussed earlier with Monroe, namely how to move to a state of war.As the administration's newspaper in Washington, the *National Intelligencer*, pointed out on 30 May, the term of the sixty-day embargo that the administration had sought in early April was about to expire and the administration remained pledged by its earlier statements that required it to carry out its measures of preparedness if Great Britain did not lift its orders. Admittedly, there remained many doubts about the adequacy of the preparations for war, but it was also unlikely that any of them would be resolved so long as uncertainty about the larger question of war or peace persisted. Consequently, Madison finally took the step that had been implicit in his conduct since mid-July 1811. He completed his "war message" and sent it to Congress on 1 June 1812.

---

[12] See Madison to Jefferson, 25 May 1812, ibid., 4:415–16.

VIII

The House quickly disposed of the message. The select committee on foreign relations – under the leadership of Calhoun after Porter had retired to his district on the western frontier of New York to take care of local business – presented on 3 June a report (written largely by Monroe's chief State Department clerk, John Graham) that echoed and reinforced all Madison's concerns. The next day, 4 June, a war bill passed by seventy-nine votes to forty-nine, not an overwhelming endorsement of the president's policies but a sufficient one nonetheless. The majority consisted wholly of Republicans drawn from all parts of the nation. The minority included every House Federalist; a substantial number of "malcontent" Republicans who later in the year would oppose Madison's reelection by supporting the candidacy of DeWitt Clinton (the mayor of New York City and nephew of George Clinton); and a smaller handful of Republicans who decided against war for largely personal or idiosyncratic reasons, including the fear that the conflict would be a bad business from which the nation could derive no advantage.

The story was very different in the Senate. The senators did not even commence debate until 9 June, and for a week thereafter the Federalists and the "malcontent" Republicans made last-ditch efforts to obstruct a president whose policies and person they heartily despised. They did not, however, attempt to defeat a declaration of war outright and preferred to concentrate on three alternative courses of action: postponing hostilities pending further preparations, a maritime war confined to the high seas, and war with both France and Great Britain. All these alternatives were voted down, albeit by narrow margins, until by 16 June there remained only the decision to vote up or down on war itself. The next day, 17 June, the Senate opted for war by nineteen votes to thirteen. A dozen or so of the administration's most reliable supporters formed the basis for the majority, with the critical votes for its victory coming from four of the more prominent "malcontent" Republicans: Giles, Leib, Samuel Smith, and Andrew Gregg of Pennsylvania. As was the case in the House, the Senate opposition consisted of all the Federalists, about one-half of the "malcontent" Republicans, and a few other Republicans who had local or personal reasons for their decision. That some "malcontent" Republicans, after having persistently criticized and opposed the president for years, should have joined the majority seemed surprising to some observers, but these Republicans had been accusing Madison for so long of being weak in his defense of neutral rights that they could hardly come out against war now unless they wished to proclaim that motives other than patriotism and a concern for national honor had governed their behavior all along.

Immediately after the Senate vote, Monroe summoned Foster to the State Department, where, in an awkward conversation over a pot of tea, he communicated the American requirements for peace. These were the repeal of the Orders in Council and a settlement of the problem of impressment. The first was to be resolved by Great Britain's signing a treaty containing "a definition of blockades according to the [Anglo-] Russian treaty" of 1801 – an agreement in which London, under pressures of the moment, had relaxed its more stringent notions about policing neutral trade in the Baltic. The second was to be placed beyond the realm of controversy by a mutual agreement, to be written into American and British law, that the two nations would forgo the employment of each other's nationals in their merchant marines.[13] The next day Madison signed the war bill, and on 19 June he issued a proclamation announcing that a state of hostilities existed between the United States and "the United Kingdom of Great Britain and Ireland and the dependencies thereof." The president then donned "a little round hat [with] a huge cockade" and visited the Navy and War departments in Washington, exhorting their officials, and the public at large, to support "all measures which may be adopted . . . for obtaining a speedy, a just, and an honorable peace" with Great Britain.[14]

[13] For an account of this meeting, see Augustus John Foster, Journal Entry, 18 June 1812, Augustus Foster Papers, Library of Congress.

[14] For the description of Madison, see Richard Rush to Benjamin Rush, 20 June 1812, Benjamin Rush Papers, Library Company of Philadelphia; for the text of the proclamation, see *Madison Papers: Presidential Series*, 4:489–90.

2

1812

I

Madison's decision to seek a declaration of war against Great Britain suggested that he had ideas about how he might defeat his enemy. This was certainly true, but it was to be more than unusually difficult for the president and his administration to translate their plans into effective action. The resulting conflict was a ragged one, marked on the American side more by military fiascoes than successes on land and interspersed with occasional naval victories at sea that, though gratifying to the nation's tender sense of pride, were inconsequential in terms of its larger outcomes. By the end of 1814 the prosecution of the war had become so fraught with obstacles that it would be no exaggeration to say that the American republic had reached the effective limits of its capacities as a war-making state. The nation was then rescued from an embarrassing predicament not so much by divine providence – as many of its clergy claimed – as by the skills of its diplomats, who were able to negotiate a not unsatisfactory peace treaty in the new international environment that emerged with the ending of the Napoleonic Wars in Europe. As a consequence, the fact that the United States had survived the war at all without incurring any significant losses became a good enough result to permit Americans to transform it into a triumph in its own right.

It was taken for granted by most Americans that the war effort would be directed largely against Canada. The republic had only a miniscule navy – sixteen vessels of all sizes – which ruled out an invasion of the British West Indies, to say nothing of the British Isles. Nor was the U.S. Army a more significant force. Since 1808 its authorized strength stood at

48

ten thousand officers and men, but in 1811 the ranks contained little more than one-half of that number. However, the United States enjoyed an enormous superiority over Canada of nearly fifteen to one in manpower; in 1810 their white populations were more than 6 million and little more than four hundred thousand, respectively. Provided that this numerical superiority could be mobilized into functional militia and volunteer units, all the advantages should have been with the Americans. Overall, Great Britain certainly had larger naval and land forces – a fleet of nine hundred vessels and a standing army of more than 250,000 – but in Upper and Lower Canada it could muster little more than 5,600 regulars, and British army officers had little confidence in the Canadian militias, totaling about 86,000 men, as a supplement. And in light of the situation in Europe, where Napoleon was about to invade Russia with six hundred thousand men, the ministry in London was in no position to send reinforcements to North America.

Early hints about the likely American war strategy were provided by the administration newspaper, the Washington *National Intelligencer*, in late November and early December 1811. "It would be the duty of the government of the United States," the paper declared, "to lose no time in reducing the whole [of Canada] above Quebec," for which task "about 20,000 men would be proper, two thirds of whom might be volunteers and one third regulars." These troops should be directed to three points, "principally to the region of Montreal – the outlet of [Lake] Ontario – and across the Niagara river." These suggestions were more or less in harmony with the preparedness measures proposed by the president himself and endorsed in late November by the House committee on foreign relations. As for Quebec, where most of the British regular forces were concentrated, its immediate capture was not deemed to be necessary, as the garrison would be cut off from the rest of Canada and would be of "no service to Great Britain" until such time as American forces could take it by a "regular siege." Upper Canada, where the British army had barely 1,200 troops dispersed across a long frontier, presented a much easier target. Provided that the invasion of the region between Montreal and Lake Ontario could be executed quickly, the entire province could be reduced "with little bloodshed."[1] In these matters it would not be necessary to occupy or annex large amounts of Canadian territory; the capture of a few strategic places and the surrender of small handfuls of

---

[1] See the editorial letters published under the heading of "The Canadas" on 23 and 28 November and 3 December 1811.

enemy troops would ensure the collapse of British rule to the west of Quebec.

Over the next few months, these preliminary ideas were to be modified almost beyond recognition as the administration adjusted its priorities in response to unforeseen contingencies and pressures from Congress and the states where interested parties assessed the probable impact of the war on their concerns. In the first instance, serious delays arose from the unwillingness of Congress to provide for the regular army and volunteers in the manner that the president had requested, as well as from the reluctance of the administration itself to carry out measures it regarded as unworkable and too costly. The war strategy was then subjected to a more searching critique by the governor of the Michigan Territory, William Hull, in March 1812. Hull rejected the assumption that the occupation of the region between Montreal and Lake Ontario would entail the fall of Upper Canada. Even the remnant of a British force at Detroit, he argued, would be sufficient to allow the enemy to seize much of the American Northwest. Consequently, the governor argued for more troops at Detroit, both to defend its inhabitants from possible attack and to secure the surrounding region against restless Indian nations. Hull also objected that the administration had not provided for the construction of naval vessels on the Great Lakes, particularly on Lake Erie. These were points he had made on several occasions since his appointment as territorial governor in 1805, but his case for them in the spring of 1812 was reinforced by the widespread sense of panic throughout the Northwest following the Battle of Tippecanoe in November 1811.

That engagement had resulted from the desire of the governor of the Indiana Territory, William Henry Harrison, to destroy an emerging confederation of the northwestern Indian nations headed by the Shawnee Prophet, Tenskwatawa, and his brother, Tecumseh. Beginning in 1805 the Prophet had established himself as the spiritual leader of a movement to revitalize Indian culture through a return to traditional ways of Indian life and the repudiation of accommodations that Indians had made with American customs in the decades after the Revolution, such as the adoption of sedentary agriculture and the wearing of manufactured clothing. Following Harrison's negotiation of a controversial land cession at Fort Wayne, Indiana, in 1809, which extended American control into the lower Wabash Valley, Tecumseh had coupled his brother's message with the argument that Indians should adopt a policy of common property in their lands to halt American encroachments. In reality, the situation on the ground was more complicated than the activities of the Shawnee brothers led many Americans to believe. The Prophet could not restore a golden age from the past; instead, he created an unstable syncretism between Indian traditions and American technology and Christianity. For example, he experienced apocalyptic visions and never renounced the use of guns. Tecumseh also fell short of establishing the united confederation he had called for. He did, however, produce a significant coalition of factions of varying degrees of strength, consisting mainly of younger warriors drawn from the Ottawa, Potawatomi, Shawnee, and Winnebago peoples who had become disillusioned with the status quo in their relationships with the Great Father in Washington. Harrison wished to destroy this coalition, both to further the advance of the American frontier and to hasten the progress of Indiana Territory toward statehood.

The administration did not want an Indian war, but it did concede that security for settlers in the Northwest was deteriorating and the secretary of war, William Eustis, had authorized Harrison in July 1811 to assemble a small army of about 1,200 regulars, militia, and volunteers, drawn largely from Kentucky, to ensure that the Indians remained at peace. Harrison accordingly advanced on Prophetstown, located on the Tippecanoe River, from where he drove the Prophet and his followers after a short battle on 7 November. The governor claimed a victory, but whether he had improved the security of the frontier was uncertain. Prophetstown was destroyed and its inhabitants dispersed, yet they were far from vanquished as a military threat. Consequently, Madison invited Hull, in April 1812, to take another army, two thousand men strong and made up of regulars and volunteers from Ohio, to reinforce Detroit and to take whatever measures were necessary "to secure the peace of the country."[2] It was not clear, though, whether those measures included an invasion of Upper Canada, and that issue became a matter of serious disagreement between Hull and the administration. The governor, appointed to the rank of brigadier general in the Northwest Army, was to maintain that his force was never intended for an invasion and certainly not without the construction of a fleet on Lake Erie. For its part, the administration contended that Hull had assured them that an army based in Detroit would be adequate for an invasion, even without the assistance of naval vessels. This confusion and lack of clarity over strategy and tactics led to Hull's downfall. It would also become a recurring characteristic of later American campaigns in the war.

---

[2] Eustis to Hull, 9 April 1812, Letters Sent Relating to Indian Affairs, Records of the Bureau of Indian Affairs, RG 75, National Archives of the United States.

At the same time that Hull accepted his assignment to Detroit, the ranking major general in the U.S. Army, Henry Dearborn of Massachusetts,
whom Madison had nominated to his position in January 1812, was
drafting a more comprehensive war strategy. His plan retained the original emphases on seizing the region between Montreal and Lake Ontario
and the attack across the Niagara Peninsula but supplemented them with
incursions into British territory from Detroit and into New Brunswick.
Hull, whether or not he acknowledged it, was to be responsible for the
invasion from Detroit; the case for an attack across the Niagara River was
reinforced by pressure from Peter B. Porter of the House foreign relations
committee, who had business interests in the region he wished to secure
against British counterattacks; and the addition of the New Brunswick
front reflected Dearborn's concern to protect the District of Maine, where
he had business interests of his own, by compelling the British to bottle
up their maritime resources in Halifax. Dearborn also understood that
the success of these invasions depended on their rapid execution, after
which the victorious Americans could proceed at their leisure to Quebec. Privately, the general was less optimistic than he seemed. He had no
doubt the United States would ultimately triumph, but he was apprehen-
sive about the difficulties of mobilization. As he told Thomas Jefferson,
he expected the nation to commence the war "clumsily" and only over
time would its performance improve.[3]

II

Dearborn's concerns were to be realized more fully than he anticipated.
They began with problems in financing the war and were to extend
to every detail connected with the recruitment, supply, and training of
troops. The issues of war finance had long preoccupied the secretary of the
treasury, Albert Gallatin, not because he was eager for a conflict so much
as he was fearful of its disruptive effects on his plans to retire the national
debt remaining from the Revolution in a regular and orderly fashion by
1817. In principle, Gallatin believed the United States might finance a
war primarily through loans, provided that government revenues during
its course remained equal to its ordinary peacetime expenditures plus the
costs of servicing an enlarged wartime debt. Had war with Great Britain
come during the Embargo crisis, for example, Gallatin had calculated that

---

[3] See Dearborn to Jefferson, 10 March 1812, *The Papers of Thomas Jefferson: Retirement
Series* (7 vols. to date, J. Jefferson Looney et al., eds.; Princeton, NJ, 2004–), 4:545.

he could meet its costs through revenue surpluses accumulated through the highly profitable years of neutral trade before 1807 in combination with loans made from the first Bank of the United States. With luck, these revenues might have sufficed to avoid the imposition of taxes.

By 1811 these options were no longer available. Government revenues had declined as a result of the policies of commercial restriction after 1807 and were lagging behind ordinary expenses; small loans had already become necessary to adhere to the schedule of debt repayments. Even if there were to be no war in 1812, Gallatin knew that "moderate" internal taxes would be necessary to balance the budget. Moreover, after the expiration of the charter of the Bank of the United States in 1811 – an outcome produced by a combination of the hostility of many Republicans toward banking and debt, as well as by internal party factionalism – borrowing from that source was no longer possible. And because of the expansion of the war in Europe, loans could not be raised in international markets, as the United States had done to finance the Louisiana Purchase in 1803. Instead, the Treasury would have to seek loans in an untested national capital market, supplied by "monied men" and local banks of varying degrees of soundness and offer them interest rates that would serve the administration's needs while also maintaining public confidence in the nation's credit.

Gallatin's first effort to address these problems led him to request Congress, in January 1812, to double all customs duties; to revive an old duty on imported salt; to raise some direct and indirect internal taxes; and to authorize a loan of $10 million, with the Treasury having the discretion to set the interest rate. Many in Congress were shocked by the cost and scale of Gallatin's proposals, but starting in February 1812, the legislature approved most of his requests in principle, departing from them only in the matter of the loan, which was set at $11 million with an interest rate of 6 percent. When the time came to vote on each bill for raising the revenue, however, the administration encountered considerable resistance, and the bills increasing both duties and taxes were passed only with the proviso that they would not go into effect until after war had been declared. The upshot was that the Treasury was left to seek loans at an interest rate Gallatin suspected was too low – he favored 8 percent personally – in a market where lenders might worry that the government would not give them a reliable return. When the loan was floated in April 1812, just over $6 million was subscribed; and by the end of June 1812, when Gallatin finally estimated that government expenditures for the year would total $26 million, the Treasury could calculate on having only just over

$16.6 million in hand. To make up the shortfall, Congress doubled some of the duties again and provided for the anticipation of future revenue through the sale of treasury notes, a fiscal device that Gallatin deplored.

The situation was not necessarily as bad as these shortfalls suggested – especially if the war should prove a success – but uncertainties about the supply and flow of money were always to hamper recruiting. This began in December 1811 with War Department orders to fill the existing ranks, but recruiting for the new forces created in January 1812 did not get under way until the spring, and then only after the administration had persuaded Congress to allow it to raise fifteen thousand regulars for eighteen months rather than the full twenty-five thousand men for five years. There were also similar delays with the measures establishing staff departments for the army. A bill for a new Quartermaster's Department was passed in December 1811, but its operations were hampered by difficulties in obtaining personnel; another bill for a new Commissary General of Purchases did not pass until the end of March 1812; and the superintendent for a new Ordnance Department did not commence his duties until mid-July. And even with these additions to the military bureaucracy, it still could not be said that the United States would go into war with a well-organized staff of general officers, comparable to those that had been established by most European armies at the time.

To organize the new troops, it was first necessary to appoint their officers. This was no easy task. There was, as Richard Rush pointed out, "a real dearth of capable military men in the country."[4] The cuts in the U.S. Army implemented by the Jefferson administration in 1802 had reduced the pool of available talent and the Military Academy at West Point, with only eighty-nine graduates by 1812, had not yet been operating long enough to expand it. And officers who had acquired military experience during the Revolution were too old to be of any use, as the wartime careers of Dearborn and Hull were about to demonstrate. Between December 1811 and March 1812, Eustis and Madison pored over the names of hundreds of candidates for army commissions that they had received, either from the state congressional delegations or from interested individuals and parties throughout the nation. Some of the recommendations were enlightening. From one correspondent the president learned that Robert LeRoy Livingston of New York – a Federalist

---

4 See Rush to Charles Jared Ingersoll, 25 January 1812, Charles Jared Ingersoll Papers, Historical Society of Pennsylvania.

congressman also known as "Crazy Bob" – would make "a most excellent Lieut. Colonel . . . if throwing Decanters and glasses were to be the weapons used" in the war.[5] By February 1812 the president was ready to nominate some of his selections but learned that the Senate was unwilling to consider any of them until they had all been made. That delayed the nomination and confirmation process until April 1812, and the allocation of the new officers to their respective regiments was not completed until May.

By the end of 1812, Madison had offered commissions to more than 1,100 officers, 15 percent of whom declined to accept them, usually giving personal rather than political reasons for doing so, and a further 8 percent resigned them after only a few months in the service. To the extent that historians have been able to uncover information about the origins of these newly created officers, it would seem that the higher ranks (i.e., major and above) were drawn predominantly from the legal, mercantile, and political elites of the nation's state and local communities, whereas men from agricultural backgrounds – farming and planting – were relatively underrepresented in proportion to their numbers in the total population. A smaller subset of the higher officers, fewer than 20 percent of the total, came from the broad middling spectrum of American society, including such groups as artisans, manufacturers, and merchants. Most of the higher ranks were probably already established in their occupations or professions and were, on average, in their late thirties to midforties when they entered the corps. The junior officers, those who held the ranks of captain, lieutenant, and ensign, were more mixed in their backgrounds. For the most part, they were much younger men; captains were in their early thirties, whereas the ages of ensigns and lieutenants ranged, on average, from eighteen to twenty-five. Many of the junior officers seem to have been the younger sons of prominent and well-connected families in their localities who had yet to settle on a profession or a vocation while others were scattered across a wider range of occupations, such as clerks, law students, schoolteachers, and storekeepers. There were also several instances where experienced or promising noncommissioned officers in the enlisted ranks were promoted as ensigns and third lieutenants.[6]

---

[5] See "No Trimmer" to Madison, 14 April 1812, *Madison Papers: Presidential Series*, 4:320. This evaluation notwithstanding, Livingston was commissioned as a lieutenant colonel, but he lasted less than a year in the army before resigning.

[6] These figures are drawn from William B. Skelton, "High Army Leadership in the Era of the War of 1812: The Making and Remaking of the Officer Corps," *William and Mary Quarterly*, 3d ser., 60 (1994): 253–74. Statements about the junior officers are based on

In June 1812, the War Department implemented a law reducing the size of the regiments in the new regular forces to one thousand officers and men; it had been set at two thousand officers and men in the law of January 1812, a number that promised to cause serious administrative and organizational problems, and on that basis the Adjutant and Inspector General, Alexander Smyth, recommended a distribution of the new army that concentrated a main force near Albany, New York, while dispersing the remainder at forts and barracks in New York City; Burlington, Vermont; Portland, Maine; Warrenton, Winchester, and Norfolk, Virginia; and Columbia, South Carolina. The regiments and companies of the older army remained where they were already located, and with the creation of this organizational structure, officers and men could be assigned to regiments in readiness for training and active service.

The recruits who could provide the backbone for this paper skeleton were slow to arrive. For the purposes of recruiting, the office of the Adjutant and Inspector General had divided the nation into six departments, usually consisting of two or three states, under a high-ranking superintending officer who received substantial sums of money to cover his costs. Quotas for the number of men to be raised were also set; for example, Brigadier General Joseph Bloomfield, who was also the governor of New Jersey, was expected to raise twenty-nine companies in Pennsylvania, eight in his home state, and two in Delaware. Thereafter, it was up to other officers to organize recruiting parties in the towns and countryside to persuade men to offer their services. There were few restrictions on who might be enlisted other than the requirements that recruits should be white male citizens between eighteen and forty-five years of age and free from serious health problems. After 1812, the citizenship requirements were ignored, but minors younger than twenty-one and apprentices were not to enlist without the consent of their parents, guardians, or masters. In return for joining the ranks, the men received a bounty of $16, a full set of clothes, pay of $5 per month, and 160 acres of land upon discharge.

Recruiting methods varied widely. Some officers appealed to popular patriotism by printing handbills and delivering speeches, accompanied by martial tunes from hired musicians; a few took their men to church on Sunday to exhort others to serve; and many set up in taverns to ply

research by the author into 373 cases drawn from eight infantry regiments distributed throughout the major regions of the nation – New England, the Middle Atlantic, Virginia, the Carolinas, and the West. Throughout the war infantry regiments were based in clearly demarcated states or regions.

men with liquor, a practice that caused many complaints, usually from wives who found that they and their children had been abandoned. The Adjutant General, however, refused to intervene in such cases, remarking that to do so "would prevent half the enlistments."[7] And, in truth, the army had more serious problems to overcome. The later recruiting commenced, the less likely it was to succeed, largely because the availability of men tended to fluctuate with the cycle of the agricultural year. Transient young male agricultural laborers offered potentially rich pickings for recruiters, but if they had contracted for a season's employment before the army could reach them, they would not become available again until the end of their contracts. Urban areas did not present such problems, but officers there often had to deal with petty obstructions, most notably attempts by aggrieved parents, wives, and masters to use writs of habeas corpus to have men discharged for wrongful enlistment. The army could not cope with these tactics. In Philadelphia, for example, Colonel Richard Dennis of the Sixteenth Infantry protested that his officers were "much harassed by the pettifogging lawyers and half-vamp'd judges of this place" for their failure to honor the writs. One judge even jailed officers for noncompliance, leading Dennis to petition for his removal as a "public nuisance."[8]

Equally detrimental to enlistment efforts were delays in providing the troops with uniforms, pay, and equipment. The army's recruiting practices assumed that men would be more likely to enlist to satisfy certain material needs – such as money, clothes, and land – rather than on hope that pure patriotism would fill the ranks. But the supply departments of the army were never able to maintain a steady delivery of money, clothing, and equipment to officers on recruiting duty, and in many parts of the nation, especially in the northeastern states, army pay also lagged well behind the wage rates offered to agricultural laborers. Throughout 1812, army officers constantly complained that shortages of money and clothing gave many recruits a sense of grievance, which, once it was widely known, became an obstacle to continuing enlistments. The spectacle of ragged, barefoot, and otherwise poorly clad and seemingly destitute troops often brought the army, the government, and ultimately the war itself into public disrepute.

---

[7] See the letter to George McFeeley, 29 June 1812, Letters Sent by the Adjutant General, Records of the Adjutant General's Office, RG 94, National Archives.

[8] For Dennis's difficulties, see his 17 November 1812 report to the Adjutant General in Letters Received by the Adjutant General, Records of the Adjutant General's Office, RG 94, National Archives.

Under such circumstances, how successful was recruiting for war? By the end of the year, the army had enlisted nearly fourteen thousand new troops, which, when combined with the men recruited before 1812, made for a force totaling nineteen thousand men – considerably less than the preparedness legislation had called for. Moreover, many of these new men had joined up in the second half of the year and too late for participation in the opening campaigns of the war. And although recruiting had been undertaken in all parts of the nation, there were marked regional and occupational differences in the men's backgrounds. Nearly one-third of them had been born in New England, even though that region contained barely one-quarter of the nation's white males between sixteen and forty-five years of age. The Mid-Atlantic and South Atlantic regions, in contrast, provided only slightly more of the men (64 percent) than their percentage of the same age group in the population might have suggested (59 percent), whereas the western states and territories, with 3 percent of the force, provided significantly fewer men from their 15 percent of that age group. This last result reflected, in part, the difficulties of organizing recruiting in more geographically remote areas, but men in frontier regions, where the threat of conflict with the Indians was the greatest, also preferred to step forward for shorter terms of service in local volunteer and militia corps rather than make a long-term commitment to the regular army.

Nearly one-half of the men, however, were not recruited in their places of birth but in states to which they had migrated. Most of these men were enlisted in New England, New York, and Pennsylvania – a result that might be explained by the army's concentration of effort in those regions nearest to enemy territory and particularly in locations from where the invasions of Lower and Upper Canada would be launched. Overwhelmingly, the new recruits were native-born Americans (87 percent), and these included small handfuls of free blacks, but 13 percent of them were immigrants, largely from Great Britain, and most of these were Irish. Because it was easier to recruit in urban as opposed to rural areas, men from farming backgrounds were underrepresented in the ranks in comparison with men joining from artisan backgrounds (39 percent and 37 percent of the total force, respectively). Laborers were not markedly conspicuous (only 14 percent), but seamen were (5 percent) – an outcome that probably reflected instability in the conditions of their employment between 1807 and 1812, as well as the failure to expand the navy in the first year of the war.

In terms of their ages, the men were not so young; their average age was nearly twenty-seven years. However, men from farming backgrounds tended to be more youthful; their median age was only twenty-two years, which might suggest that they were not landowners themselves but the younger sons of farmers who were attracted to the service by the promise of land bounties. Nevertheless, the army that began to emerge in 1812 was significantly different from the establishments that had been raised in 1802 and 1808. Those forces had been drawn much more from the southern states, were substantially older, and contained many more immigrants and poorer laborers. In that sense, the administration did make a start on creating a force that over the course of the war would become more representative of the social structure of the nation's white male population than the prewar army had been.[9]

Yet even as men were being recruited, there were continuing difficulties with their organization and training. The establishment of the regiments themselves did little to improve prospects for a successful war; if anything, it made them worse. Voluntary enlistment in the army was widely regarded as a personal contract between the officers and their men, with both parties assuming that recruits would serve with their enlisting officers who would guarantee them the contract. The War Department did not share this attitude and instead disposed of bodies of men where it saw fit. Because some officers were better recruiters than others, the placement of men into regiments inevitably separated many of them from the officers who had raised them. That annoyed the officers, especially when they saw their men being transferred to the command of less enterprising recruiters. Above all, it shocked the colonels of the army who had presumed that their own regiments were well on the way to

[9] Figures on enlisted men are taken from J. C. A. Stagg, "Enlisted Men in the United States Army, 1812–1815: A Preliminary Survey," *William and Mary Quarterly*, 3d ser., 43 (1986): 615–45; Stagg, "Soldiers in Peace and War: Comparative Perspectives on the Recruitment of the United States Army, 1802–1815," *William and Mary Quarterly*, 3d ser., 57 (2000): 79–120. The number of blacks who served in the army is difficult to calculate, largely because recruiters did not consistently record their racial backgrounds. There may have been, however, about one thousand blacks in the wartime army – approximately 1.6 percent of the total number of men enlisted – which is a far lower number and percentage of blacks than had served in the Continental Army during the Revolution. Free black men were to make their major contribution to the war effort not in the army but in the navy and on privateers, where it remained the practice to employ them in significant numbers. As for the Irish, it is a fallacy to assume that they flocked to the ranks to fight against Great Britain; in fact, the percentage of Irish immigrants in the army between 1812 and 1815 declined from the levels that had been established in the prewar years.

completion. It became apparent, though, that with one or two exceptions, many of the companies that were assigned to the regiments were
only at one-third to two-thirds of their full strength. The preference of
the colonels was to delay action until the regiments were completed and
their training more advanced. The administration had other priorities,
and the War Department spent the second half of 1812 detaching companies from their regiments, marching them to the northern frontier, and
then reassembling them as invading armies.

Events were to reveal not only that these improvised forces were inadequate for victory but also, and perhaps more important, that they failed
to establish the basis for a functioning army. As the regiments were fragmented, their officers found it impossible to complete their organization,
let alone to attend to their equipment and training. In fact, most of the
troops received no proper training at all before being sent into action, and
because the campaigns of 1812 brought only capture, defeat, and sickness to the forces, the regiments were left as hollowed-out shells of what
they should have become. The problem was compounded by the policy
of using local militia and volunteer forces to supplement the army, and
because these forces also had their full share of organizational problems,
they were to contribute as well to the military fiascoes that followed. It
was, therefore, a cruel irony that as the wartime army struggled to come
into existence, the administration, driven by its own exigencies and the
pressure of events, destroyed its institutional basis. That meant that the
efforts of the first year of the war would have to be repeated in subsequent
years to keep troops in the field.

III

The first campaign of the war got under way when Hull arrived in Cincinnati, Ohio, in early May to take command of 1,200 state volunteers who
had been raised by the Republican governor, Return Jonathan Meigs.
The governor had encountered little difficulty in raising these men. The
residents of Ohio were largely united in their support for the war, at least
to the extent that they assumed war was necessary to deal with the Indian
threat on the frontier, and the quota had been filled in little more than a
month. While waiting for Hull to take up his duties, Meigs had placed the
force under the control of three of Ohio's most prominent Republican
leaders – Lewis Cass (a lawyer and U.S. marshal for the state), James
Findlay (the mayor of Cincinnati and a local militia officer), and Duncan
McArthur (a wealthy landowner and former congressman). The regulars

of the Fourth Infantry Regiment, now increased in size to eight hundred men after the Battle of Tippecanoe and under the command of Lieutenant Colonel James Miller, were not ready until 10 June, by which time Hull had already started his march to Detroit.

Originally, Hull had intended to avail himself of water routes by marching up the Auglaize River to the U.S. Army post at Fort Defiance and then along the Maumee River to Miami of the Rapids and the northwestern shore of Lake Erie. After learning that low water levels in the rivers would create problems with transporting supplies, he chose instead to open a new road from Dayton through central Ohio to the southern shore of the lake. Hull had previously argued for the construction of such a road to improve communications with Detroit, but to cut it now was no small matter, as it required him to cross the Black Swamp, a vast wetland that stretched across to the northwestern border of Ohio, in rainy weather. This decision delayed his progress, and he did not reach Detroit until 5 July. Outwardly, the general seemed confident and optimistic, but the march to Detroit exposed several problems that were to undermine his command. His Ohio troops were not well equipped or well disciplined; one company mutinied over the details of a clothing allowance while still in the state. The Ohio colonels, moreover, quarreled over issues of seniority and precedence – a dispute eventually won by McArthur – before they then united to insist that they be given precedence over Lieutenant Colonel Miller, a demand that was contrary to federal law. The Ohio colonels, backed by Meigs, persisted with their demands, to the point of threatening to disband the army if they did not get their way. Hull was powerless to solve the problem, and it left him with a force whose hybrid composition and internal politics, as he later recalled, was "peculiarly calculated to create mistrust."[10]

Even worse was Hull's failure to win the confidence of the rank and file. Despite his reputation and his experience in the Revolutionary War, Hull's character was weak and his behavior often quite unpredictable. His abilities may also have been impaired by a stroke he had suffered in the previous year – a fact of which Madison was unaware and after which Hull "never appeared to be the man he was before," as Dr. Benjamin Waterhouse recalled.[11] The Ohio colonels were quick to sense this.

---

[10] Hull made this point on 17 March 1814, in remarks he offered in his defense during his court martial; see "Documents Relating to Detroit and Vicinity, 1805–1813," *Michigan Historical Collections* 40 (1929): 630.

[11] See Waterhouse to Madison, 30 June 1825, James Madison Papers, Library of Congress.

Regarding him as an outsider, they dismissed him as irresolute. Such opinions soon percolated down to the troops. Indeed, the entire army observed Hull in great embarrassment when, on parade before leaving for Detroit, the general lost control of his horse, his stirrups, his balance, as well as his hat, and frantically clutched the mane of his mount to save himself. Only decisive and vigorous action in battle could restore the standing of such a general in a society where military leadership depended not only on technical skill but also on popular perceptions of the strength and moral character of the commander.

But the circumstances under which combat began would have been discouraging to all but the most intrepid of generals. The War Department inexplicably failed to inform Hull promptly of the declaration of war, with the result being that the British authorities in Upper Canada learned of it first. The British then exploited this advantage to seize an American schooner, the *Cuyahoga*, which was carrying baggage and the medical supplies for Hull's army as well as Hull's military papers from Miami of the Rapids to Detroit. The Americans also learned that Tecumseh and about 1,800 of his supporters from various northwestern tribes had crossed over into Upper Canada at Fort Malden to make an alliance with the British. This was a development the administration had tried to prevent, specifically by summoning two Indian councils to meet at Piqua, Ohio, and at Kaskaskia, in the Illinois Territory, over the coming summer, during which time they might be persuaded to remain neutral. The councils were delayed, however, because of difficulties in transporting presents. This gave the British the upper hand. Officials of the Crown had experienced many difficulties in restoring good relations with the Northwestern Indians after abandoning them at the end of the Revolution in 1783, but ever since the *Chesapeake* affair of 1807, they had been working hard to cultivate them and to restore some of their former influence in the Great Lakes region. Neither the number of settlers in Upper Canada nor the nature of British land policy there pressed on the Indians in ways that had given rise to serious discontent, nor did the British, as many Americans casually assumed, incite Indians to attack frontier settlements. As a consequence, the British were in a position to reap the benefits of Tecumseh's decision to ally with them as the best way to advance his goals.

Nevertheless, on 12 July Hull crossed over into Upper Canada at Sandwich – to the north of Fort Malden – though not, it would seem, with any clear intention of assaulting the fort. The British could command more naval vessels on Lake Erie and in the Detroit River than the Americans, and Hull had recently been informed by Eustis that the supporting American invasions of Canada at points to the east were likely to be delayed. Consequently, Hull did little more than build a fortified camp and issue a proclamation, on 13 July, promising the people of Upper Canada liberation from British "tyranny," provided that they remained peacefully at home and did not take up arms with the British and the Indians.[12] He then spent the next two weeks in training his men and going through the motions of preparing his artillery to attack Fort Malden, which – despite the numerical inferiority of its defending force – was a strong post, well stocked with cannon. Hull was not sure his artillery was up to the task. After learning by 2 August that the British had captured the small American post at Michilimackinac at the head of Lake Huron, his nerve began to crack. He asked a council of his officers to consider the withdrawal of his army back to Detroit to improve its communications with Ohio and to prevent it from being cut off by Indians. The dangers Hull faced were not unreal, but at the moment they were still more hypothetical than imminent, and he might have been able to stave them off by decisive action.

Hull's officers refused to support him. There ensued a week of unseemly disputes, during which the officers called for an immediate attack on the enemy. Hull equivocated, pointing to the limitations of his artillery and his undisciplined troops. The troops soon learned of the general's reservations, and they, in turn, denounced him as a coward and an "old lady."[13] Hull's anxieties about the Indians were reinforced when the Wyandots at Brownstown in Michigan Territory joined the British, thereby threatening to sever American communications with Miami of the Rapids. The general sent a small detachment to keep the road open, but it could manage no more than an indecisive skirmish at Brownstown on 5 August. Three days later, without consulting anyone, Hull withdrew the bulk of his army to Detroit, leaving only three hundred men at Sandwich as a token of his intent to return later. Once in Detroit, Hull began to talk of withdrawing to Miami of the Rapids. He also implored the War Department and the governors of Ohio and Kentucky to send him reinforcements. Further detachments sent from the army, this time under the command of Miller, to keep the road to Ohio open were also unsuccessful,

---

[12] For the text of the proclamation, see "Documents Relating to Detroit and Vicinity," 409–11.

[13] Quoted in Robert C. Vitz, "James Taylor, the War Department, and the War of 1812," *Old Northwest* 2 (1976): 117. Taylor was serving as quartermaster general to the Northwestern Army.

producing another inconclusive encounter at Maguaga in Michigan on 9 August. That outcome heightened the defensive cast of Hull's thinking. On 11 August he withdrew all remaining American forces from Upper Canada to Detroit, where he was then trapped, paralyzed by his fear of the Indians and his lack of confidence in his own men.

Hull's vacillations gave the British an opening. Their forces in Upper Canada were under the command of the provincial administrator, Major General Isaac Brock, an officer with more than twenty-five years' service, although he had not had a great deal of combat experience. He was nonetheless bold and willing to take risks. For much of 1812 he was confined to York, where he had labored to prepare for war by strengthening the defenses along the Niagara River and trying to discipline the militia. Like many British officials in Canada, Brock did not have much confidence in the provincial settlers. By 1812 nearly 60 percent of this population of about eighty thousand was of American origin. Most of them were not Loyalists from the 1780s but more recent migrants from marginalized minority groups in the United States who had taken up free land the British had offered to build up settlements. The border between Upper Canada and the United States signified little in their daily lives, and some of them had property and relatives in both locations. Living for the most part in isolated and scattered communities, they regarded themselves as unaffected by the disputes that had produced the war. They seldom turned out for militia duty, and more often than not, they deserted when they did. Their representatives in the provincial assembly also rejected Brock's requests for a loyalty oath and the suspension of habeas corpus, though probably more from an instinctive distrust of military rule than from any marked sympathy for the American cause. It was for these sorts of reasons that British officials had frequently wondered whether it might not be better to abandon Upper Canada in a war with the United States in order to concentrate on holding Lower Canada at Quebec. But Brock appreciated that its people had become sufficiently important and numerous to Canada's future to require defending against an invasion.

Brock was unable to travel to Fort Malden before 13 August, but once he arrived, he lost no time in meeting with Tecumseh and planning measures to take advantage of the American retreat. He knew a lot about the force opposing him – British scouting and raiding parties had captured a good deal of American correspondence – and he realized that Hull was already acting in overly cautious ways. From batteries on the Canadian shore opposite Detroit, he opened fire on the Americans without drawing any significant response, either from Hull's artillery or his infantry. Then, after learning that Hull had detached more of his men to maintain communications with Ohio, Brock decided to attack. Dressing his militia forces and Indian allies in British uniforms, he paraded them before Detroit and on 15 August called on Hull to surrender to avoid an "unnecessary effusion of blood."[14] At first, Hull rejected the demand, but his fears of an Indian massacre that would spare neither women nor children drained what little was left of his will to resist. His behavior became erratic; his speech was blurred; and he was reported to be dribbling tobacco onto his vest and jacket while crouching in a corner of the fort. The next day he surrendered Detroit and all the American forces in its vicinity.

Unsurprisingly, this British victory produced a widespread sense of panic, both throughout the Northwest and in Washington. Settlers abandoned the frontier, and the governor of Ohio was swamped with demands to bolster the defenses of the state. In the nation's capital the cabinet had dispersed for the summer, with Madison home at Montpelier while Gallatin visited New York on Treasury business. Monroe, Eustis, and Rush, who were on the spot, quickly concluded that Hull's weakness alone was responsible for the disaster, and they plotted to bring Jefferson out of his retirement and back to the cabinet to permit Monroe to leave for the Northwest and raise troops to retake Detroit. The president, initially, vetoed these suggestions. He saw no need to disturb Jefferson's retirement, nor was he convinced that the immediate recapture of Detroit was necessary. The remaining plans for the invasion of Canada, if successful, would suffice to nullify the effects of the loss in Michigan. Madison then reconsidered and realized that the restoration of order and security in the Northwest would require some centralized direction; otherwise the Treasury would be overwhelmed by the costs of paying for a series of uncoordinated responses to the British advance. By the end of the first week in September Madison agreed that Monroe might take command on the northwestern frontier.

At that juncture, however, the administration lost the initiative to Harrison. After Tippecanoe, Madison had not allowed any role for Harrison in offensive operations, but as the news of Hull's retreat and surrender spread throughout the Northwest, Harrison went to Frankfort, Kentucky, where he met with the governor, Charles Scott, and an informal caucus of Republican leaders, including Henry Clay, for discussions on the threat posed by the British-Indian alliance. The Kentuckians agreed that

---

[14] See Brock to Hull, 15 August 1812, "Documents Relating to Detroit and Vicinity," 451.

Harrison should be commissioned as a major general in the state militia and raise a force of three thousand men, ostensibly for the relief of Detroit. But Harrison was less interested in recovering Detroit or invading Upper Canada than he was with preventing the fall of Fort Harrison and Fort Wayne in the Indiana Territory as the best way to secure the frontiers of Ohio and Indiana. The administration was reluctant to sign on to this strategy; aside from sending out Monroe, the only other measure it had considered for the defense of the frontier was to direct U.S. Army Brigadier General James Winchester of Tennessee to raise a force of two thousand local regulars and militia and march them toward Detroit. Upon learning that two armies were being raised in the region, Monroe abandoned his own military ambitions and retired to Virginia. Madison would have preferred that Winchester take the overall command, but when Harrison and Winchester met in Cincinnati to make their plans, Winchester withdrew his pretensions in favor of Harrison. Somewhat unwillingly, Madison, realizing that Harrison was the more popular of the two generals, accepted the situation. In mid-September the War Department confirmed Harrison's command over all the forces in the Northwest, directing him to protect the frontiers and to take what measures he could "with a view to the conquest of Upper Canada."[15]

As the new major general had predicted, parties of Indians moved quickly to attack the forts in Indiana, but both were relieved by the efforts of their local commanders – one of whom was Captain Zachary Taylor (at Fort Wayne), cousin of President Madison and later to become the twelfth president himself. Nevertheless, Harrison continued to direct throughout September and October 1812 a series of raids against the Indian townships along the rivers in Indiana Territory to destroy their winter food supplies and to reduce their capacity to wage war the following spring. He then based himself at Franklinton, Ohio, where for the following three months he worked frantically to organize and equip his troops. These consisted of a mixture of regulars and Kentucky and Ohio militia volunteers, which the administration supplemented with two detachments of Pennsylvania and Virginia militia volunteers, totaling three thousand men. All in all, Harrison had nearly ten thousand men under his command – far more than Hull had ever had – but he also had sole responsibility for redeeming all the harmful consequences of Hull's failure.

[15] See Eustis to Harrison, 17 September 1812, Letters Sent Relating to Military Affairs, Records of the Office of Secretary of War, RG 107, National Archives.

The general did not relish his situation, although he could hardly afford to admit as much, at least not before the public whose confidence in him was premised on his ability to retake Detroit and to launch another invasion of Canada. His main difficulties were those of supply. The material needs of the enlarged army were enormous, and competition between local merchants and suppliers, on the one hand, and federal supply agencies, on the other hand, drove up the costs of clothing, food, timber, horses, and wagons. Consequently, Harrison constantly lectured the administration on the importance of sparing no expense in the prosecution of the war. His staff officers, similarly, alternated between imploring and threatening Eustis not to embarrass them, but by March 1813 one of them was to admit that the cost of Harrison's army had come to exceed $3 million. There were also continuing problems in Harrison's relationship with Winchester. The latter, after another round of disputes over rank and precedence, had become a division commander in the Northwest Army, and he was already advancing toward Fort Defiance and Miami of the Rapids, where, it was assumed, Harrison would eventually concentrate the other divisions of the army before deciding on his next move.

As to what that move might be, Harrison believed it should not be to retake Detroit but simply to seize Fort Malden. He had no desire to bypass the enemy fort and march along the shore of Lake Erie toward Detroit so long as the British had the advantage of being able to shift men and supplies on water more rapidly than he could on land. But whatever Harrison's intentions were, they were defeated by logistical problems. Like Hull, he had to cross the Black Swamp, but he was badly hampered by unusually cold and wet conditions. It was simply impossible to transport men, animals, and artillery through vast expanses of icy water, two to four feet deep, with the ground beneath full of holes. Harrison exhausted himself and his men in trying, and by the end of December he had to report that he could advance no further until the waters in both the Black Swamp and Lake Erie had completely frozen over, developments that he did not expect to occur before January in the new year. To say this much was to admit failure, which Harrison was loath to do, but the general tried to escape from his dilemma by presenting the administration with a choice – either to back to the full a winter attack on Fort Malden or to postpone the campaign until such time as the United States had gained control of Lake Erie. By then, the administration was more than a little displeased with Harrison's all-too-obvious preference for defeating the Indians before he implemented its Canadian strategy, and it declined to indicate a preference until the general himself finally declared, in January 1813, that it would be "prudent" to suspend operations altogether.[16]

That should have been the end of the northwestern campaign. That it was not was due to Winchester. On 10 January 1813 the Tennessee general reached Miami of the Rapids, where he learned that a British and Indian force under Colonel Henry Proctor had left Fort Malden to intercept his advance by occupying Frenchtown in Michigan. Winchester was not popular with his men – the Kentucky volunteers disliked his "aristocratic" pretensions and style – and they had endured conditions of almost unbelievable hardship while on the march. Their terms of service, moreover, were about to expire, and Winchester, realizing that only ongoing operations that held out a chance for success would hold his force together, decided to meet the British and the Indians at the river Raisin near Frenchtown. There they engaged the enemy twice, on 18 and 22 January, winning the first encounter but losing the second, after which Winchester surrendered his army to avoid further loss of life. On 23 January, a party of Wyandot Indians, most of them intoxicated, killed about sixty Kentucky prisoners of war in retaliation for atrocities committed by Kentuckians against Indians taken in earlier encounters.

The "massacre at the Raisin" outraged Americans throughout the Northwest, but the defeat and the highly emotional reaction to it obscured awareness of the fact that Harrison had also failed to accomplish anything. Seeking to salvage something from the situation, Harrison took about three hundred troops and artillery to Miami of the Rapids, where he requested the governors of Kentucky and Ohio to send him more men so that he might cross the ice to attack Fort Malden. Both governors protested that the request was "morally impossible" to fulfill in the middle of winter.[17] Harrison then contemplated a raid to burn a British vessel on its stocks, but in February 1813 his army dissolved around him as the volunteers demanded their discharge to return home to plant crops in the spring. Harrison withdrew his force to Ohio, where he built a post – named Fort Meigs, near Miami of the Rapids – to await future developments. Quite unfairly, he claimed that had it not been for

---

[16] See Harrison to James Monroe, 6 January 1813, in *Messages and Letters of William Henry Harrison* (2 vols.; Logan Esarey, ed.; Indianapolis, 1922), 2:300.

[17] See Isaac Shelby to Harrison, 30 January 1813, William Henry Harrison Papers, Library of Congress.

Winchester's defeat, he might have taken both Detroit and Fort Malden, but the administration knew better. In the coming year, it would try different policies from those that had failed in 1812.

IV

While the misfortunes of Hull's campaign were playing out, the United States was unable to take significant military action against Lower Canada. For this failure, Dearborn was largely responsible, the strategy he had devised in April 1812 notwithstanding. The general was a reluctant warrior and had only grudgingly left his position as U.S. customs collector at Boston, to where he had retired after resigning as secretary of war in 1808. Worse, by 1812 he was a gentleman of sixty-one years of age who had become quite portly. He even needed a little trolley to permit him to mount a horse and both his thoughts and his movements were sluggish, if not torpid. He was, nonetheless, an important Republican leader in Massachusetts who had acquired some military experience during the Revolution – he had participated in the unsuccessful American assault on Quebec in 1775 under Brigadier General Benedict Arnold – and his political influence was expected to be an important factor in raising large numbers of troops in the regions closest to the border with Lower Canada.

To facilitate the invasions of both Lower and Upper Canada, the War Department had chosen the town of Greenbush, outside Albany, New York, as the main headquarters for the army. From there, roads and rivers led directly to the valley of Lake Champlain, to Sackett's Harbor (at the eastern end of Lake Ontario), and to the Niagara Peninsula. It was, therefore, a convenient location to assemble regulars and volunteers from both New England and New York before sending them on the offensive, but it also had its disadvantages. Albany and the upstate New York region was the center of the Clintonian opposition to Madison's reelection in 1812, and the mobilization for war there was to become entangled in the factional and partisan complexities of state politics. Important interest groups – both mercantile and agricultural, Republican and Federalist – had reservations about the war, if for no other reason than it promised to be bad for business, especially the grain trade. That difficulty was felt most severely in the regions closest to Canada, particularly to the south and the east of the Niagara Peninsula, where the rapid growth of recent settlement had been dependent on American farmers being able to transport their produce, mainly grain and potash, on Lake Ontario and down the St. Lawrence River to Montreal. Income from this commerce was essential to permit the settlers to repay the mortgages and other debts they had incurred to the landlords of upstate New York, including the Holland Land Company, which held 3.3 million acres in the region. It was this same trade that had also contributed so much to the increasing value of Canada to the British Empire, and one effect of the war would be to end it.

Consequently, the responses to mobilization were confused and chaotic. In April 1812 the administration had requested the governor of New York, Daniel D. Tompkins, to place militia reinforcements along the northern and western frontiers, but the governor was uncertain whether these were for defensive or offensive operations. Personally Tompkins supported the war, but he was well aware that powerful Republicans, including DeWitt Clinton and Judge Ambrose Spencer, were ambivalent at best and that the Federalists were hostile. Nor did Tompkins get any help from Dearborn; the general repeatedly stated that his concerns lay further to the east, in Lower Canada, and he left the governor to his own devices in taking care of New York. Tompkins's task was next complicated by the death, in early July 1812, of Major General Peter Gansevoort, the ranking officer in the state militia, and the fact that the administration suggested that Gansevoort's successor, at least on a temporary basis, should be Major General Stephen Van Rensselaer, a prominent Hudson Valley landlord and Federalist. "The Patroon," as he was known, was no advocate for the war, and he had no military experience. Although he was willing to do his patriotic duty, he remained suspicious of the wisdom of Republican policies and the motives behind them. But to assist Tompkins and Van Rensselaer, the War Department dispatched to Greenbush reinforcements of 1,650 regulars under Brigadier General Alexander Smyth of Virginia – then acting Inspector General of the army – and 2,000 Pennsylvania militia volunteers.

Throughout this period, Dearborn was in Boston and contributed nothing toward organizing and training the troops at Greenbush. He did not even return to Albany until the end of July, when his next decision was to accept a proposal for an armistice offered to him on 8 August by Lieutenant General Sir George Prevost – the Captain-General and Governor in Chief of all the British Canadian provinces – after Prevost had learned that Great Britain had lifted the Orders in Council. Madison repudiated the armistice and directed Dearborn to get on with invading Canada. At that point Dearborn abandoned the business to Van Rensselaer and Smyth. The former had arrived on the Niagara Peninsula, where he and his staff officers, largely Federalist in their politics and led by the general's extremely abrasive cousin, Colonel Solomon Van Rensselaer, were already at odds over the war with their predominantly Republican officers and volunteer militia. Their quarrels were exacerbated by the news of the fall of Detroit and Brock's decision, as he returned to Fort George (at the western end of Lake Ontario), to parade his American prisoners of war along the Niagara River as they were being sent to Montreal. Smyth's reinforcements did not reach Niagara until 29 September, but the Virginian disdained Van Rensselaer's militia forces and declined to meet with him to make invasion plans. Smyth's decision, in effect, divided the army into two camps – one at Buffalo above Niagara Falls and the other below the falls at Lewiston – and that organization posed a strategic dilemma that their commanders were unable to surmount. The British positions opposite Lewiston were lightly manned but protected by the extremely turbulent current of the Niagara River; the defenses opposite Buffalo, where the river was easier to cross, were considerably stronger.

Under pressure to avoid imputations of cowardice, Van Rensselaer decided to upstage Smyth by taking three thousand men across the Niagara River. His goals were to redeem Hull's disgrace, to undermine British morale by cutting their communications between Lakes Erie and Ontario, and to position his army for further advances. After some difficulties in obtaining boats with the requisite number of oars, Van Rensselaer, in the early morning hours of 13 October, moved a force of about five hundred men from Lewiston to Queenston Heights, on the opposite side of the river. During this action Brock was killed as he impulsively tried to recapture a small field battery located near the town. At that juncture, however, the British were aided by a detachment of the Iroquois Indians from the Grand River region in Upper Canada under the command of the Scottish-born, half-Cherokee John Norton. To that point, the Iroquois, who had settlements on both sides of the Niagara River and the Great Lakes, had sought to sustain an ambivalent, albeit rather fractured, neutrality in the war, but after Hull's surrender Norton was able to convince the Canadian branch that a British victory would be more favorable to their interests than an American one. The intervention proved critical. It terrified the Americans as they observed their dead and wounded being carried back across the river, with the result that Van Rensselaer could not persuade more than a fraction of his remaining forces on the American side to cross over and hold the ground at Queenston. After British reinforcements under Major General Roger Sheaffe, who had succeeded Brock, rounded up the stranded Americans, taking nine hundred prisoners as he did so, Van Rensselaer surrendered and agreed to a month's truce. He was disgusted and convinced that he had been betrayed.

Throughout these unhappy events Van Rensselaer received no aid from Smyth. Nor did he get any from Dearborn, who confined himself to advising the two generals to cooperate and avoid unnecessary risks. But it fell to Smyth to redeem the failures of Van Rensselaer. In a series of pompous speeches he promised to do so, but the aspersions he cast on the "undisciplined rabble" of the militia and the "degenerated race" of New Yorkers served only to anger local political leaders, especially Peter B. Porter, whom Smyth had asked to raise additional volunteers for an invasion.[18] At the end of November, the general twice went through the motions of putting advance parties across the Niagara River to attack Fort Erie (at the eastern end of Lake Erie) and calling on its commander to surrender. He had to withdraw the parties because his own officers, concerned about the alarming spread of sickness among their men, to say nothing of their inadequate equipment and training, refused to follow him. Smyth then terminated the Niagara campaign and dismissed the volunteers and militia. These became so resentful at their treatment that the general was compelled to maintain a personal guard for his safety as he retired to Virginia.

As had been the case with Van Rensselaer, Dearborn did nothing. Indeed, he washed his hands of all responsibility for the Niagara invasions by returning to New England in the first week of November. He had already passed much of the summer in the region, where he was supposed to use his influence, along with that of other New England Republicans, to raise troops before proceeding to invade Lower Canada. By the fall he had abandoned any idea of attacking New Brunswick as local volunteers for that enterprise could not be obtained. Whether he then invaded Canada across the Niagara River or up the Champlain Valley toward Montreal, the administration had left to his discretion. But instead of focusing on the administration's goals, Dearborn became distracted by the opposition to the war stirred up by the Federalists. Its intensity caught him off guard, especially after the Federalist governors of Massachusetts, Connecticut, and Rhode Island refused to honor his requests for militia detachments

---

[18] For Smyth's proclamations to the army on 10 and 17 November 1812, see Frank H. Severance, ed., "The Case of Alexander Smyth," *Publications of the Buffalo Historical Society* 18 (1914): 226–29.

to be placed on the coast for defense. The governors asserted that they could see no threat of an invasion and that the requirement of the 1795 law for taking the militias into federal service had therefore not been met. Local New England Republicans, led by the outgoing governor of Massachusetts, Elbridge Gerry, who had been nominated to serve as vice president for Madison's second term, took alarm, concluding that their Federalist opponents were plotting with the British to bring about the secession of the northern states from the Union.

The War Department told Dearborn to ignore the Federalists, but he could not, as their opposition to the war far exceeded anything the administration itself had anticipated. Republican congressmen who voted for the war were assaulted, Congregationalist clergy preached sermons against it, public meetings and fast days were held to protest it, the president was hanged in effigy, flags were flown at half-mast, men who attempted to enlist were harassed with suits for debts and their officers with writs of habeas corpus, and talk of secession conventions and plots circulated freely. Dearborn consequently came to believe, along with his fellow New England Republicans, that their task was not so much to facilitate the invasion of Canada as to secure their states from British incursions and Federalist treason. Even when Dearborn did make efforts to raise more volunteers later in the fall, it was not for offensive purposes but to encourage the local Republicans to organize and turn out for the November presidential election. It was to no avail; with the exception of Vermont, the Federalists, in alliance with Republicans who supported DeWitt Clinton, carried every New England state, thereby creating serious political and organizational problems for the administration in the months to come.

After the failure of Van Rensselaer and the Federalist victories in New England, Dearborn made a belated effort to launch a winter campaign against Montreal. He went to Plattsburg, New York, where he expected to find nearly ten thousand regulars and militia volunteers. In fact, about only one-half of that number was there, and many of the militia believed they could not be compelled to serve outside the United States. To attack Montreal was then out of the question, and instead Dearborn, in the third week of November, opted to march a limited distance into Lower Canada and establish a forward base camp for future operations. He attacked a small outpost held by some British troops and local Indians at La Cole Mill but withdrew in confusion after his regulars had fired on his militia volunteers. He then discharged the latter and went into winter camp. Thus ended the campaigns of 1812 – as the Pennsylvania congressman

Charles Jared Ingersoll later recalled – in a "miscarriage without even the heroism of disaster."[19]

V

For a war that was fought in the name of "free trade and sailors' rights," the U.S. Navy played a limited and ultimately ambiguous role. The navy had never been a favored object of Jefferson's administrations, and there was considerable controversy within Madison's cabinet over whether it should play any part in the war at all. In his November 1811 message calling for preparedness, the president barely mentioned the navy, beyond assuming that Congress might make some provision for it. Neither Eustis nor Gallatin, however, contemplated any significant contribution from the navy; indeed, the latter dismissed it as "a substantial evil" – because he could not see how it justified its costs – and this view was endorsed by the House foreign relations committee when chairman Porter called for "a public war on land and a war by private enterprise at sea."[20] In other words, the United States should make no effort to contend with the Royal Navy on the high seas, and it might do little more than allow privateers to prey on enemy commerce.

Career naval officers had long resented such attitudes, and they persuaded the secretary of the navy, Paul Hamilton of South Carolina, to submit to Congress a far more ambitious proposal that called for the construction of twelve ships of the line, to carry seventy-four guns each, and twenty frigates of thirty-eight guns each. The cost was estimated at the prohibitively high sum of $4.5 million, but a House committee, chaired by Hamilton's fellow South Carolinian Langdon Cheves, nonetheless endorsed the call for the frigates and supplemented it with requests to stockpile timber and build a dry dock to allow the navy to gain undisputed control of American territorial waters. The Jefferson administration, after 1806, had attempted to meet this last goal by the construction of 165 gunboats that could operate in shallow waters and rivers in conjunction with militia forces on land, but Cheves and Hamilton called

---

[19] Charles Jared Ingersoll, *Historical Sketch of the Second War with Great Britain* (2 vols.; Philadelphia, 1845), 1:99.
[20] For Gallatin's remark, see his memorandum to Madison, ca. 1 November 1811, *Madison Papers: Presidential Series*, 3:537; for Porter's view, see his 6 December 1811 speech in the House of Representatives (*Debates and Proceedings of the Congress of the United States, 1789–1824* (Joseph Gales, comp.; Washington, D.C., 1834–56), 12th Cong., 1st sess., 414).

for their defunding and separation from the navy altogether. This was too much for most Republican congressmen to tolerate; in response they would vote for no more than repairing the existing force and stockpiling timber.

The subject of the navy, to say nothing of a naval strategy, then languished for several weeks. The administration continued to assume that the prospect of victories on land made it unnecessary to grapple with naval issues, and any program of naval expansion, of course, would have been not only costly but also time consuming and very slow to take effect. By June 1812, however, as Congress debated the case for war, it was apparent that most of the land forces were in no position to take the offensive, thus raising the question of how the United States might be able to commence hostilities at all. It was in this context that the prospect of employing the navy in the war reemerged for more serious consideration. Some "malcontent" Republican senators, who were lukewarm supporters of the war at best, argued that the nation should attempt no more than maritime war against Great Britain (and possibly France as well), and it is possible that navy captains William Bainbridge and Charles Stewart also convinced Hamilton that it would be better to allow the fleet to sail rather than to keep it at home, either laid up in ordinary or confined merely to harbor defense. But it is more likely that the administration's financial needs were instrumental in finally opening up a role for the fleet. Still facing a shortfall in his budget and belatedly aware that a substantial number of American merchantmen would return home with cargoes in the following few weeks, Gallatin conceded that the navy could go to sea – to protect this commerce for revenue purposes and to see what else it might do.

Consequently, naval strategy for the remainder of 1812 was more a matter of improvisation than of careful calculation. Beginning in June 1812, Hamilton and the senior naval captains debated the merits of allowing the fleet to sail in small squadrons or whether vessels should operate singly or in pairs. In fact, the captains were to pursue both strategies according to circumstances, with generally satisfactory results in each case. Commodore John Rodgers, in command of a squadron of five vessels headed by the USS *President*, sailed from New York in search of an enemy convoy en route from Jamaica to Great Britain. Rodgers never found his quarry, but his actions prevented the British commander on the Halifax station, Vice Admiral Herbert Sawyer, from posting his cruisers before American ports to seize merchant vessels and cargoes returning from Europe. Most of the latter reached home safely, thereby boosting the revenue from customs. The British, in searching for Rodgers, were also unable to attack American merchantmen and consequently took very few prizes.

There were also significant accomplishments by individual officers. Isaac Hull of the USS *Constitution* (and the nephew of the commander of the Northwest Army) encountered five enemy vessels from the Halifax station, which he succeeded in evading for several days by executing the laborious tactic of kedging (dropping anchors ahead to haul his vessel over shallow waters without wind). Subsequently, in mid-August 1812, he met up with HMS *Guerrière* and disabled it so badly within thirty minutes that he had to sink it rather than take it to Boston as a prize. (It was during this engagement that a British cannonball bounced off the side of the *Constitution*, thereby immortalizing it as "Old Ironsides" in the mythology of the U.S. Navy). Two months later, in October, Stephen Decatur of the USS *United States* came across HMS *Macedonian* west of the Canary Islands. After damaging it extensively, he took it to Newport, Rhode Island, where it was recommissioned as an American vessel. And in December 1812, the *Constitution*, now under the command of Bainbridge, sank HMS *Java* off the coast of Brazil. Several smaller American naval vessels also defeated small British vessels, and American privateers, operating mainly from Bristol, Rhode Island, and Baltimore, Maryland, captured British vessels and cargoes worth nearly $2 million.

These striking American naval successes, in contrast with the failures on land, provoked much debate over the reasons that lay behind them. Americans were, understandably, elated and surprised; they attributed their success to superior virtue and seamanship. And there is no doubt that the U.S. Navy, small though it was and often starved for funds, was well trained, in part as a consequence of prior experience obtained in the Quasi-War with France and the Barbary Wars in the Mediterranean. It was also strongly motivated, whereas its British counterpart in North America tended to take too much for granted and had lost some of its edge as a result of too many years of unchallenged control of the seas. But it must also be pointed out that the Americans, vessel for vessel, were usually larger and more heavily armed than the British, thanks to the frigate designs laid down by the Philadelphia shipwright Joshua Humphreys in the 1790s. The Americans could throw a heavier weight of shot from a greater distance, and that advantage accounts for much of the damage American frigates could inflict in a short space of time. Consequently, the British, who were mortified by these setbacks, complained that the contests were unfair. How else could they explain being bested by "a few fir-built frigates, manned by a handful of bastards and outlaws?"[21] Yet despite all the controversy, these individual American victories did not alter the balance of naval power in the war – as the events of 1813 and 1814 would shortly prove.

Nor were these successes any sort of strategic or tactical equivalent for the defeats on land. It took Hull's surrender of Detroit to underscore for the administration the point Hull himself had made about the difficulties of trying to invade Canada without naval support. Up to that point the British had been able to furnish more small naval and merchant vessels on the lakes than the Americans, although the naval forces in question were manned not by officers and men from the Royal Navy but by the Provincial Marine of Upper Canada, which one historian has scorned as "little more than a transportation service under the Quartermaster-General branch of the army."[22] Consequently, it was not until the end of August 1812 that Hamilton directed Commodore Isaac Chauncey, then in command of the New York Navy Yard, to relocate to Sackett's Harbor and Buffalo with a view to building naval vessels that would give the United States command of both Lakes Erie and Ontario. He was to strip the New York Navy Yard of whatever men and equipment might be necessary for him to accomplish this task. Shortly thereafter, on 11 September, after learning of the arrival in Washington of an experienced Lake Erie mariner, Daniel Dobbins, Hamilton appointed him as a sailing master and assigned him to assist Chauncey with the construction of vessels at Presque Isle (now Erie), Pennsylvania. Two weeks later, the navy lieutenant Thomas Macdonagh was dispatched to Plattsburg, New York, on a similar mission and to aid Dearborn with whatever prospects remained for an invasion of Lower Canada.

Considering the inauspicious circumstances under which these assignments were commenced, it is remarkable they accomplished anything at all. On Lake Erie, an enterprising naval lieutenant, Jesse D. Elliott, by taking two barges manned by a mixed force of sailors and soldiers, was able to seize by surprise at night two British brigs, the *Detroit* and the *Caledonia*, near their base at Fort Erie. Dobbins, however, achieved very little. He quarreled with Elliott over the very possibility of constructing warships on Lake Erie, and he was otherwise hampered by a lack of clear

---

[21] This remark originated in the London *Evening Star* and was widely reprinted in the American press (see the New York *National Advocate*, 16 December 1812).

[22] See W. A. B. Douglas, "The Anatomy of Naval Incompetence: The Provincial Marine of the Canadas," *Ontario History* 71 (1979): 3–26.

authority to assemble his workforce and supplies. Chauncey arrived at Sackett's Harbor in the first week of October, and by tremendous exertions he did create a small fleet that, five weeks later, could chase British vessels back to their base at Kingston on the northern shore of Lake Ontario and even attempt a blockade. To that extent, the United States could be said to have obtained a tenuous control of Lake Ontario by the end of 1812. Macdonagh, at Lake Champlain, began planning to build vessels for a campaign but was unable to match the small British naval force that was already there.

None of these activities was of any military value in 1812. Neither Van Rensselaer nor Smyth nor Dearborn could turn them to advantage, and they were, moreover, commenced too late in the year to be effective. By the end of November, on Lake Ontario particularly, the winter storms and ice made water navigation all but impossible. That situation effectively favored the British. Chauncey was to pass the winter in constant fear that a well-organized force sent from Kingston across the ice would be able to destroy the preparations he had been making. That threat was enhanced by the parlous state of the American land forces along the frontier with Canada. The defeats and failures of 1812 had left the American army in too weakened a condition to be able to mount any sort of defense against a winter invasion, should it have materialized. For the future, the United States would have to find better ways of coordinating land and naval forces than it had in 1812.

3

1813

I

In his annual message to Congress on 4 November 1812, Madison put the best interpretation he could on the events of the previous five months, notably by drawing attention "to the providential favors which our Country has experienced, in the unusual degree of health dispensed to its inhabitants, and in the rich abundance with which the Earth has rewarded the labors bestowed on it." As he did so, he admitted that the loss of Detroit had been "painful" and that the outcome of Van Rensselaer's Niagara campaign was "deeply to be lamented." Naturally enough, the president could be more positive in praising his naval officers for giving the American flag "an auspicious triumph" in their encounters with the enemy's frigates; and for the enemy he had only harsh words of condemnation, both for Great Britain's failure to offer a negotiated settlement to the war and for using the Indians – "that wretched portion of the human race" – as allies. For the future Madison promised a "vigorous prosecution" of the war, including filling the ranks of the military establishments, reforming their staff departments, raising the pay of enlisted men, establishing "auxiliary" forces for frontier defense, and enlarging the navy, both on the Great Lakes and on the high seas.[1]

This was easier said than done. Congress was not blind to the need for change, but its members had no confidence the cabinet could manage it, and in December pressure from the legislators compelled both Eustis and Hamilton to tender their resignations. Madison struggled to find their

---

[1] For the message, see *Madison Papers: Presidential Series*, 5:427–33.

replacements. Monroe was willing to step into the War Department, but after listening to advice from his son-in-law that a capable administrator could only lay the foundations for a victory that would be credited to a general, he hesitated. He told Madison he would take the War Department on a temporary basis only, almost certainly in the hope that he would later enter the army and become that general. The president then offered the position to Dearborn and Senator William Harris Crawford of Georgia, respectively. After they had both declined, Gallatin pointed out that the vacancy should be filled by a New Yorker, a consideration that narrowed the field to Governor Tompkins, who was seeking reelection to a third term, and John Armstrong, the U.S. minister to France between 1804 and 1810. On purely personal grounds Tompkins was the better choice, but it seemed unwise to remove him from Albany and risk his being replaced by a Federalist in the upcoming state elections. Armstrong was a more controversial figure. In 1783 he had come close to inciting the Continental Army to mutiny in a series of disputes over how to compensate its officers, and more recently, it had been rumored that the reason for his return from France in 1810 was to organize opposition to Madison's reelection in 1812. The former diplomat, however, had supported both the president and the war. And as an old officer who regarded himself an expert on military affairs, he was also willing to accept a cabinet post. Replacing Hamilton was more straightforward. Madison offered the Navy Department to William Jones, a Philadelphia merchant who could easily claim more familiarity with maritime matters than his predecessor.

As Madison reconstructed his cabinet, Monroe and Gallatin established the parameters within which the campaigns of 1813 would be fought. Both secretaries realized that in future it would not be sufficient for the United States to concentrate on offensive operations while neglecting problems of defense. The defeats of 1812, coupled with the realization that Great Britain might wage a more aggressive war than it had done so far, mandated comprehensive planning for defense. Monroe accepted Gallatin's suggestion that the nation be divided into nine military districts, each with its own body of regulars and an adequately staffed commanding officer who would coordinate defensive measures in conjunction with state governors and their militias. That plan would employ at least ten thousand regulars from the army, thereby creating a shortfall in the numbers that would be available for offensive operations. And Monroe's plans for the offensive were not modest. He wanted not only to retake the ground that had been lost in 1812 but also to occupy within the year all of Canada between Fort Malden and Halifax. He even contemplated the occupation of East Florida, on the grounds that the Spanish Regency in Cádiz would probably allow its British ally to use the territory as a base for attacks against the United States.

For all this Monroe reckoned he might need another thirty-five thousand men (thus creating, on paper, a regular army seventy thousand strong), but he also knew that this would overstrain the budget. He therefore proposed that the volunteer laws of 1812 – which had proved unworkable because the War Department lacked the power to control the men they raised – be replaced by an act to allow the president to raise twenty thousand troops in the states adjacent to Canada for one year's service. This was still too much for Gallatin, who declared that the $24 million he estimated as the cost for these schemes was excessive and risked destroying confidence in the public credit. Monroe accepted the Treasury's limitation and amended his plan to raise for one year only that number of troops, not exceeding twenty thousand, which would be necessary to fill the existing establishments. The measure passed into law in January 1813, as did bills to raise the pay of enlisted men to $8 per month, along with increases in the bounties and premiums offered to both enlisted men and the officers who recruited them.

The future direction of naval policy proved more complicated. Before he resigned in December 1812, Hamilton – under heavy pressure created by widespread criticism of his well-known drinking problem – had repeated the calls he made a year earlier for a very substantial increase in the oceangoing fleet, claiming that more frigates would protect both commerce and the coasts. In so arguing, he seemed to be oblivious to the need to expand naval construction on the Great Lakes, and his proposal was too costly for Congress anyway. The Senate reduced it by passing a bill to construct only ten additional vessels at a cost of $2.5 million, but this was still too much for most Republicans in the House. They refused to tax their constituents for a program from which they would derive no benefit. The bill only became law when a minority of House Republicans broke with the majority to join with a solid block of Federalists in its support. Gallatin then tried to urge further cost-cutting measures on Jones as he took up his duties, but his efforts revealed that there were limits to economies in expenditure that could not be achieved without ending the war itself. Jones, too, desired the construction of more frigates, and the most he would consider was the abolition of the gunboat division along with reforms in departmental administrative practices.

Gallatin was worried primarily about the escalating costs of the war. Even if the military and naval establishments of 1812 were not expanded, the secretary believed that he would have to find nearly $20 million more than the anticipated revenues for 1813. His means for doing so were limited until he was able to grasp at an unexpected windfall in government receipts. The nation had received a flood of imports in 1812, after Great Britain had repealed the Orders in Council. The importers, believing there would be no war, had acted in good faith, but legally their cargoes were forfeit under the nonintercourse policy imposed in 1811. To confiscate these goods now would cause much resentment in mercantile and banking circles, but to remit the penalties of the law would allow these same groups to make enormous profits in a market starved for British goods. Gallatin therefore proposed that he might raise $10 million from doubling duties on the imports in return for the importers lending the government the equivalent of one-third of their value. That would leave him to raise a balance of about $9.5 million from loans and treasury notes, a task not too dissimilar from the one he had accomplished in 1812. And if successful, it would also allow the administration to postpone recourse to direct taxation, a step that was still extremely unpopular in Congress.

This policy required legislation to remit the penalties of nonimportation, but Republicans in Congress quarreled over the expediency and morality of passing it. In the House it proved impossible to form a majority for either remitting or enforcing the penalties, whereas the Senate could agree only on a bill to remit the penalties altogether. This bill eventually passed the House, but as had been the case with naval policy, it did so only after a minority of Republicans joined with the Federalists against a majority of their fellow partisans. Its passage required Gallatin to raise $21 million in revenue, nearly twice as much as he had initially calculated. That sum would require the imposition of war taxes, and Congress would have to meet in an extra session over the coming summer to pass the necessary legislation. But, worst of all, it revealed that the Republicans in Congress could no longer form stable coalitions to support the war and its policies.

All these matters were vexing the administration before it could grapple with the problem of what sort of diplomatic and military strategies might lead to a successful conclusion to the war. On that front there were few grounds for optimism. Because the Orders in Council had already been repealed, it would be difficult for the administration to insist that they be permanently outlawed in a peace treaty, and the British ministry itself was in no mood, and under little pressure, to make further concessions to the

United States. Had Napoleon succeeded with his 1812 invasion of Russia, it would not have been implausible to suppose, as Madison did, that Great Britain and its navy would have been subjected to enormous difficulties in coping with an enemy who would have almost total domination over the European continent. The news from Europe in early 1813 suggested, however, not merely that Napoleon had failed but also that, after losing five hundred thousand men in eastern Europe, he was facing a disaster of epic proportions, unlike any other that had occurred since the resumption of the European wars in 1803.

That change in the European balance of power raised the question of whether a dispute over impressment alone would sustain American support for the war. To answer it, the administration proposed in January 1813 the so-called Seamen's Bill – a seemingly simple solution for an otherwise intractable problem that required the United States to exclude foreign-born seamen from its merchant marine in return for Great Britain renouncing the "right" to impress from neutral vessels on the high seas. The idea was not a new one; it had been put forward in the past, and Great Britain had not responded positively. But for both domestic and diplomatic reasons, the administration needed to find justifications for continuing the conflict by redefining the issues at stake. Congress accordingly debated the measure for much of February 1813. The bill passed the House, but again by a coalition of Republicans and Federalists, with more than thirty Republicans in opposition, most of them strong supporters of the war who regarded it as a needlessly weak concession to the enemy for its tacit admission that the United States should not exercise the sovereign power of naturalizing foreign-born mariners. In the Senate, the voting reproduced the long-standing divisions among administration supporters, "malcontent" Republicans, and Federalists that had done so much to hobble war preparations in 1812.

That the war was even less popular by the spring of 1813 than it had been in June 1812 was reflected in the response to the loans floated by Gallatin in February. Seeking $16 million, the Treasury received barely $3.75 million. By March the situation was so desperate that Gallatin informed Madison that there were scarcely enough funds to carry on the government for a month, let alone a year, and he hinted that military operations should be postponed until the finances were on a firmer footing. The secretary had also approached some wealthy financiers, mostly notably the fur trader and merchant John Jacob Astor, about the possibility of forming a consortium to borrow $10 million (the sum he had originally proposed to raise in exchange for the remission of the penalties for nonimportation). Astor replied that the government interest rate of 6 percent was too low to be attractive and that investment in the war was a bad prospect anyway when the chances for American success seemed so remote. The best Astor could suggest was that Gallatin might charter a new Bank of the United States – an idea that was bound to offend many Republicans – and borrow $30 million from it to carry on.

Gallatin was reluctant to accept such advice. He was saved from having to do so by the fortuitous intervention of Alexander I of Russia. Facing a French invasion in 1812, the Russian emperor had no desire to see his British ally divert resources across the Atlantic to Canada, and certainly not when the emperor also had considerable sympathy for Madison's position in the Anglo-American dispute over neutral rights. In September 1812, therefore, he presented himself as an honest broker between Great Britain and the United States and offered to mediate a settlement. The offer reached Washington at the end of February 1813, and Madison had accepted it by 8 March. If nothing else, the mediation opened up the prospect of a decent withdrawal from the war on terms that could be better than the military performance of the United States would have otherwise justified. Moreover, the administration had just redefined its terms for peace in the Seamen's Bill, and some members of the cabinet, notably Monroe, even remained willing to believe that the United States would succeed with its invasions of Canada in 1813. That optimism did not mean that the administration sought Canadian territory as a goal of the war. In drawing up instructions for the mediation, Monroe did not exclude the possibility that Great Britain might transfer Upper Canada to the United States, but he stressed that the restoration of peace would not require the cession of Canadian territory if Great Britain was reasonable in settling the disputes over maritime rights. The American mediators – to meet in St. Petersburg – would necessarily be headed by the minister to Russia, John Quincy Adams. He was to be assisted by Senator James A. Bayard of Delaware – a Federalist who could testify that the administration was acting in good faith – as well as by Gallatin himself, who was by then weary of his administrative duties after twelve years in Washington.

Gallatin also sought the appointment to Russia because the mediation allowed him to solve the problems of financing the war for the coming year. After news of the offer had arrived and after raising the government interest rate to 7.5 percent, Gallatin persuaded Astor to lend $2.5 million to the Treasury, and two other financiers, David Parish, who had extensive land investments on the New York–Canadian frontier, and Stephen Girard, a Philadelphia banker and merchant, agreed to provide another $8 million. These financiers received a handsome discount for their money – they had to pay only $0.88 on the dollar – but the war was funded for the year. And Gallatin was more than willing to testify to Alexander I that the United States sincerely sought an honorable end to the war. As the campaigns of 1813 commenced, therefore, the prospects for their success seemed rather brighter than they had done only two months earlier, but these hopes rested on slender bases. It was by no means certain that the United States could recover the ground it had lost in the Northwest, much less make significant inroads into Lower Canada. And the administration remained weak at home and had no more than a year in which to achieve its goals in an international environment that had come to favor British interests more than it did American ones.

II

Serious planning for the campaigns of 1813 started when Armstrong took up his War Department duties on 5 February. Within three days he had seized the initiative from Gallatin and Monroe by presenting a note to the cabinet. The new secretary realized that the army would be in no condition to attack Montreal by the spring, seemingly leaving him with a choice between remaining on the defensive for a long period or attempting a more limited goal. Armstrong opted for the latter – in the form of an assault on the British naval base at Kingston, to be followed by supplemental operations against York and Fort George. The proposal had its merits. It promised to give the United States naval control of Lake Ontario by the spring, and it would sever enemy lines of communication between Upper and Lower Canada. There was also the additional, if unspoken, advantage that an early American victory could have a beneficial outcome on the spring elections in New York, a state Madison had failed to carry in the presidential election of 1812. Consequently, the cabinet approved the note, and Armstrong instructed Dearborn, who remained in command for the lack of an alternative, to gather four thousand men at Sackett's Harbor for the attack on Kingston and three thousand at Buffalo for the operations against York and on the Niagara Peninsula.

Having laid out his strategy, Armstrong allowed himself to be diverted from it, largely in response to representations from Chauncey and Dearborn, who believed that the British position at Kingston was extremely strong – so strong in fact that they feared an enemy assault on their own naval base at Sackett's Harbor – and that it would be better to take York and Fort George before risking more at Kingston. The secretary acquiesced but reminded Dearborn of the importance of ensuring that the first encounter with the enemy should be a successful one, "the good effects [of which would] be felt throughout the campaign."[2] Armstrong also underlined the political considerations behind this decision by arranging that the troops employed would be drawn from Maryland, New England, and Pennsylvania rather than from New York, so that New York troops could be sure of turning out at the election. Otherwise, the preparations went reasonably smoothly. Sizable purchases of local produce and supplies by quartermasters and army contractors eased potential discontent among New York farmers who had worried about the economic disruptions occasioned by the war. The troops were ready by early April, and once Lake Ontario was free of ice, the army departed for York on 23 April, four days before the polls opened for the spring election, in which the Republican Tompkins was reelected as governor.

The campaign started well. York, although the provincial capital, was not strongly fortified, and its commander, Major General Sheaffe, had barely seven hundred men of all descriptions – regulars, militia, dockworkers, and a few Indian allies – to defend it against more than twice that number of Americans, who arrived on sixteen vessels from Chauncey's fleet on 26 April. Armstrong had encouraged Dearborn to command any attack in person, but the general preferred to immerse himself in staff work while complaining of various ailments at the same time. Dearborn turned the task of leading the assault over to Brigadier General Zebulon Montgomery Pike, one of the army's more enterprising officers, who had already won fame as an explorer. Aided by fire from Chauncey's schooners, the Americans encountered relatively little resistance as they came on shore on 27 April, especially after the British suffered a number of casualties from an accident that also destroyed one of the two small batteries defending the approach to York. Realizing he was badly outnumbered, Sheaffe gave orders to withdraw toward Burlington Heights, Ontario, and to blow up the Government House in the course of doing so. As Pike pressed his advantage, he was killed when the British magazine, with two hundred barrels of gunpowder and other munitions, exploded. The Americans thus took York – albeit briefly – but the enemy escaped in the confusion surrounding the explosion. And although the Americans lost few troops in the fighting itself, the explosion, which killed 38

[2] Armstrong to Dearborn, 29 March 1813, Letters Sent Relating to Military Affairs.

and wounded 222, raised their total casualties in the operation to nearly one-fifth of their force.

To the east, a number of factors conspired to delay the attack on Fort George for another month. Among them were bad weather, a lack of suitable winds for sailing, outbreaks of sickness among the troops, difficulties in communication between Chauncey and Dearborn, and the time consumed in Chauncey's moving additional forces from Sackett's Harbor to the western end of Lake Ontario. By 25 May, some 4,700 men had been concentrated to the east of the American post of Fort Niagara, with a view to moving them to Fort George and attacking it from the rear. To defend the fort, Brigadier General John Vincent had about 1,500 men, most of them regulars, supplemented by 300 militiamen and a small detachment of Indians under John Norton. American artillery had already commenced a destructive bombardment of Fort George on 25 May, and two days later Colonel Winfield Scott led ashore a combined force of artillery, infantry, riflemen, marines, and naval vessels. After two assaults they overwhelmed the British, who could withstand neither the heavy artillery and naval fire nor the American superiority in numbers. Vincent accordingly ordered the garrison at Fort George to spike its guns, to blow up the magazine and stores, and to retreat toward Beaver Dams (about eighteen miles northwest of Queenston).

Scott prepared to pursue the enemy but was prevented from doing so by his superior officers, Brigadier Generals John Boyd and Morgan Lewis, who, along with Dearborn, feared he might be ambushed and defeated by the British and their Indian allies. The Americans thus won only a local victory at Fort George, at the cost of allowing Vincent to escape. Had he been captured, the British could not have replaced his force; the Americans would have achieved a more secure footing on the Niagara Peninsula and thereby avoided the loss of their tenuous grasp in the region later in the year. In Washington, Armstrong was quick to realize the implications of this failure, and he reprimanded Dearborn by pointing out that "battles are not gained when an inferior and broken enemy is not *destroyed*."[3] And to underscore just how limited the American control of Lake Ontario was, while Chauncey was moving troops out of Sackett's Harbor, the British commanders at Kingston – Sir George Prevost and Commodore Sir James Lucas Yeo RN (one of a number of naval officers the British moved in to replace the Canadian provincial marine) – launched an attack on the American naval base on 29 May. The Americans, including a local

[3] Armstrong to Dearborn, 19 June 1813, Letters Sent Relating to Military Affairs.

militia force commanded by Jacob Jennings Brown, blunted the attack, after which Yeo broke it off, apparently because he feared that the cost of failure in its pursuit would be too high; it would leave Kingston almost completely defenseless.

After the escape of the British army from Fort George, Dearborn became depressed and fell seriously ill. His moods, to say nothing of his lethargy, annoyed his fellow officers, some of whom began to agitate for his removal. In a belated effort to remedy his failure to pursue the enemy, Dearborn, in the first week of June 1813, dispatched Brigadier Generals John Chandler and William Winder, along with about 2,500 troops – a force rather larger than that commanded by Vincent – to round up the British on the northwestern shore of Lake Ontario. On 5 June they encountered a detachment of Vincent's army at Stoney Creek – about fifty miles west of Fort George – and drove it from the field in a brief skirmish, after which they encamped for the night. Chandler attempted to take precautions against a night attack, but instead of arranging his troops in battle formation, he divided them into three sections and failed to ensure that their campfires were extinguished. Although outnumbered, Vincent's second in command, Lieutenant Colonel John Harvey, took 750 men on a night raid, which succeeded in penetrating the American lines. In the course of a chaotic encounter, the British captured the American artillery as well as Chandler and Winder, who had become confused about how to locate and rally their own men.

Mortified, the Americans retired to Fort George, where they remained cooped up by British and Indian raiding parties operating to their west. At the same time, the morale and the numbers of the men in the fort began to decline from widespread sickness, produced by a combination of unusually wet summer weather and the consumption of contaminated provisions. Their officers, too, had their grievances, especially against Armstrong's promotion policies, which elevated and reassigned them without regard for their assumptions about rising through the workings of the seniority system. In protest, large numbers of officers in the lower grades at Fort George resigned their commissions. In an attempt to break out of these deteriorating conditions, Boyd, in the third week of June, ordered Lieutenant Colonel Charles Boerstler, with nearly six hundred men, to drive the enemy raiding parties off the Niagara Peninsula, but he was ambushed at Beaver Dams on 24 June by a party of Kanawake Indians who had been sent to Upper Canada from the Montreal region by the British Indian Department. Boerstler, running low on ammunition and fearing the prospect of a massacre, decided to surrender. In doing so, he gave the Indian allies of the British their most important victory over American troops in the war.

This fiasco was the last straw for Dearborn's campaign. Throughout these unfortunate proceedings, the general, writing from his sickbed, pleaded the difficulty of his circumstances – the sickness of the troops, the weather, the resignations of the officers – as extenuations for his lack of decisive results. But after Beaver Dams, even Dearborn's supporters gave up on him. Deputations of frustrated officers and angry congressmen waited on the War Department to demand that Dearborn be relieved, and given the state of the general's health alone, Madison was in no position to resist. He therefore consented to Armstrong's ordering Dearborn into retirement on 6 July, while the secretary, who by then had to abandon his hopes for an attack on Kingston, ordered the army to remain on the defensive and take no further risks. The only exception he allowed here was in the event of Chauncey winning a decisive victory over Yeo for the naval control of Lake Ontario. But Chauncey, too, had adopted the same defensive attitude. He spent the remainder of the summer of 1813 trying to prepare for a great battle that he was never able to initiate.

III

While Dearborn's campaign was running its course, the administration had to consider how to resume the offensive in the Northwest, where Harrison's forces remained encamped at Fort Meigs. Armstrong had little respect for Harrison – dismissing him on one occasion as an "artificial general" raised to high rank by public opinion rather than by merit – and he was no more enthusiastic about how the general had managed his affairs over the previous fall and winter.[4] The general's efforts to assemble large forces on land had proved both unreliable and too costly, and even before Gallatin had imposed a limit on all War Department expenditures of $1.4 million per month, Armstrong realized that they would have to be curtailed. Accordingly, in March 1813 he offered Harrison one of the six major generalships in the new army of twenty thousand men to be raised in the coming year. Acceptance of the offer would restrict the freedom of action Harrison had enjoyed as a major general in the Kentucky militia and make him directly accountable to administration priorities. Armstrong followed the promotion with an abrupt order directing

---

[4] See Armstrong to William Duane, 16 March 1813, "Selections from the Duane Papers," *Historical Magazine*, 2d ser., 4 (1868), 62.

Harrison to hold fast at Fort Meigs pending the construction of an army base at Cleveland and the building of a fleet at Presque Isle to attack Fort Malden by water. To supervise the former, he dispatched the army captain Thomas Sidney Jesup to Cleveland, and to assist Dobbins with the latter, Master Commandant Oliver Hazard Perry was sent to Presque Isle. Finally, Armstrong wished to prevent an undue reliance on militia volunteers, so he limited Kentucky's quota in the new twenty-thousand-man force to merely one regiment.

Harrison relished the promotion but not his orders. He could hardly deny that naval control on Lake Erie would be of value in a campaign, yet he also wished to preserve the preparations he had already made, in case such control never materialized. Moreover, he was alarmed by the possibility that Cleveland might replace Fort Meigs as the main base for the army. What was at stake here was that, if Cleveland should be preferred over Fort Meigs and the headwaters of the Maumee River, not only would all of Harrison's previous efforts be slighted, but also significant areas of the western states and territories could be exposed to future attacks by the British and the Indians. That consideration, as Harrison well knew, would carry most weight in Ohio and Kentucky, whose governors were already complaining that the administration was not doing enough to protect the frontiers. Harrison reinforced these complaints by pointing out that the War Department was overconfident about the army's ability to raise regular troops in the Northwest; large numbers of "auxiliaries" would also be necessary, he declared, both to ensure victory and to maintain public confidence in the war.[5]

Armstrong stood his ground. He minimized the dangers from the British and the Indians, claiming that they were in no position to take the offensive in the spring. Nor did he believe that large numbers of troops were necessary to take Fort Malden. Control of Lake Erie could accomplish that more effectively, but Armstrong became so angry in arguing these matters with Harrison that he neglected to respond to the general's point about where his army would be based. Not until May did he make it clear that he did not intend to remove the troops to Cleveland and that troop transports would follow an American fleet either to Sandusky or to the headwaters of the Maumee to pick up the men there. Reluctantly, Harrison acquiesced; and he waited while Perry constructed brigs and sloops at Presque Isle for an American naval force on Lake Erie. But Harrison was right about the difficulties of raising regulars in the Northwest.

[5] Harrison to Armstrong, 28 March 1813, *Letters and Messages of Harrison*, 2:404–6.

Army recruiting was sluggish, as young men were unwilling to commit to long terms of service, and even after the pay for enlisted men had been increased, it still remained uncompetitive with the wages laborers could receive elsewhere. Harrison was also right about dangers from the British and the Indians. On two occasions, in May and July 1813, they tried to drive the Northwest Army from Fort Meigs, but Harrison had anticipated the attacks and dealt with them in his own way, usually by relying on locally raised volunteers to a greater extent than the War Department would have liked.

Consequently, by the end of July, when Perry was ready to embark his fleet on Lake Erie, Armstrong's plans for a better-organized land force in the Northwest had not materialized. At that point, Harrison had barely 2,500 regulars at his disposal, and it was necessary for him to call for more militia and volunteers. Representative Richard M. Johnson of Kentucky, who had raised a force of 1,200 mounted riflemen earlier in the spring, was more than willing to attach them to the Northwest Army, and Harrison then called on the governors of Kentucky and Ohio for additional troops to make up the force of 7,000 that the War Department would allow. Few of these men would come from Ohio – because Harrison and Meigs were unable to agree on the terms of payment for their services – but Governor Isaac Shelby of Kentucky, a hero of the Battle of King's Mountain during the Revolutionary War, personally volunteered to lead five thousand men to the headwaters of the Maumee River. In fact, he was only to raise 3,500 and they were hardly a well-organized or well-disciplined force. Even Madison, from his summer retreat at Montpelier, began to worry about the accumulating expenses of such volunteer militia to the United States, predicting that unless they won some "conspicuous successes," they would become a topic of "great animadversion" and the source of much "fiscal embarrassment."[6] Nevertheless, by such ad hoc means, Harrison was able to assemble a force of seven thousand men throughout August 1813.

During that interval Perry jostled with his British counterpart, Commodore Robert H. Barclay RN, for position on Lake Erie before finally engaging him at the Battle of Put-in-Bay on 10 September. This was a five-hour encounter – an unusually long one by the standards of the time – in which the Americans enjoyed a slight advantage in the number of vessels (nine to six) and a greater one in the weight of shot they could throw (1,528 pounds to 883 pounds). But much would depend on how closely

---

[6] Madison to James Monroe, 19 August 1813, *Madison Papers: Presidential Series*, 6:543.

the two fleets could engage and which one held the weather gauge – the position of one vessel being upwind from another – before these factors could prove decisive. Perry won the weather gauge, but both fleets suffered considerable damage. The British battered Perry's flagship the USS *Lawrence* to such an extent that he decided midway through the battle to abandon it and relocate himself on the USS *Niagara* under the command of Jesse D. Elliott (who had already won renown on the lake the previous fall). To this point, Elliott had hardly attacked the enemy at all, because he was unwilling to break the line of battle to do so, and his apparent caution here was to become a source of great acrimony between him and Perry in the future. Perry was nonetheless able to attack the center of the British line and do such extensive damage to its two largest vessels – HMS *Detroit* and the *Queen Charlotte* – that Barclay had to surrender. Perry then scrawled a hasty note to Harrison: "We have met the enemy and they are ours: Two ships, two Brigs, one Schooner, and one Sloop."[7]

Two weeks later, Perry transported Harrison's army to the Canadian shore to the south of Fort Malden, where the British commander, Henry Proctor – who had been promoted to major general after his success at the river Raisin – concluded he could no longer retain either Fort Malden or Detroit. He was badly outnumbered, although he still had a sizable force of Indian allies – at least one thousand – in whom he had little confidence and even less ability to supply. Some of the Indians, principally the Chippewa, Ottawa, and Wyandot, were beginning to defect. Proctor therefore abandoned his positions on 27 September and retreated around the northern shore of Lake Erie, finding as he did so that the Indians were reluctant to follow suit. Some seventy miles from Detroit, he paused at the river Thames, and Harrison, on 2 October, set out after him with a force consisting largely of Johnson's and Shelby's Kentucky volunteers. Proctor's situation was untenable. He needed to join up with other British forces at the head of Lake Ontario, but Tecumseh and the Indians were unwilling to go beyond the Thames. The British-Indian alliance, which had been vital to the defense of Upper Canada, was unraveling from the inability of its parties to reconcile their differing needs. Proctor, nevertheless, decided to make a stand at Moraviantown on the Thames. The encounter was a brief one, no more than

---

[7] See Oliver Hazard Perry to Harrison, 10 September 1813, *The Naval War of 1812: A Documentary History* (3 vols. to date, William S. Dudley et al., eds.; Washington, 1985–), 2:553.

forty-five minutes, and it was decided when the Kentucky mounted volunteers broke through the British and Indian lines with the British being unable to fire more than a single volley in response. During the battle Tecumseh was killed, although whether by Johnson, as some witnesses claimed, is impossible to settle conclusively. But with his death, the power of the confederated Indians in the Northwest was broken, forever, as it proved. And the United States had regained the ground lost by Hull in 1812.

IV

The victories of Harrison and Perry in the Northwest certainly altered the balance of power there in favor of the United States, but they had relatively little impact on developments further to the east. British positions of greater strategic consequence had still to be taken and the means to do so found. It was for that purpose that Madison summoned an early session of the Thirteenth Congress to Washington in the last week of May. The session might have been a short one. There were only two items on the agenda – the passage of tax bills to finance the war and the Senate confirmation of the nominations of Bayard and Gallatin to the mediation in St. Petersburg. However, the session proved to be quite lengthy, nearly ten weeks. By its conclusion, the administration, although it had obtained much of what it desired, had also suffered some setbacks, all of which undermined the precarious foundations on which the war effort rested.

The nominations for the Russian mediation, to which Madison added a request for the appointment of Jonathan Russell (the American chargé d'affaires in London before the declaration of war) as minister to Sweden, were sent in on 31 May. Three days later, Jones, who was to be acting secretary of the treasury during Gallatin's absence, forwarded to the House a report on the finances, including a list of nine direct and indirect taxes that Gallatin regarded as essential to balance the budget and maintain the government's credit in 1814. As the House Ways and Means Committee began deliberating, the Federalists, strengthened by their recent electoral victories, seized the initiative. Led by Daniel Webster of New Hampshire, who was at the beginning of his long career in national politics, they launched an examination into the grounds on which Madison had justified his recourse to war. Their pretext was the publication in the United States of the so-called Decree of St. Cloud, bearing the date of 28 April 1811, in which Napoleon had announced the "definitive" repeal of his Berlin and Milan decrees. The document bore all the hallmarks of

a postdated fraud – it had not been sighted in London, Paris, or Washington before May 1812 – but it embarrassed the administration, as Madison
had previously based his demand for the removal of the Orders in Council
on the repeal of the French decrees as outlined in the Cadore letter of 5
August 1810.

Webster's attack took the form of five resolutions requiring the administration to release correspondence on all aspects of the publication of the
Decree of St. Cloud and inquiring whether it had ever demanded an
explanation from France for its conduct toward the United States after
August 1810. The president could hardly answer without incriminating
both himself and the French emperor, nor could he refuse to answer
without suggesting that he had something to hide. Monroe sat on the
resolutions for as long as he could before denying that the State Department had received any information about the St. Cloud document before
May 1812. He followed this denial with a long and complicated report
on Anglo-American and Franco-American relations as they bore on the
coming of the war. Its arguments were frequently tortuous, but essentially
the secretary of state asserted that the case for war against Great Britain
stood on its own merits, regardless of if or when France had repealed
its antineutral decrees. He also maintained that France, nevertheless, had
repealed its decrees in August 1810. The debate dragged on through
mid-July, and the Republicans could not even agree among themselves
on whether to support a resolution approving Madison's diplomacy as
described in Monroe's report. They thus left the grounds and the purposes
of the war, as the Federalist senator Rufus King remarked, in a state of
"great obscurity."[8]

As the House concentrated on Webster's resolutions, the Senate opened
an attack on the effort to end the war through the Russian mediation.
Opposition senators requested the correspondence on the acceptance of
the offer of Alexander I and inquired whether and how Gallatin might
perform his Treasury Department duties while in Europe. Republicans
declined to support the call for the Russian correspondence, but they
were willing to investigate Gallatin. They also agreed to another request
for information surrounding the circumstances of Russell's nomination to
Sweden. Madison declined to cooperate, responding that Gallatin would
remain in the Treasury even as Jones performed his duties for him in

---

[8] For King's notes and memoranda on the first session of the 13th Congress, see *The Life
and Correspondence of Rufus King* (6 vols., Charles R. King, ed.; New York, 1894–1900),
5:337.

Washington; but the president did release letters confirming that the court of Sweden had suggested an exchange of ministers. The administration, it can be presumed, agreed to the proposal in the belief that additional diplomatic representation in the Baltic region would strengthen its case in the Russian mediation. The Senate was not satisfied. Some of its members sought meetings with Madison, but on 15 June the president fell seriously ill with an attack of "bilious fever." For several weeks he was unable to attend to his duties and reports circulated that he was near death.

The president's opponents did not wait on his recovery. As he fell ill, they resolved that Gallatin's Treasury duties were "incompatible" with those of a diplomat, and in early July they voted that it was "inexpedient" to send a minister to Sweden. Contributing greatly to these outcomes was the intensity of the debate over taxes. The House Ways and Means Committee reported recommendations for Gallatin's tax bills, totaling $6.365 million, on 26 June, but its chairman, John Wayles Eppes of Virginia, a son-in-law of Thomas Jefferson, declined to support them in debate. He denounced the measures as no better than the controversial taxes levied by the Federalists in the Quasi-War of 1798–1800 and pointed out that they had not been apportioned according to the provisions of the Constitution. Other committee members followed Eppes's lead, with the result that by mid-July the Republicans had become so divided that it was necessary to call an emergency party caucus to sort the quarrels out. The caucus did not produce a clear consensus, but Republicans thereafter began to vote for the taxes, if for no other reason than a grudging awareness that they had no better alternative. After the taxes were passed, the Senate finally rejected, by one vote, Gallatin's nomination to Russia.

These outcomes, especially in the Senate, were the culmination of several years of factional infighting within the Republican Party. But some embarrassment, especially that relating to Gallatin, might have been avoided if the president had been in better health or able to be more flexible. There was an implied bargain in the Senate's behavior to the effect that Gallatin might go to Russia if he relinquished the Treasury. And Gallatin had no desire to retain his cabinet position, although he had failed to make that clear to the president. In that sense Madison suffered a needless defeat. And he continued to try the loyalty of his supporters. The day after Gallatin's rejection, Madison requested from Congress an embargo on American exports. He had, of course, always been a strong believer in the value of economic coercion, but there were also other considerations in play. Commercial and naval developments along the

Atlantic coast were not going as well for the United States as they had
in 1812. The only major encounter of the summer between an American
and a British frigate – the 1 June engagement between HMS *Shannon*
and USS *Chesapeake* off Boston – was a British victory, in less than fifteen minutes. The Royal Navy had also commenced a blockade along the
coast south of New England, but its presence did not dissuade Americans
from trading with the enemy, both in Canada and off the shores.

Even worse, British forces were looting and raiding in the Chesapeake
region, including an attack on the village of Hampton, Virginia, that had
culminated in a much-publicized series of rapes of local women. Madison wished to curtail these activities, and he also sought to discourage
British governors in the West Indies from granting special licenses to
American merchants to bring their cargoes into the Caribbean to supply
the plantations of the British West Indian colonies. The House passed the
embargo, but the Senate defeated it, largely through the efforts of the long-
established alliance between the Federalists and some "malcontent"
Republicans. The administration was annoyed but it was not to be
deflected. On 29 July the secretary of the navy issued orders to all vessels
to interdict trade with the enemy, in the hope of achieving the benefits of
an embargo by these means.

But these measures could not conceal the reality that the larger international context continued to shift in ways that did not favor American
policy. By August 1813 it was known unofficially in Washington that
Great Britain had declined the Russian mediation. The ministry's reasons
went beyond its suspicion that Alexander I did not favor British notions
about maritime rights; the more important reality was that the power of
their mutual enemy, France, was clearly on the wane. Even as Napoleon
rebuilt his armies after the losses of 1812, he could no longer inflict defeats
on his enemies in central Europe in the manner he had done previously,
as the outcomes of the Battles of Bautzen and Lützen in May 1813 indicated. The French emperor claimed them as victories, but he suffered
more casualties than his Prussian and Russian opponents, and he was
even constrained to accept a brief armistice as a preliminary to more general peace negotiations that might be held in Prague. Just as serious was
the defeat of the French armies in Spain at the Battle of Vitoria in June.
The British forces in the Iberian Peninsula, under the Duke of Wellington,
were now able to threaten an invasion of France itself. Monroe professed
hopes that a Franco-Russian peace would advance American efforts to
obtain greater international recognition for its neutral rights, but this was
shallow optimism indeed. It would still be up to the United States to see

how much of Lower Canada it could occupy in the remainder of the campaign.

V

Armstrong's plans to attack Montreal in 1813 looked devious. In early March, before Dearborn's campaign had even started, he summoned to Washington a comrade in arms from the days of the Revolution, Brigadier General James Wilkinson, and suggested that together they might "renew the scene of Saratoga."[9] The imagery was hardly appropriate – the point of a successful campaign would not be to defeat an invading British army on American soil – and Wilkinson was not the obvious choice to accomplish it, even though Armstrong offered him promotion to the rank of major general. He had been the ranking general in the army for several years, but he had never commanded a force in battle, and no thought had been given to the possibility that he might have done so in 1812. Moreover, his reputation had long been clouded by rumors that he was an agent in the pay of Spain; by his ambiguous conduct throughout the Burr conspiracy of 1806–1807; and by a court martial in 1811 in which he was doubtfully acquitted of negligence in the loss of more than one thousand troops to disease near New Orleans in the summer of 1809. There was, therefore, no reason to suspect that Wilkinson would be an able and inspiring leader of men.

Later in the spring, Armstrong formed some notions about strategy that would shape his conduct for the remainder of the year. Assuming that Great Britain would lose its positions on the Niagara Peninsula, he concluded the enemy would then be faced with a choice between defending Kingston at all costs or of abandoning it in favor of withdrawing to Montreal. In the former case, Armstrong believed the United States should sever communications between Kingston and Montreal by sending an army across the St. Lawrence River at some point between Ogdensburg and the eastern end of Lake Ontario and storm the British base from the rear, in conjunction with naval forces. In the latter, the secretary held out the prospect of bypassing Kingston altogether and attacking Montreal directly, either by approaching the city from a route leading north from Lake Champlain or by moving down the St. Lawrence to attack the right flank of the force defending it, as Lord Jeffrey Amherst had done in 1760.

[9] Armstrong to James Wilkinson, 12 March 1812, James Wilkinson, *Memoirs of My Own Times* (3 vols.; Philadelphia, 1816), 3:342.

Between those alternatives, Armstrong's preference was for the latter, on the grounds that Montreal was more vulnerable by the river route, which would also allow for greater ease of movement by water. But in either event, Armstrong presumed that Kingston would be neutralized, one way or another, before American forces entered Lower Canada.

Dearborn's campaign failed to establish a basis for pursuing either option. There was little Armstrong could do about this immediately, although by April it was clear that he was contemplating a visit to the Canadian frontier over the summer, at which time he might "supervise" the movements of the army. That prospect alarmed Monroe, who feared that Armstrong would be a rival for the presidency in 1816 and that he would not scruple to combine the duties of the War Department with those of a commanding general to serve this ambition. The secretary of war did not revisit the matter until late July, when he sent Madison a letter about future campaigning. Assuming that Chauncey and his fleet might control Lake Ontario, he outlined, initially, two plans. The first differed little from his earlier thinking, that is, that the United States might either take complete control of the Niagara Peninsula or attack Kingston. He discounted the former in the belief that if Harrison should take Fort Malden, his success would suffice both to secure Upper Canada and to control Britain's Indian allies. For his latter option Armstrong proposed a direct assault by army and navy forces, to be supplemented by another American advance from Lake Champlain toward Montreal. If the British should weaken Montreal to shore up their defenses at Kingston, Armstrong then suggested that Montreal itself might also be attacked.

Those operations promised to be complicated enough, but Armstrong also entertained a third possibility – that American forces move from Sackett's Harbor down the St. Lawrence River to Madrid in upstate New York, cross the river at that point, and establish a base there from which to march on Montreal in tandem with the army moving north from Lake Champlain. This tactic was much riskier. It assumed that the United States would control not only Lake Ontario but also the length of the St. Lawrence at least to Madrid, if not to points as far east as Lake St. Francis, with no more than a few gunboats and barges. The secretary knew he could not safely make that assumption, as he had already noted that American naval forces might hold the "ascendancy" on Lake Ontario "but for a short period." And all of Armstrong's plans assumed that he could find two generals, one at Sackett's Harbor and the other at Lake Champlain, who could coordinate their movements over the considerable distances involved. For these reasons he made no final choice about where to concentrate the American forces for the remainder of the campaign.[10]

Wilkinson arrived in Washington on 31 July. At first, he disapproved of trying to attack either Kingston or Montreal – on the grounds that the United States did not control Lake Ontario. Instead, he wished to concentrate on the Niagara Peninsula and even go west from there to Fort Malden, if Harrison should fail to take it. He next stipulated conditions that limited the ability of the secretary of war to correspond with subordinate officers under his command; he also demanded the right to remove from his army any person who seemed disposed to excite "discontents."[11] Such steps were by no means uncommon for Wilkinson, who was always obsessively jealous of his authority, but on this occasion he was strongly motivated by concerns about how Armstrong might behave in the event of his visiting the Canadian frontier and by the knowledge that the secretary had chosen Major General Wade Hampton – a martinet from South Carolina – to command the forces at Lake Champlain. The two generals had long detested each other, and there was little reason to expect that they could work together.

Armstrong tried to finesse the problem of the relationship between Wilkinson and Hampton by telling the former that Hampton would "operate cotemporarily with him and under his orders in the prosecution of the plan of the campaign." To the latter he gave the impression that his command was an independent one. Such ambiguity was not good enough for Hampton, who promptly tendered his resignation to take effect at the end of the campaign. The secretary was only somewhat clearer about the goals of that campaign. He vetoed any operations west of Kingston, which he told Wilkinson was "the *first* and *great* object of the campaign," and he gave the general the choice of attacking it "directly" or "indirectly." This choice, he claimed, was explained in the note he had recently sent to Madison, which he interpreted to mean that the army should go down the St. Lawrence to Madrid, fortify that place, and then move on "to take a position which will enable you to secure what you gain."[12] The vagueness of this last remark exposed a suspicion that the army might well conclude the campaign short of Montreal, but it is also

---

[10] Armstrong to Madison, 25 July 1813, *Madison Papers: Presidential Series*, 6:467–68.

[11] See Wilkinson to Armstrong, 6 August 1813, Daniel Parker Papers, Historical Society of Pennsylvania.

[12] See Armstrong to Wilkinson, 8 August 1813, Letters Sent Relating to Military Affairs; Armstrong to Wilkinson, 9 August 1813, Daniel Parker Papers.

possible that what Armstrong had in mind was an extended pincer movement of land and naval forces that would compel the British in Kingston to surrender the base for want of supplies or to risk fighting their way back to Montreal. In either event, though, the point of concentration for the American forces remained obscure.

At that point Armstrong and Wilkinson left Washington and made their separate ways to the New York frontier. The general went to Sackett's Harbor, inspected his troops, and promised vigorous action, either against Kingston or in the St. Lawrence. But to his senior officers, including Lewis, Brown, and Chauncey, he confessed that he lacked the means to make a decisive blow anywhere. He sought advice on whether to delay until the issue of naval control on Lake Ontario was settled or whether to risk more by attacking either Kingston or Montreal. The officers voted for Montreal, but Wilkinson continued to vacillate. Even Madison, recuperating at Montpelier from his summer illness, could detect the problem, but he hoped that a victory by Chauncey on Lake Ontario would permit the United States to take at least Kingston and then secure a strong position from which to commence the next campaign. The president also warned Armstrong to ensure that the mutual hatreds of Wilkinson and Hampton did not undermine the campaign.

For a brief moment in September it appeared that Chauncey might blockade the British in Kingston, but Yeo escaped, and the two fleets chased each other around the northern shore of Lake Ontario without any result. Armstrong urged his generals to accelerate their preparations, but more ominously the weather began to deteriorate and the troops assembled at Sackett's Harbor fell ill, from consuming bread made from contaminated flour and from drinking polluted water. Even Wilkinson took ill, becoming "feeble to childhood," and he retired to his bed "with a giddy head and a trembling hand."[13] By mid-September he had recovered sufficiently to announce that he would move on Kingston, though without precluding the possibility of also moving into the St. Lawrence. He continued to gather troops at Sackett's Harbor until he had a force of eight thousand, organized into four brigades. At that point, in the first week in October, he met up again with Armstrong, who came to Sackett's Harbor. The general and the secretary then squabbled, quite publicly, over the merits or demerits of attacking Kingston and Montreal. Armstrong was still inclined to the former, whereas Wilkinson implied he could

[13] See Wilkinson to Armstrong, 16 September 1813, printed in *American State Papers: Military Affairs*, 1:467.

attack the latter as the "chief object" of the campaign. While they quarreled, the British reinforced Kingston with 1,500 men from Montreal, a development that ruled out an attack on the British base. Accordingly, on 19 October – and after the American army had begun to load men and supplies onto transports – Armstrong directed Wilkinson to go down the St. Lawrence toward Montreal.[14]

Wilkinson was trapped – and he knew it. He realized only too well that Armstrong had never strongly favored moving down the St. Lawrence without first taking care of Kingston, and to the general his latest orders could be only an invitation to an advance that might end in humiliation. Armstrong also knew that the campaign was, for all intents and purposes, finished, a fact that he tacitly admitted – on 16 October, three days before he ordered Wilkinson to advance and without informing him – by directing Hampton to prepare winter quarters for his troops. But neither Armstrong nor Wilkinson could admit this failure to themselves or to a public, which would only ask awkward questions about the abandonment of a campaign before it had ever started. So, the campaign went on, not with any real expectation of victory but to enable its leaders to arrange for its termination under the least embarrassing circumstances. Accordingly, Wilkinson continued to embark his army, and on 21 October he headed for Grenadier Island at the entrance to the St. Lawrence. The movement was not completed until 3 November, during which period gale-force winds and heavy sleet scattered many of the boats and damaged substantial quantities of army stores. As Wilkinson finally entered the St. Lawrence two days later, Armstrong departed for Albany, leaving Hampton and Wilkinson to manage as best they could. He corresponded with them both, assuming that they had each "seized on all advantages that the errors of an enemy may have given."[15] And in Albany, on 15 November, the secretary announced to a crowd of bystanders that it was his belief that the army was then in Montreal.

If the remainder of the campaign was more of a charade than it was a serious military enterprise, it was one that had truly unfortunate consequences for the men condemned to participate in it. To approach Montreal Wilkinson had to travel 150 miles down the St. Lawrence and run five major rapids, all on the strength of supplies that would last no more than fifteen days. By 7 November, the army had reached Ogdensburg,

[14] Armstrong to Wilkinson, 19 October 1813, *Documentary History of the Campaigns upon the Niagara Frontier in 1812–1814* (9 vols.; Welland, ON, 1896–1908), 8:81–82.
[15] Armstrong to Wilkinson, 12 November 1813, Letters Sent Relating to Military Affairs.

where its officers, for want of a better alternative, voted to continue. Their situation, however, was a dangerous one. Wilkinson fell ill again and took to treating himself with large quantities of whiskey and laudanum (a tincture of opium). Whatever this medication did to lift his spirits – he was reported as being "very merry, and sung, and repeated stories" – it did nothing to enhance his judgment.[16] Even worse was the fact that Chauncey had failed to prevent a detachment of British sloops and gunboats under the command of the Royal Navy captain William Mulcaster from slipping into the St. Lawrence to follow the Americans, who were compelled to fight rearguard actions even as they advanced. Wilkinson, nevertheless, muddled on, and he ordered Hampton to meet him at St. Regis on 9 November to prepare for an assault on Montreal. Armstrong, at a distance, endorsed these orders, although he was almost certain that Hampton would not obey them.

Armstrong was right. Hampton was experiencing his own difficulties that would preclude a union of the two American armies. Although the United States had gained a degree of naval control on Lake Champlain by the end of 1812, it was to forfeit it to the British following a brief encounter in June 1813 that sunk two American vessels. Macdonough had to start over again with the construction of his fleet, but as he did so Hampton would have to maneuver on land without the benefit of water transportation. To comply with Armstrong's wishes that he move toward Montreal from the south, Hampton marched his army from Burlington to Cumberland Head and then to Four Corners on the Chateauguay River, where he was repulsed in battle on 26 October. In doing so, he violated an explicit directive from Armstrong to "hold fast" and not take any action until he could coordinate with Wilkinson.[17] And Hampton's army, although about four thousand strong, was by no means ready for battle. Its men were raw recruits with little knowledge of military discipline, and their officers were too unfamiliar with their duty to provide it. Opposing it was an admittedly smaller force of about 1,600, consisting mainly of Canadien Voltigeurs under the command of Lieutenant Colonel Charles-Michel d'Irumberry de Salaberry. The Voltigeurs were, in fact, a well-trained volunteer light infantry force that was eager to defend their homeland. Hampton might have continued after the check at

[16] Harrison Ellery, *The Memoirs of General Joseph Gardner Swift* (Worcester, MA, 1890), 116.

[17] Armstrong to Wade Hampton, 25 and 28 September 1813, printed in John Armstrong, *Notices of the War of 1812* (2 vols.; New York, 1836–1840), 2:189–90.

Chateauguay, but he did not do so, as he received after the battle Armstrong's orders that he prepare his troops for winter quarters. He interpreted the order as proof that the campaign was over, and he promptly reaffirmed his decision to resign. But he hardly complied with Armstrong's directive to go into winter camp just inside Canadian territory; instead, he moved back toward Plattsburg, thereby increasing rather than reducing the distance between the two American armies.

Hampton replied to Wilkinson's summons to St. Regis with a refusal, telling him at the same time that he lacked the additional supplies that Wilkinson had counted on to continue his advance. That meant that Wilkinson would have to proceed at his own risk. By 10 November he had reached the vicinity of John Crysler's farm on the north bank of the St. Lawrence, where he decided he would give battle to the enemy forces at his rear as well as to a British detachment of eight hundred men under Lieutenant Colonel Joseph Morrison that was harassing him from the shore. Morrison took a position at Crysler's farm, from where three American brigades, under the overall command of Boyd and about five thousand strong, attempted to expel him on 11 November. (Wilkinson remained too ill to command in person.) It was a dreary and rainy day; the British defenses were relatively strong; and the Americans had great difficulty in maneuvering in the cold, wet, and muddy conditions. Boyd could scarcely control the battle, he was unable to coordinate his artillery and infantry units, and he attacked the enemy piecemeal rather than by making a concentrated assault. Nor were the Americans well disciplined, to say nothing of their morale being quite low. At the end of the day, Crysler's farm was still in the hands of the British. Somehow, Wilkinson tried to claim this outcome as a victory of sorts. The next day he advanced to the junction of the St. Lawrence and the Salmon rivers, where he set up a winter camp at French Mills, just below the boundary with Lower Canada. All that remained were the recriminations.

VI

As Hampton and Wilkinson indulged in their recriminations, a serious crisis arose on the southern frontiers of the nation, one that involved American, British, Indian, and Spanish interests in ways that would eventually have a major impact on the final phases of the war. It centered on the Creek (or Muscogee) Indians, a loose but formidable confederation that occupied much of the territory that was bounded in the north by the Tennessee River, by the Gulf of Mexico in the south, in the west by the Tombigbee River, and the Oconee River in Georgia in the east. Some Creeks had extended their settlements into the Florida Peninsula, but most of them were concentrated in townships between the Chattahoochee and Coosa rivers. Their territory was thus extensive, fertile, and well watered, but because it no longer abounded in game, many Creeks had concentrated on sedentary agriculture, a development that had led them to adopt American and British customs, even to the point of intermarrying with Europeans and employing black slave labor on their farms. The Creek Nation also met annually in a general council, although it seldom acted as a unified body, and its towns were split between "red" and "white" kinship groups (or clans), a division that corresponded roughly with a geographical line between the upper and lower Creeks, with the lower towns being located in the region between the Chattahoochee and Flint rivers and the upper Creeks between the Coosa and Tallapoosa rivers.

Surrounded by expanding American settlements in Georgia, Tennessee, and the Mississippi Territory, the Creeks, even more so than the Indian nations of the Northwest, had experienced many of the difficulties of cultural contact, including the loss of land and the spread of alcoholism and disease. Much of the discontent arising from these causes was concentrated in the upper townships, and after July 1811 it was compounded by the decision of the United States to cut a road from the Tennessee River to Mobile Bay. The lower townships were more accommodating of American ways, and they were more exposed to the influence of the U.S. agent to their nation, Benjamin Hawkins of North Carolina, who encouraged them to accelerate their assimilation to American agricultural and political practices. However, the Creeks had also been exposed to the influence of Tecumseh – whose mother was a Creek – and who had visited the southern Indians in the summer of 1811 to broaden the base of his own confederation against American expansion. Tecumseh had little success with the neighbors of the Creeks – the Chickasaw, the Choctaw, and the Cherokee nations – but his message opposing the adoption of American culture won some acceptance among the Creeks themselves, especially in the upper townships. Consequently, Tecumseh's visit inspired the rise of local Creek prophets, otherwise known as the Red Sticks (for the red sticks they carried to indicate their opposition to American ways), among them being Josiah Francis, Paddy Walsh, Peter McQueen, and High-Headed Jim.

Some of these prophetically inspired Creeks, led by Little Warrior of Wewocau on the Coosa River, had even joined Tecumseh at Fort Malden, and on their return to the south in the spring of 1813, they attacked some isolated American settlements, an action that caused an outcry in Tennessee and led Hawkins to request that the Creek National Council turn over Little Warrior and his supporters to the United States for punishment. Somewhat reluctantly, the Creek leadership agreed, and even though Little Warrior and his companions evaded arrest, they were hunted down and executed. Although the Creek leaders intended these actions to settle the problem, they only made matters worse. The Red Stick prophets demanded revenge for the executions, and they attacked the Creek council town of Tuckabatchee (which was also the home of Big Warrior, who had taken the lead in seeking the arrest of Little Warrior). Events thereafter rapidly led to conflict between members of the red and white clans and the residents of the lower and upper towns, a development that led Josiah Francis and Peter McQueen to visit Pensacola in Spanish West Florida to seek powder and ammunition from its governor, Mateo Gonzalez Manrique. The governor, who was torn between the need to avoid trouble and his desire to exploit the situation, gave the Creeks a limited supply only – about three hundred pounds of powder and a similar amount of shot. As the Indians returned home, they were ambushed at Burnt Corn Creek on the Alabama River on 27 July 1813 by a detachment of Mississippi territorial militia under the command of Colonel James Caller, who assumed that the Indians intended to wage war on Americans. The attack failed, and its failure transformed what had been a civil war among the Creeks into a wider war against the United States.

Hawkins, predictably enough, suggested to the War Department that the situation might require a "military corrective," but the administration had already anticipated the request.[18] On 13 July, two weeks before the engagement at Burnt Corn Creek, Armstrong directed the governors of Georgia and Tennessee to raise 1,500 troops apiece to suppress the hostile Creeks. His reasons for doing so, however, went beyond the need to restore order on the frontier. There had long existed in the southern states strong sentiment to expand the boundaries of the nation to include the Gulf Coast and the Florida Peninsula, at the expense of the local Indians and Spain. The administration shared this sentiment, provided it could be accomplished in a legitimate manner. Madison had already authorized the occupation of Spanish West Florida as far east as the Perdido River between 1810 and 1813, and as late as the spring of the

---

[18] Starting in early June 1813, Hawkins sent several letters to the War Department describing the dissensions within the Creek Nation. Extracts from this correspondence can be found in *American State Papers: Indian Affairs*, 1:844–51.

latter year he had still been entangled in problems caused by his agent George Mathews and some overzealous settlers from Georgia, who had provoked an ill-conceived revolt in Spanish East Florida as a means of acquiring that province as well. But because Great Britain was allied with the Spanish Regency government in Cádiz, there had always been the possibility after June 1812 that the regency would permit British forces to use its Gulf Coast settlements as a base against the United States. For these reasons, Indian policy, national security, and expansionist wishes were fused in the directive to suppress the hostile Creeks. The defeat of the Indians would justify further land cessions from them, and if the Spanish authorities should openly assist the Indians, there could be grounds for seizing Spanish territory as well.

Waging an Indian war for these purposes was by no means easy. The secretary of war had headed for the border with Canada, the president was recuperating at Montpelier, and there were few troops ready for immediate action in the south. By default if for no other reason, Madison realized he would have to leave the problem of the Creek Indians to the states nearest at hand, trusting that their citizens and governors would fully appreciate the dangers arising from alliances among Great Britain, Spain, and the Indians. He did assume, however, that Georgia would carry the burden of the war on the Creeks, and he hoped that its governor, David B. Mitchell, would step forward as its most important leader. But Mitchell chose to retire from politics instead, leaving a vacuum that was to be filled by Tennessee. The Indians also shifted the focus of the war to the west by attacking blockhouses and stockades along the southwestern frontier in the course of seeking their revenge for the ambush at Burnt Corn Creek. Their most striking success came on 30 August 1813 with the destruction of Fort Mims on the Alabama River. The commander of the fort underestimated the danger of his situation and failed to take the most elementary precautions, including closing the gate of the fort. The result was a heavy loss of life on the American side, probably between 250 and 300, but rumors circulating throughout the region placed the death toll as high as 600.

Such rumors inspired public meetings in Nashville to call for "a hurried campaign" against the upper Creek towns.[19] That plan won the endorsement of both Andrew Jackson, the commander of the West Tennessee militia who was recovering from wounds he had received in a recent duel

---

[19] For a description of these meetings, see William Martin to Lyman Draper, 12 September 1844, Tennessee Papers XX 3, Lyman C. Draper Collection, State Historical Society of Wisconsin.

with Thomas Hart Benton, and the governor, Willie Blount. Blount was already trying to raise the 1,500 men requested by Armstrong in July, and both the governor and the Tennessee legislature, on 24 September, agreed to increase the number of state troops to 5,000 and voted up to $300,000 to cover the costs of their new operations. Some of Jackson's militia had already been embodied for a year's service since December 1812, and their commander, along with his kinsman John Coffee, was eager to enter the Indian country before the Creeks might have the opportunity to inflict further damage on the frontiers of Tennessee and the Mississippi Territory. Jackson and Coffee accordingly assembled a force of 2,500 men at Fayetteville in October, and they entered Creek territory, where they advanced to build a supply base at Fort Deposit on the southernmost point of the Tennessee River on 24 October.

Jackson then marched further south to construct a second post, Fort Strother, on the Coosa River. From that point, his army fought two engagements with the Creeks, at Tallushatchee and Talladega, on 2 and 9 November, respectively. Coffee commanded one division of the Tennessee troops, about one thousand strong, at Tallushatchee, while Jackson led the remainder to Talladega to relieve a friendly Creek town that was under attack from the Red Sticks. Both actions were victories for the Tennessee forces, with the Creeks suffering heavy casualties. Problems of supply then forced Coffee and Jackson to return to Fort Strother, where they expected to receive fresh supplies. Jackson considered his next move in light of the other campaigns against the Creeks that were supposed to be waged from East Tennessee, Georgia, and the Mississippi Territory at the same time.

Cooperation between these various American forces in the Southwest failed to materialize, partly because of difficulties with supply, but mainly because no means existed to coordinate their movements. A small force from Mississippi under Brigadier General Ferdinand Claiborne, the brother of the governor of Louisiana, did manage to penetrate to the heart of the Creek country at the Holy Ground by Christmas 1813, but its numbers were too few to affect the course of the war at that stage. Cooperation with the East Tennessee militia, under the command of John Cocke, was hampered by misunderstandings and personal rivalries; Cocke was a political ally of the Tennessee leader and Congressman John Sevier, one of Jackson's oldest and bitterest enemies in state politics. In late November 1813, East Tennessee forces even attacked the Hillabee towns of the upper Creeks, which unbeknownst to Cocke had agreed to enter into peace negotiations with Jackson. And Georgia failed to contribute much to these campaigns at all. Some of the state militia, under the command of Brigadier General John Floyd, constructed a post, Fort Mitchell, on the Chattahoochee River, from where they marched west to defeat a Creek force at Autosee on the Coosa River on 24 November, but both the Georgians and the Creeks incurred large numbers of casualties, and Floyd had insufficient numbers to hold his position in country that was still overwhelmingly hostile. He therefore withdrew back to Fort Mitchell to make better preparations before taking further action.

These developments left Jackson's army at Fort Strother as the tip of the American offensive against the Creeks. But Jackson was to encounter difficulties of his own. The supplies that he expected to be delivered to Fort Strother from Fort Deposit failed to arrive, and his men refused to forage off the countryside or, as Jackson himself did, live on a diet of acorns. The militia companies among them therefore attempted to return home. Jackson, who was unwilling to give up ground or to remove his sick and wounded, persuaded them to stay by promising that supplies would arrive within two days. When they did not, he consented to withdraw to Fort Deposit. While en route, the army met with a supply train, and the men received their provisions. Nevertheless, many of them still wished to march to Tennessee rather than return to Fort Strother. There then ensued a dramatic confrontation between Jackson, assisted by his aide John Reid and Coffee, and the troops, during which Jackson threatened to shoot the first man who attempted to move. By sheer force of personality, he prevailed, and he took immediate steps to improve the flow of supplies into the Creek country.

Supply, however, was to be the least of Jackson's problems. A more serious dispute resulted from the expiration of the year's service that his volunteer militia had agreed to in December 1812. These forces believed that they were entitled to their discharge and that they had the letter of the law on their side. Jackson disagreed, arguing instead that their service had been broken and that they were required to remain until June 1814. There followed another ugly confrontation, in which Jackson threatened to rake the line of volunteers with the two cannon that made up his entire artillery. Jackson summoned Cocke's troops to Fort Strother and attempted to raise fresh volunteers in Tennessee. But the men, both Cocke's and Jackson's, continued to insist on their discharge, and company by company they walked out of Fort Strother. As 1813 gave way to 1814, Jackson's army dissolved around him, and by January 1814, he held his position in the Creek country with no more than 130 men.

4

1814

I

As Jackson's campaign against the Creeks stalled, Madison met the second session of the Thirteenth Congress in Washington. In his annual message, delivered on 7 December 1813, the president played up the recent victories in the Northwest while glossing over the disappointments and failures of the year. Wilkinson's lack of success on the St. Lawrence he attributed to "adverse weather of unusual violence" and to delays "attending the final movements of the army that the prospect, at one time so favorable, was not realized." Even less could be said about the Creek War, beyond Madison's observing that the Indians, "infuriated by a bloody fanaticism," had become "the unfortunate victims of seduction," but he predicted that the various campaigns in the southwest would eventually succeed in proportion to the "martial zeal" with which they had been commenced. Otherwise, most of the message was devoted to criticizing the British, both for their refusal to end the war by accepting the mediation of Russia and for their threat to expatriate British-born American prisoners of war to try (and execute) them for treason. Should that policy be implemented, Madison promised to retaliate on British prisoners in like fashion, but he offered little more with respect to the future. Indeed, the only policy measure in the message was the suggestion that Congress revise the militia laws to permit the administration to mobilize that force more efficiently.[1]

[1] For the text of the message, see *The Writings of James Madison* (9 vols.; Gaillard Hunt, ed.; New York, 1900–1910), 8:265–74.

The president was not as bereft of ideas as his message suggested. Two days later, he called on Congress to pass an embargo on all American exports, coupled with a ban on all imports of British origin. As had been the case in July, the request reaffirmed Madison's belief in commercial restriction and the need to deal with the ongoing problem of Americans trading with the enemy. By the end of 1813 this traffic had grown to scandalous proportions, both along the Atlantic coast and across the borders with Canada and Spanish East Florida. There were even reports that Boston merchants had sent thirty thousand barrels of flour to Canada in November 1813. Because most of the supplies going to Canada would be consumed by the British army, some of the Republican "malcontent" senators, who had opposed administration policies in the first session of the Thirteenth Congress, had been censured by their state legislatures for their unpatriotic obstructionism. This public "switching" of the critics of the administration, as one congressman noted, was not without effect, and as a result, the president had his way.[2] The House and the Senate passed the legislation within the week, with most of the "malcontent" Senate Republicans now voting for a measure they had previously rejected.

But the main reason Madison had not outlined more initiatives on 7 December was the continuing absence of Armstrong from the capital. The secretary of war, in fact, did not return to Washington until 24 December, and in the interim he had said nothing about the failure to take either Kingston or Montreal. That he was deeply embarrassed by those episodes was clear to the army officers who were members of his entourage, and almost inevitably, the secretary had turned his thoughts to how campaigns in the coming year might redeem his reputation. Armstrong's prescription for future success was simple – American military and naval forces for the conquest of Canada would have to be vastly increased. That notion embraced an expansion of the fleets on Lakes Champlain and Ontario; replacements for Hampton and Wilkinson; and most important, an enlargement of the regular army to fifty-five thousand men, with these troops to be raised not by the usual methods of voluntary enlistment but by "classification" of the state militias, a form of conscription that required the younger members of that force to furnish a specified number of men for national service. The proposal was a drastic one, but the times were desperate. The army was on the point of

---

[2] See Joseph Desha to Isaac Shelby, 18 December 1813, Miscellaneous Mss., New York
   Historical Society.

dissolution, because in the coming months the five-year terms of men enlisted in 1808–1809 as well as the one-year and eighteen-month terms of those enlisted in 1812–1813 were all due to expire, and the recruiting record in the war to date, to the extent that Armstrong and his contemporaries could measure it, did not suggest that these men could be replaced by voluntary enlistments alone.

Despite the impending manpower crisis, Armstrong's call for a conscripted army generated little support. Republican newspapers were generally indifferent or unsympathetic, and the House of Representatives would consider nothing more than bills to increase bounties and wages for military service to induce men whose terms were about to expire to reenlist. The most hostile reaction, however, came from within the cabinet. Monroe, with his eye still on the election of 1816, had been troubled by Armstrong's conduct during the campaigns of 1813, so much so that he had taken the questionable step during Madison's summer illness of having War Department papers routed to the State Department for his examination, even as he opened a personal correspondence with the generals on the northern frontier. Yet not even Armstrong's failures in the campaigns against Kingston and Montreal had assuaged Monroe's anxieties about his own future prospects. Rumors were circulating that the campaigns in 1814 should be directed by a lieutenant general of the army, a new and exulted rank for which the secretary of war might still be regarded as the best candidate. But now that Armstrong seemed vulnerable, Monroe decided to strike. He urged the president to remove his rival from office, citing Armstrong's incompetence, his corrupt administration of army patronage, and what Monroe described as his dangerously unconstitutional schemes to take over the militias, as sufficient grounds for doing so.

Madison, well aware of the self-interested nature of Monroe's request, ignored it. The president did not, however, display any great enthusiasm for Armstrong's plans for the army, and he left his cabinet colleague on his own as he tried to implement them. The result was that Armstrong was subjected to constant pressure to modify, if not abandon, those plans. Within a week of his return to Washington, Armstrong offered Congress the choice between classifying the militia and continuing with the existing methods of voluntary enlistment, but given that choice, Congress hardly hesitated. By the end of January 1814, both the House and the Senate had passed, by strict party votes, bills to raise six more rifle regiments, to reenlist all the short-term troops for longer terms, and to continue with voluntary enlistments for the future. The only new incentive offered these men was an increase in the monetary bounty – to $124 – for those who would enlist either for five years or for the duration of the war.

Armstrong was disillusioned, even resentful, at these outcomes, and shortly thereafter he contacted Senator Jeremiah Mason of New Hampshire to discuss the prospects for making an alliance with northern Federalists to cast the Virginia dynasty from power in 1816. He also feared there would not be enough troops to carry on the war with vigor, and he predicted, correctly as it proved, that merely increasing the monetary bounty – and paying most of it to the men before their service began – would dramatically increase the rate of desertions in the coming year. The army was thus condemned to several months of turmoil arising from the problems of rapid turnover as large numbers of men left the ranks and had to be replaced. It was not until September 1814 that the situation began to stabilize as the number of reenlistments and new enlistments exceeded the departures from the ranks. By the end of the war in February 1815, some forty-eight thousand men were on the rolls, but almost all of these men were raw recruits, and the army had still to overcome the difficulties in previous years with their organization and training.[3]

Another reason Armstrong feared there would be too few troops for victory was Madison's decision, made in the first week of January 1814, to accept an unexpected offer from Great Britain to hold peace negotiations at Gothenburg in Sweden. The British had made the offer in large part to mollify their Russian ally after refusing its mediation of the previous year, and the ministry of Lord Liverpool was as yet far from thinking of concessions to meet American requirements for peace. But the mere fact that peace talks had been offered and accepted was sufficient to encourage many, Federalist and Republican alike, to hope that another year of campaigning might be avoided. And the projected costs for another year's fighting were more than enough to encourage that line of thought. In mid-January 1814, the acting treasury secretary Jones estimated that the total cost for the army and navy establishments for 1814 would exceed $45 million, an increase of more than one-half the amount that had been required in 1813. Yet the revenue for 1814 would cover little more than the ordinary costs of the civil list and debt servicing, whereas the taxes voted by Congress in the summer of 1813 promised to produce barely two-thirds of their estimated yield of just more than $6 million. Even after Jones had doubled the customs duties, it was clear that most of the war

---

[3] For the fluctuations in army size, see Stagg, "Enlisted Men in the U.S. Army, 1812–1815," 621–22.

revenue would have to come from another loan for the unprecedented sum of nearly $30 million. The obvious difficulty of that task also led Jones to seek relief from his Treasury duties on the grounds that he could not fulfill them while also running the navy, and Madison had to beg him to stay a little longer until a permanent replacement could be found.

One solution for the problems of war finance was to recharter a national bank to replace the Bank of the United States that had ceased operations in 1811. The restoration of such a bank would reduce the need for the Treasury to rely on a rapidly proliferating number of small banks of varying degrees of reliability to manage its own transactions and to draw on their funds as a source of loan capital. The government's difficulties in locating fresh sources of capital had, moreover, been compounded by the decision of the Royal Navy to exempt New England from its blockade of the Atlantic coast. The effect of that policy was to drain the nation's limited supply of specie into banks in the Northeast and into Boston banks in particular, some of which then began exerting pressure on banks south of New England as a way of discouraging them from subscribing to government loans.

Yet the creation of a second national bank would be difficult. It would require a permanent head in the Treasury Department, a problem Madison addressed by nominating the Tennessee senator George Washington Campbell in February 1814 to the position finally vacated by Gallatin (and Jones). Campbell's nomination was confirmed easily enough, but there was good reason to doubt that he was qualified for his duties; one New England Federalist jeered that the appointment of "GWC" openly proclaimed that the "Government Wants Cash!"[4] There remained as well the issue of the constitutionality of a national bank, coupled with the political realities that many Republicans were hostile to banks of all descriptions and that they would oppose returning to any measure that had been espoused by Alexander Hamilton in the 1790s. To get around that problem, the administration backed a proposal to incorporate the bank in the District of Columbia, where the authority of Congress would be less open to question, but the legislators failed to take any action on the matter before the session ended on 18 April 1814.

In desperation, Campbell opened a short-term loan for $10 million in the first week of April. As had been the case in 1813, John Jacob Astor

---

[4] See Samuel Taggart to John Taylor, 15 February 1814, George H. Haynes, ed., "Letters of Samuel Taggart, Representative in Congress, 1803–1814," *Proceedings of the American Antiquarian Society* 33 (1923): 428.

and David Parish – though not Stephen Girard – expressed interest in subscribing, but they withdrew after learning that Campbell had commenced dealing with Jacob Barker, a Quaker merchant from New York, who had offered to put up $5 million. The problem was that Barker did not really have that sum at his disposal; rather, he was acting as an agent for a number of state and local banks who were offering to lend money in return for the Treasury transferring its business to them. Campbell could not meet this condition without violating agreements the Treasury had made previously with other banks – as the chief departmental clerk, Daniel Sheldon, reminded him with some asperity. Eventually, Campbell prevailed on Barker to part with the $5 million in return for vague promises about the Treasury moving some of its business to the banks represented by Barker. The secretary was then able to fill the outstanding $5 million from some forty individuals and banks in Boston, New York, and Philadelphia.

But not even that proved sufficient to permit the administration to limp along. In the spring of 1814, the international situation moved dramatically against the United States, and from that point onward, the initiative in the war passed to Great Britain. At the time Madison had accepted the offer of peace talks, the administration was aware that Napoleon had recently suffered another major defeat – at the Battle of Leipzig in October 1813 – and that the French emperor was on the defensive. Even so, few Americans were prepared for the subsequent news that by March 1814 the European allies had invaded France across its southern and eastern borders and that immediately thereafter they would occupy Paris on 31 March 1814, leading to Napoleon's abdication twelve days later. With the total defeat of France and a radical shift in the international balance of power in prospect, it made little sense to persevere with policies such as the embargo and nonimportation as a way of supplementing the war effort. As Napoleon's Continental System collapsed, Great Britain would be able to trade openly with Europe, and it would be essential for the United States to do likewise, especially if it wished to encourage vessels from neutral European nations to challenge the British blockade to enter American ports. From his post in the Navy Department, Jones made these points forcefully in a memorandum to the president, even going so far as to call for the abandonment of efforts to conquer Canada and going instead on the defensive by land while resuming trade and waging a naval war at sea. If nothing else, Jones added, the resumption of trade would permit the Treasury to raise more revenue from customs receipts than it was likely to do through loans.

Madison paused to consider his options, but he was unable to deny the logic of Jones's arguments. On 1 April he called on Congress to repeal both the embargo and nonimportation. His most loyal supporters were dismayed. They worried that lifting the trade restrictions would be too great a concession to Great Britain before peace negotiations had even begun; they also complained that the immediate beneficiary of the policy change would be the British army in Canada. A hard core of Republicans, therefore, refused to follow the president's lead, but the remainder, in an embarrassing moment of agreement with the Federalists and "malcontent" Republicans, voted to end the embargo and nonimportation on 12 April. Moreover, the decision to reopen trade added weight to the view that the war might conclude without another campaign. Madison and Monroe did not disagree. They authorized Brigadier General William Winder – then on assignment to the British authorities in Montreal to arrange for prisoner of war exchanges – to seek an armistice, with the proviso that the British would apply it to their forces on both the Canadian frontier and the Atlantic coast. As a way of stopping the fighting in advance of the peace talks, the proposal failed. Neither Sir George Prevost in Montreal nor Vice Admiral Sir Alexander Cochrane on the North American station in Bermuda had the authority to commit each other's forces to an armistice, and Cochrane did not see any benefit in doing so anyway. The Royal Navy then pressed home the advantage by extending its blockade to all of New England, and rather more alarmingly, Cochrane issued a proclamation inviting the slave and free black populations of the American South "to emigrate from the UNITED STATES," either to join the British naval and land forces or to be relocated in other British colonies as "FREE Settlers."[5] If the United States had been prepared to scale down the fighting at this juncture, it was clear that Great Britain was not.

II

The circumstances that shaped the planning for campaigns in 1814 were not promising. Whatever ideas Armstrong might have had for another invasion of Lower Canada, they were immediately derailed by events on the Niagara Peninsula. On 10 December 1813, New York militia forces occupying Fort George abandoned the post in a moment of panic, burning the town of Newark (now Niagara-on-the-Lake) as they did so. This

---

[5] For Cochrane's proclamation, dated 2 April 1814 at Bermuda, see *The Naval War of 1812: A Documentary History*, 3:60.

retreat, coupled with the attack on a civilian population, led British forces under the direction of the newly appointed commander in Upper Canada Lieutenant General Gordon Drummond to respond, first by seizing the American post of Fort Niagara on 19 December and, beginning on 24 December, by sending out raiding parties to lay waste to the towns of Buffalo, Black Rock, Lewiston, and Niagara. The success of these British incursions starkly exposed the defenseless nature of the American frontier between Sackett's Harbor and Detroit, and the War Department was inundated with demands from Governor Tompkins and other New York Republicans for the organization of a counterattack within the month. As a New Yorker, Armstrong could not dismiss these pleas out of hand – to do so risked incurring serious military and political consequences in the months to come – but to commit limited and precious resources to western New York so early in the year could also foreclose future strategic options with respect to progress eastward in Lower Canada. Nevertheless, the secretary tried to do something: he ordered troop concentrations at Plattsburg and Niagara and urged that William Henry Harrison be sent back to the Northwest to carry out raids, using Indian auxiliaries, against British settlements in Upper Canada. Madison, however, would not approve any recourse to "savage" methods of warfare, and he decided against an immediate offensive.[6]

News from the Creek country was somewhat better. Over the winter months in early 1814 Jackson rebuilt his army at Fort Strother. The War Department authorized Governor Blount in Nashville to raise more volunteers; regulars from the Thirty-Ninth Infantry were also assigned to the general's command. By March his force was 3,500 strong, but there were still delays in the delivery of the supplies that would permit him to resume the offensive. And the volunteers from Tennessee were enlisted for no more than sixty days, so there remained the possibility that the force could dissolve in ways similar to those that had occurred in December 1813. But Jackson was determined not to run that risk. Assuming that the regular troops would obey him in all circumstances, he took the unprecedented step in mid-March of executing a disobedient volunteer, John Woods, to set a stern example to the men from Tennessee. He then advanced fifty miles to the south of Fort Strother, where he built another post, Fort Williams, and attacked the Creek stronghold at Horseshoe Bend on the Tallapoosa River on 27 March. The Creek casualties were so heavy – they were to amount to the loss of nearly 2,500 warriors in

[6] See Ingersoll, *Historical Sketch of the Second War*, 2:80.

the conflict with the Americans – that their will to continue fighting was broken. The survivors from Horseshoe Bend fled to Spanish territory in Florida rather than risk another encounter.

After the Battle of Horseshoe Bend, Jackson constructed a fort bearing his name at the junction of the Coosa and Tallapoosa rivers, from where six months later he dictated a harsh peace treaty that was to break forever the power of the prophets in the Creek townships and eliminate their confederation as an obstacle to American expansion toward the Gulf Coast. Indeed, so severe were Jackson's terms that even Indians who had fought with the Americans against the Red Sticks were compelled to cede territory to the United States. In all Jackson seized more than 23 million acres of land, much of it, as he boasted, the "cream of the Creek country," which in time would become the heart of the cotton belt in the antebellum Deep South.[7] Admittedly, events later in the year would reveal that the threat to the southern frontier had not been entirely eliminated – a British army would yet attempt to invade through Spanish Florida – but Jackson's victory over the Creeks made it far easier for him to repel that attack when it culminated in the Battle of New Orleans in January 1815.

As Jackson resumed the offensive in the south, Armstrong wrestled with the problems of invading Canada. To avoid the mistakes made in 1813 and to compensate for the weakened American position on the Niagara Peninsula, the secretary sought to launch a rapid campaign across the ice against Kingston in February 1814. The way he went about this, however, only ensured its failure. As he gathered troops at Sackett's Harbor, he also tried to deceive the British by ordering Jacob Jennings Brown to march toward Batavia, New York, as if he were heading for the Niagara Peninsula. Influenced by Chauncey, who believed the British were too strongly entrenched in Kingston, Brown misunderstood Armstrong's stratagem and he actually went to Batavia, where he remained for several weeks. By the time the confusion was sorted out, the American forces remained divided, and it was too late to attack the British naval base. Armstrong thus accomplished nothing, but over the winter months he did improve the high command of the army by replacing many of the unsuccessful generals of 1813 with younger officers whose careers would reshape the force over the next forty years. Dearborn and Lewis were given assignments in which they could do relatively little harm, Hampton resigned, and Wilkinson – after bungling a poorly considered attack on

---

7 See Andrew Jackson to John Overton, 10 August 1814, John Overton Papers, University of North Carolina.

a British post on the Lacolle River in February – was relieved pending a
court-martial. Their replacements included Brown, George Izard, Alexander Macomb, Eleazar Ripley, and Scott. The only discordant note was
the resignation of Harrison, as a result of disputes with Armstrong over
military protocol and the settlement of his accounts, and the secretary –
too eagerly as it proved – replaced him by promoting Jackson to the rank
of major general.

Further campaign planning, however, was delayed while Madison
retired to Montpelier for the month of May to improve his still precarious health and to attend to estate and family business. During that
interval Armstrong and Jones debated inconclusively whether the enemy
would confine its operations to Lake Ontario and the Niagara region or
whether it would attempt to restore ties with its Indian allies further to the
west in Upper Canada. That issue was rejoined when Madison returned
to the capital and summoned a cabinet meeting on 7 June, directing its
members to attend with as much information as they could gather on the
strength of American and British forces. Their reports told a sorry story:
according to figures provided by the adjutant general there were now
some thirty-one thousand men in the army, although only twenty-seven
thousand of them could be regarded as "effectives"; and behind those
figures other grim reports compiled by army inspectors depicted a force
that was badly supplied with food and clothing, that was still lacking in
almost all of the basic elements of hygiene and military discipline, and
was organized in regiments that were seldom at full strength. The navy
was in better shape, but Jones had no additional resources at his disposal.
The secretary believed that the United States might command a slight
majority on the Great Lakes and Lake Champlain in vessels of all sizes,
but it lacked the seamen to exploit that advantage. There were seamen
enough on the Atlantic coast, but there the Royal Navy was far superior
in the number of frigates and ships of the line. There had, moreover, been
no more American victories over British frigates, and in the spring of 1814
the navy had sustained another defeat when the USS *Essex* surrendered to
the British at Valparaiso, Chile, after making a successful voyage into the
western Pacific Ocean and capturing more than a dozen British whalers.

As for the enemy in North America, Armstrong believed that there
were twelve thousand British regulars in Canada, but given the recent
developments in Europe, it was obvious that the London ministry would
be able to reinforce them in the coming months by amounts that could
hardly be reliably estimated. On the diplomatic front, the ultimate fate
of Napoleon and the future of France were still unknown, but there

seemed to be few grounds for optimism or to expect that Russia or any other neutral European nation would actively take America's side while the state of the continent was being settled. The president was almost inclined to take these matters personally; he lamented that the nations of Europe had abandoned their own best interests by not standing up for notions of international maritime rights, especially when such inaction would only increase British influence in European affairs.[8] In response, he could only counsel patience to see what future events would bring, but he was doubtful that the negotiations scheduled for Gothenburg now would produce a peace.

In this slough of despond, the cabinet decided to resume the offensive in Canada, if for no other reason than to prevent the British from deploying their forces elsewhere to American disadvantage, coupled with a wishful prayer that developments in Europe might also work in ways to limit the extent to which enemy reinforcements might be sent across the Atlantic. Two joint army-navy operations were planned: one on Lake Huron, under the navy commander Arthur Sinclair, to take the enemy positions at Michilimackinac and St. Joseph Island to prevent the British from reestablishing links with the Northwest Indians; the other, under Jacob Jennings Brown, to enter Upper Canada from Lake Erie in an attempt to reduce all the British positions below Burlington Heights. Depending on Brown's success there and assuming that in the interim Chauncey might gain control of Lake Ontario, Brown would then advance on York and reduce the remaining enemy positions on the northern shore of the lake. To prevent the British from moving forces westward, Brigadier General Edmund Pendleton Gaines at Sackett's Harbor was ordered to build armed vessels to control the entrance to the St. Lawrence River (and cut communications between Kingston and Montreal), and Izard, at Plattsburg, was instructed to make "demonstrations" toward Montreal.

No one in the cabinet was completely satisfied with these decisions, and all members were aware that the thrust of the invasions pointed to the west rather than at Lower Canada. In that sense, the campaign, even if successful, would be little more than a holding operation to consolidate the American victories of the previous year while waiting on news from Europe and any movements by British forces from Lower Canada. Armstrong was particularly critical of the Lake Huron expedition, pointing out that if the campaigns on Niagara and Lake Ontario were successful, the security of regions farther west could be taken for

---

[8] See Madison to Ingersoll, 28 July 1814, James Madison Papers, Library of Congress.

granted. (His doubts about the Lake Huron expedition were confirmed by the end of July when Sinclair's force had failed to achieve any of its objectives.) But before the campaigns could even begin, the prospects for their effectiveness, as a way of supplementing the nation's diplomacy, were undermined by further developments in Europe. Throughout June 1814, American newspapers reported increasing amounts of detail about the fall of France, including the restoration of the Bourbon monarchy in the person of Louis XVIII, all of which served only to bolster the position of Great Britain. On 23 and 24 June, Madison asked his colleagues to consider three alternatives: the United States should make the British abandonment of impressment an ultimatum in a peace treaty, a peace treaty could be signed without reference to impressment, and impressment and other outstanding commercial disputes should be referred to postwar negotiations. The cabinet voted for the third, believing that the nation had upheld its honor by resisting impressment until the end of the war in Europe and that peace should be made on that basis.

Four days later, though, after receiving more news from Europe, particularly from Bayard and Gallatin, who had left St. Petersburg and made a private visit to London, the cabinet reconsidered its decision. The envoys anticipated that a "general peace" was at hand in Europe. They reported that the enemy would be free to direct "all its forces" across the Atlantic, mentioning at the same time that British public opinion was running strongly against the United States and wished to see the upstart republic punished for its temerity in going to war. Rumors about the likely terms of a peace treaty were alarming: Great Britain would never renounce impressment; the United States should be compelled to surrender the fishing privileges in Canadian waters it had won in 1783 and prevented from navigating on the Great Lakes; the boundary lines with Canada should be redrawn to enhance the security of its provinces; and there was even talk of forcing the United States to relinquish the Louisiana Purchase and restore it to Britain's ally, Spain.[9] Accordingly, the cabinet resolved to settle for a peace treaty without an article on impressment, with the proviso that silence on the issue was not to be construed as acknowledging its legitimacy. Thus did the administration discard the last of its justifications for the war and reserve its rights for the future. What remained in the meantime was to wait on events on the frontiers and the coasts and

---

[9] See Gallatin and Bayard to Monroe, 6 May 1814, James Monroe Papers, Library of Congress.

to deal with the outcomes of what Secretary Jones predicted would be "a bloody and devastating summer and autumn."[10]

III

Of all the American commanders in 1814, Brown and Scott, newly promoted to the rank of major general and brigadier general, respectively, were the most eager to take the field. Over the winter of 1813–1814 Scott, with some two thousand troops, had been based at Buffalo, where a similar number of men from Brown's command also eventually marched following the misunderstandings arising from Armstrong's effort to attack Kingston in February. While waiting for the administration to settle its campaign strategies, Brown ordered Scott to put his "little army" through a more intensive spell of training than any of its men had hitherto received. For both officers and men, company drills were held in the morning, regimental drills in the afternoon and evening, based on Scott's adaptation of the French regulations that Alexander Smyth had prescribed in 1812. Scott also insisted that camp police, particularly in matters of hygiene, be strictly observed to reduce sickness in the ranks; and he clamped down on desertions by executing, with one lucky exception (who was shot with a blank cartridge), those who were convicted of the offense. The significance of these activities was not that Scott was the first officer to show any serious interest in training the troops, but that he had under his command a sufficiently large number of men who received advanced training in the evolutions of the line – the ability to move flexibly in formation from column to line and back again and to wheel to the left and the right – that were necessary for American regiments to meet British regulars on the battlefield.

These American regulars were supplemented by about one thousand militia volunteers from New York and Pennsylvania under the command of Peter B. Porter, as well as by some five hundred American Iroquois warriors led by Red Jacket and Farmer's Brother. On 1 July Brown, Porter, and Scott crossed over the Niagara River, intending to take Fort Erie, a lightly defended British post with ramparts on three sides but open at the rear. The Americans took it with little difficulty two days later. Acting on his understanding of the administration's campaign plans, Brown had already requested that Chauncey, still at Sackett's Harbor,

---

[10] See William Jones to William Young, n.d. [1814], William Jones Papers, Historical Society of Pennsylvania.

meet him off Fort George by 10 July, at which time he presumed that the navy would cooperate in the reduction of the fort and then transport the troops to the remaining British positions on Lake Ontario – Burlington Heights, York, and ultimately Kingston.

It was not to be. After the events of 1813 Chauncey had become suspicious of both the abilities of the army officers and their understanding of the realities of naval warfare. Concerns on those scores reinforced his normally cautious disposition, as did recurring bouts of illness resulting from the prevalence of lake "fevers" in the unhealthy environment of Sackett's Harbor. Moreover, Chauncey assumed it would be pointless for the army to attempt anything before he had wrested control of Lake Ontario from Yeo, now elevated by the British Admiralty to the position of an independent command over all British vessels and shipyards on the Great Lakes. And from Washington, Secretary Jones had made it clear that Chauncey's first priority was the defeat of the British fleet. There then ensued throughout the summer a game of cat and mouse as each fleet monitored the rate of shipbuilding and preparations in their opponent's naval bases. There was no victor in this "war of the dockyards." At the beginning of the summer, Chauncey had a slight advantage in the number of ships and the long guns (cannon) they could carry, whereas the British had the edge in the number of carronades (short guns that could throw a greater weight of shot at close distance). But the Admiralty, reacting to the loss of Lake Erie, nearly doubled the size of the British naval forces on the lakes in 1814, with the result being that, although the Americans always led the race in the number of vessels, the British more than compensated by increasing their number of long guns and their superiority in carronades, especially with the construction of the 104-gun HMS *St. Lawrence*, by far the largest vessel ever built on any of the lakes.

Consequently, Chauncey refused to relegate his fleet to the role of a transport service for the army. He informed Brown that he would not meet him off Fort George on 10 July and at one point even hinted that the United States would probably be unable to take the offensive at all during the summer. Nevertheless, Brown advanced from Fort Erie, and on 5 July he met a slightly smaller British force under the command of Major General Phineas Riall, an Irish-born veteran with twenty years' experience, on a flat plain at Chippawa, about three-quarters of a mile from the Niagara River and bounded by thick woods on the west. The engagement began early in the afternoon, with skirmishing in the woods until Riall decided to drive the American force off the peninsula, assuming that he could easily do so as he had heard that the Americans – who were wearing gray uniforms, the future color for West Point cadets – were "mere Buffalo militia" and lacking in training. The general soon realized that he had misjudged the situation. "Those are regulars, by God!" he is said to have exclaimed, and they performed well enough to drive the British from the field later in the day.[11] Both sides incurred heavy casualties – the Americans some 320 killed and wounded while the British loss was 446. The result vindicated Scott's training regime at Buffalo; the battle was the first occasion in the war on which Americans bettered the enemy in a conventional fight on an open field.

Elated, Brown advanced to Queenston and toward Fort George, but he knew he could not take that post without further supplies and heavy guns, both of which would have to be conveyed up the lake by Chauncey from Sackett's Harbor. Accordingly, Brown, on 13 July, repeated his earlier call to the commodore to meet him off Fort George, claiming that Yeo would not fight and that together they could still take Forts George and Niagara as well as Burlington Heights, York, and Kingston. Failing either to sight or to hear from Chauncey, Brown withdrew to Chippawa, where several days of light skirmishing ensued. Riall, who had been directed by Drummond not to abandon the Niagara Peninsula, mustered all the reinforcements he could until a large body of his force, more than 1,600 strong, encountered a reconnaissance party led by Scott late in the afternoon of 25 July. Rather than risk the dangers of retreat, Scott engaged the British and sent for reinforcements from Chippawa.

The resulting Battle of Lundy's Lane was fought mainly in the darkness, until about midnight, on a sloping field adjacent to Niagara Falls. After about three hours of engagement, it became apparent that the key to victory would be the British artillery, positioned on the crest of a ridge from where it could rake the field. After several attempts, the Americans took the British position and the artillery, but both armies, exhausted by the prolonged fighting and suffering casualties far heavier than those incurred at Chippawa, withdrew from the field in the dark. During the battle, Riall had been captured by the Americans, and both Brown and Scott were badly wounded and invalided out to Buffalo. The American command then devolved on Ripley, a recently promoted Massachusetts lawyer and politician. Brown directed Ripley to return to the field to secure the abandoned British artillery, but the British beat him to it. On the morning after the action, they returned to Lundy's Lane to repossess

---

[11] For a discussion of this "myth" about the Battle of Chippawa, see Hickey, *Don't Give Up the Ship!*, 72–73.

their field pieces. Both sides therefore claimed a victory – the Americans on the grounds that they had driven off the British; the British on the grounds that the Americans had also withdrawn and failed to capture the artillery. The outcome is still disputed by American, British, and Canadian historians, even though it is clear that the immediate consequences of the battle were more favorable to the British than to the Americans.

As Ripley took command, he demonstrated that he was a less able and less inspiring general than either Brown or Scott, but he was in a difficult position. He could not resume the offensive, nor could he remain where he was without reinforcements and fresh supplies, neither of which was in immediate prospect. In early August, therefore, Ripley withdrew to Fort Erie, where the army would remain for the duration of the campaign. That result and how to assign the responsibility for it gave rise to angry controversies in the American officer corps. For the retreat to Fort Erie, Brown blamed Ripley and said as much in his official dispatches, which were widely reprinted in the newspapers; Ripley took his revenge, albeit after the war was over, by impeaching the credibility of the main witnesses on whose word Brown had relied for his accounts of the campaign. But Brown also blamed Chauncey, and their quarrel was very public and unseemly. The general faulted the commodore for treating the navy as his "private property," without regard for national priorities. The commodore, insisting on his "higher destiny" to defeat the British fleet, refused to be the scapegoat for the failure of the general's unrealistic and "romantic" ambitions.[12] And the Niagara campaign was, at best, only a minimal success. Certainly, the reputation of the army was rehabilitated and upstate New York spared from further British incursions, but these results did not greatly strengthen the American position in the larger contest with the enemy.

It is difficult, however, to see how the Niagara campaign could have accomplished more, largely because Brown and Chauncey had been given incompatible assignments. Brown tacitly admitted that he could not take Fort George, much less Kingston, without the assistance of the fleet; Chauncey could not have defeated Yeo without taking more risks than he thought wise, and there was little that Brown could have done about that. In hindsight, it seems obvious that the campaign suffered from the want of a unified command that might have prevailed over interservice

---

[12] See Jacob Brown to Isaac Chauncey, 4 September 1814, and Chauncey to Brown, 10 August 1814, as published in the *Daily National Intelligencer*, 8 September and 26 October 1814.

and personal rivalries, but no nation had yet worked out how to establish such a command in joint operations. (The British had not, and in Canada both Prevost and Yeo were wrestling with the same issue, though with less serious consequences.) From Washington, Armstrong had a better sense of the problem than his colleagues, but he could do no more than implore Jones to make Chauncey accept Brown's priorities. Jones refused. Even when he agreed that Commodore Stephen Decatur might have to replace Chauncey because of the latter's illness, he did not change the orders he had originally given to Chauncey. At that point, only the president might have settled the matter, but it was not clear to Madison that he should act in that way as commander in chief; after all, the army and the navy had cooperated successfully enough in the spring of 1813, so why could they not do so again? Moreover, Madison did not want to alienate Jones. Though relieved from the burdens of the Treasury, Jones was still complaining that the personal sacrifices required by government service were too great, and he was poised on the brink of quitting.

While placating Jones, Madison sought other ways to ease the pressures on Brown, namely by suggesting that the general might coordinate his movements with Izard's army at Plattsburg, especially if the latter could detach forces to enemy settlements on the upper St. Lawrence River as a way of preventing the British from sending reinforcements up to Niagara. Armstrong was unimpressed. The scheme could probably not be executed in time to aid Brown, it was fraught with serious problems about how the armies might communicate, and the secretary was reluctant to turn so much of the campaign over to the discretion of the generals. At first, Izard had seen some merit in the proposal, but he changed his mind after realizing that to detach a significant number of troops to the west risked exposing both Plattsburg and Sackett's Harbor to counterattacks. Consequently, when he was ordered to march to Brown's assistance, he moved too slowly to prevent Drummond's force from following the American army to Fort Erie and besieging it for the following several weeks. During that interval, Brown resumed his command, greatly strengthened the defenses of Fort Erie, repelled a British assault, and in mid-September executed a sortie from the post that finally drove Drummond away. By the time Izard reached the peninsula in October, he decided it was too late for offensive operations. He put his army into winter quarters for the next campaign, and Brown demolished Fort Erie altogether in the first week of November. The Americans thus ended the Niagara campaign – as honorably as they had begun it, but without retaining a foothold on the Canadian side, even though the British still held Fort Niagara at the northern end of the peninsula.

IV

Armstrong's doubts about bringing Izard into the Niagara campaign were symptomatic of a bigger quarrel that was brewing between the president and the secretary. To be sure, Armstrong had always been difficult to work with – he was often moody and irritable – but after the decision to accept peace negotiations with the British, he had become estranged from his colleagues. For his part Madison became more skeptical about the abilities of his secretary. He also resented the manner in which Armstrong had promoted Jackson. The issue was not that Jackson should not be promoted – both Armstrong and Madison had agreed that he should be – but that Madison, who was at Montpelier at the time, wanted the business deferred until his return to Washington. Armstrong, however, had not waited and had promoted the general immediately. Thereafter, Madison began supervising War Department business more closely and was disconcerted to find that Armstrong had been implementing many policy changes without consulting or informing him. Indeed, Madison complained, the first he often learned of these matters – such as the reorganization of regiments and the summary dismissal of dueling officers from the service – was when he read about them in the newspapers! Eventually, the president's dissatisfaction climaxed on 13 August in a seven-page memorandum, reprimanding the secretary and requiring him to consult him in advance on all matters "of a higher character & importance" that in "the public understanding" involved the "just responsibility" of the president.[13] In effect Madison had decided, much more than he had been in the past, to become his own secretary of war.

The timing of the decision was unfortunate because Madison tried to enforce it in the midst of a serious crisis that centered on the defense of the nation's capital against attacks from British forces along the Atlantic coast. Rather surprisingly, the problems of coastal defense had not featured prominently in the cabinet discussions held in the first week in June, but as Madison learned about the growing hostility of Great Britain, he concluded that an attack on Washington was more than likely. Accordingly, on 1 July he created a tenth military district to provide additional

---

[13] See Madison to Armstrong, 13 August 1814, James Madison Papers, Library of Congress.

protection for the region between Annapolis and Norfolk, and especially Baltimore and Washington, and entrusted its command to Brigadier General Winder. Admittedly, Winder had not distinguished himself so far in the war. He had been captured by the British under embarrassing circumstances at the Battle of Stoney Creek in June 1813 and more recently he had mismanaged aspects of the armistice and prisoner of war negotiations with Prevost, but he was the nephew of Levin Winder, the Federalist governor of Maryland. And Maryland would have to make a substantial contribution to the defense of the new district.

Armstrong, however, did not endorse the appointment of Winder. His preference was for Brigadier General Moses Porter, a more experienced career officer, and he did not think Washington was in serious danger in any case. After all, the Royal Navy had moved almost at will around the Chesapeake area in the summer of 1813, conducting a "ruffian system of warfare" characterized by brutal raids and the seizure of supplies and slaves, without attacking the undefended capital. Even if the Royal Navy did seem intent on expanding such a policy, other more prominent cities between Boston and New Orleans presented more tempting targets than Washington. And should the British decide to attack the capital, Armstrong believed they could be easily stopped. Here the secretary was assuming that the most obvious approach by the Potomac River presented difficult navigation problems for frigates and ships of the line; the alternative approach by the Patuxent River required an army to make a considerable march across terrain that could be strongly defended. Moreover, Armstrong was unwilling to commit men and money to places he believed would not be attacked; that policy, he feared, would simply "exhaust the treasury."[14]

Madison disagreed and pressed Armstrong to prepare a comprehensive plan for the defense of the entire American coastline. The secretary responded by calling on the governors of the states affected to organize militia and volunteers to the number of 93,500 men, but he did little in particular to assist Winder. He provided the general with only a single adjutant (and a chaplain) by way of staff support; otherwise, he left him to his own devices, even though Atlantic coastal cities were becoming increasingly fearful about enemy attacks and city corporations were demanding more from the War Department in the way of troop commitments and expenditure on fortifications. Their anxieties on this score

[14] For Armstrong's defense of these decisions, see his 17 October 1814 letter to Richard M. Johnson, printed in *American State Papers: Military Affairs*, 1:538.

were reinforced when the British, in mid-July, occupied the town of East-port in the District of Maine. The occupiers seemed intent on taking up permanent residence. They required the local population to take oaths of various sorts – to George III (for the enjoyment of trading privileges as British subjects) or to keep the peace (on pain of being expelled). Many took the oaths. A small Royal Navy squadron also bombarded Stonington, Connecticut, for two days after 11 August. But such developments did little to alter Armstrong's attitudes.

The community most alarmed by this situation was Washington itself, where the citizens were powerless to take steps for their own protection. Memorials to Armstrong from the mayor and city council fell on deaf ears, despite the fact that on two occasions between the end of July and the third week in August, British forces operating from a forward base on Tangier Island in Chesapeake Bay, where they trained runaway slaves to serve in a colonial marine corps, entered the Patuxent River and carried their "ruffian" mode of warfare to within twenty miles of Washington. Such circumstances almost invited an attack on the city, and Rear Admiral Sir George Cockburn, Cochrane's second in command on the North American station, was quick to sense the diplomatic and psychological advantages that Great Britain might derive from exposing the vulnerability of the American capital. He accordingly drew up a plan that called for naval and land forces to enter both the Potomac and the Patuxent rivers, with the approach by the former route to serve as a diversion in favor of the main thrust from the latter. To that point in the summer, British coastal raids had not been intended to strike at any particular strategic object; rather, they were designed to destroy American resources in retaliation for damages inflicted by American forces in Upper Canada and to prevent the United States from moving reinforcements to the Canadian border. Cochrane was, therefore, hesitant to focus on Washington, as was the newly arrived British army commander, Major General Sir Robert Ross, a twenty-year veteran fresh from the Duke of Wellington's Peninsula Campaign, but Cockburn won them over and the movement toward the capital commenced on 20 August.

The American reaction remained confused and uncertain. For this, Armstrong was partly responsible by persisting in his belief that the British would never come to Washington, but Winder was even more at fault. The general displayed considerable energy in his movements around the Tenth Military District, but at the same time he failed to visualize ways in which the British might attack and to allocate his resources accordingly.

He compounded his difficulties by assuming that if the enemy approached by the Patuxent River, it would signify that its target would be either Annapolis or Baltimore but not Washington. And Winder was under great pressure to secure Baltimore, especially after his uncle displayed a striking lack of confidence in him by appointing Senator Samuel Smith of Maryland to a special command over the militia forces in that city. The result was that the capital was far less prepared, both militarily and psychologically, than it might have been. Within the administration, only Monroe seemed unduly alarmed. Dreading the prospect of being associated with a disaster for which he believed Armstrong alone should receive the blame, the secretary of state left his desk and became a scout for Winder. His forays along the banks of the Patuxent River, however, shed little light on the intentions of the British and at times exposed him to capture when he moved into territory that left enemy forces between him and his route back to the capital.

By the evening of August 23, though, there was no doubt that Washington would be attacked. The next morning Winder tried to improvise a last-minute defense by assembling a mixed force, nearly six thousand strong, of regulars, volunteers, militia, artillerists, flotilla men, and navy yard workers on a field at Bladensburg, Maryland, that commanded a route from the Patuxent to the capital. There they met a smaller British force of about 4,500, whose strength had been somewhat eroded by the inability of many in its ranks to cope with the humid summer conditions. The cabinet joined Winder at Bladensburg, but after a further dispute between Madison and Armstrong over whether the latter might play a role in the coming engagement, the president withdrew. Undoubtedly, he hoped the British would be stopped in a pitched battle, but the result was a fiasco, with the Americans being driven from the field in only three hours. In the event of the administration having to abandon Washington, Madison had directed the cabinet to reassemble at Frederick, Maryland, but all notions of orderly government collapsed on the retreat from Bladensburg. The president, accompanied by the secretary of the navy and the attorney general, ended up on the other side of the Potomac River, in Loudoun County, Virginia, looking for Dolley Madison; Winder marched toward Baltimore while Monroe went in search of the president; only Armstrong and Campbell managed to reach Frederick. Amid the confusion, the British entered Washington, where they burned most of the public buildings, including the president's house; and for good measure they destroyed the printing press of the *Daily National Intelligencer* as well. The extent of the damage was limited by a severe thunderstorm – possibly a hurricane – but of all the symbols of American authority in the capital, only the Patent Office was left unscathed.

V

Madison returned to Washington on the evening of 27 August to reassemble his cabinet and to restore the authority of the government. Even before the British assault, the president, on 8 August, had already summoned Congress for a session to begin on 19 September, mainly to make further provision for the Treasury but also to respond to any developments on the diplomatic front in Europe. But before these matters could be addressed, the District of Columbia still required defense, the more so after the British attacked Fort Washington on the Potomac River and, on 28 August, forced the residents of Alexandria to capitulate to avoid sharing the fate of the capital. Both Madison and Monroe tried to encourage the remaining forces in the city, as well as its citizens, to prepare themselves for further resistance; they found, instead, that the will to resist was gone and that no one was prepared to take further directions from the War Department anyway.

Armstrong returned to Washington on 29 August, at which time Madison sought him out for a painful conversation. Monroe had resumed his attack on his colleague by volunteering to take charge of the defense of the district – on the condition that Madison did something about Armstrong. The president, however, did not want to dismiss his secretary. Armstrong's unpopularity notwithstanding, Madison realized that he needed Republicans from the northern states in his administration and that there was, moreover, no obvious candidate to replace him. Nor was the president convinced that Monroe could, or should, run both the War Department and the Department of State. Inevitably, though, Armstrong and Madison fell into a quarrel over who was most responsible for the fall of Washington, after which the secretary suggested that he take a brief leave of absence and visit his family in New York. He traveled to Baltimore, apparently with the expectation that he would soon be recalled, but he quickly realized that his position was untenable. The newspapers were full of accounts about how Monroe had stepped into the breach in Washington, from which Armstrong concluded that Madison had succumbed to the demands of "a village mob stimulated by faction." On 4 September he sent the president a short and angry letter of resignation, after taking pains to publish a more extended defense of his conduct in a Baltimore newspaper the day before.[15]

Few in Washington regretted Armstrong's departure. On 1 September Madison issued a proclamation criticizing the British for their "uncivilized" ways of warfare while at the same time minimizing the extent of the damage they had inflicted. He also exhorted all civil and military officials to persevere in their duties and to be "vigilant and alert" in providing for the defense.[16] The response was not what he wished. Confidence in the ability of the administration to defend the nation collapsed completely after the burning of Washington. Local authorities everywhere leapt to the conclusion that the British were free to strike anywhere at will, and a force from Halifax did compel the surrender of Castine in the District of Maine on 3 September. State and city governments, including specially created local defense committees in Boston, New York, Philadelphia, and Baltimore, consequently flooded the War Department with demands that federal troops and federal funds be earmarked for defensive purposes only. Monroe, now acting as secretary of war, was in no position to withstand the pressure. He made the best deals he could by borrowing money from local banks on the understanding that the loans were to be made in the name of the United States and that local defense forces were also to be considered as serving in the same capacity. The precise details of calculating the respective financial obligations of state and federal authorities were postponed until after the war.

While dealing with these issues, the administration lost sight of the larger contours of the conflict. Almost forgotten in Washington in early September was the rearguard action that Brown was waging on the Niagara Peninsula, to say nothing of the fact that Izard's movements from Plattsburg toward Sackett's Harbor and beyond risked exposing upstate New York and Vermont to an invasion from Lower Canada. And Prevost, as part of a new British strategy to increase pressure on the United States, was under orders to seize the moment. Since 1812 the governor of Canada had been instructed to remain on the defensive and avoid unnecessary risks, but now the ministry wanted him to seize strategic points on the border as diplomatic bargaining chips that would improve the future

---

[15] See Armstrong to Madison, 4 September 1814, James Madison Papers, Library of Congress. Armstrong's longer defense of his conduct was published in the 3 September 1814 issue of the *Baltimore Patriot*.

[16] The proclamation appeared in the *Daily National Intelligencer* on 3 September 1814.

security of Canada. For that purpose he was sent reinforcements from Europe to the number of thirteen thousand, some ten thousand of whom he organized into a force to march down the Champlain Valley, on the west side of the lake, to take Plattsburg. Since April 1814 Izard had done much to improve the number and quality of the American troops in the region as well as its defensive fortifications, but his second in command, Brigadier General Alexander Macomb, would still have to meet the enemy with a very mixed force – consisting of regulars, militia, volunteers, and even men who were still convalescing – that was far inferior in size.

The Americans, nevertheless, fought with sufficient determination between 3 and 6 September to halt the British advance at the Saranac River, thereby inducing Prevost to wait on the outcome of a naval engagement on Lake Champlain before risking more. On the lake, navy lieutenant Thomas Macdonough had been rebuilding the small American fleet since the summer of 1813, with the result that the two naval forces were approximately equal in the number of vessels and men as well as in the weight of shot they could throw. If the British had an advantage, it was in the number of long guns, but their ability to use it would depend on whether they could maneuver for position in the winds to deliver broadsides from a distance. On 11 September, however, the winds were light, which dictated an encounter at closer quarters. This favored the Americans, whose carronades inflicted such heavy damage that they overwhelmed the British in little more than two hours. Although some of Prevost's officers thought he could still have risked an assault on Plattsburg and continued his advance, the instinctively cautious general, who might well have recalled the ultimate outcome of Major General John Burgoyne's decision to press on down the Champlain Valley toward Saratoga in 1777, decided against it. He withdrew to Lower Canada and began contemplating an attack on Sackett's Harbor.

It was, of course, more difficult for the administration to forget about the British forces still in the Chesapeake, but after disposing of Washington and Alexandria, Cockburn and Ross had set out to attack Baltimore. They did so for two reasons: the attractions of the prize money that might be had in America's third-largest city and the need to close down what had become the most important base for American privateers in the war. Given its size, it was impossible to defend all of Baltimore by land; the men, the resources, and the time available made this unrealistic, but because the British would clearly come by sea, only the most vulnerable points needed protection. And Samuel Smith, after facing down a brief attempt by Winder to reassert his control over the

Tenth Military District, was able to assemble nearly seventeen thousand men of all descriptions and occupations to man the defenses. The British fleet arrived at the mouth of the Patapsco River on 11 September, with Ross landing a force of some 4,600 men at North Point, about fourteen miles from Baltimore, and he commenced his march the next day. Advance parties of the Maryland militia were unable to stem the advance, but Ross fell to sniper fire when he had covered about half the distance to Baltimore, and the British, greatly demoralized by this loss, encamped to reconsider their tactics.

Command of the British army then devolved on Colonel Arthur Brooke, who decided to wait on the results of a naval bombardment on Fort McHenry, a star-shaped fixture that guarded a direct approach to the heart of Baltimore, before risking further casualties. The bombardment commenced in full on the evening of 13 September, and for the following twelve hours the outcome seemed to hang in the balance. The fort, however, suffered little damage, with barely one-quarter of the British bombs and shells finding their target, and only four Americans were killed. On the morning of 14 September, it was clear, in the words of Francis Scott Key, a local lawyer who had been detained on board a British vessel, that the American flag – an enormous drapery forty-two feet by thirty feet in size – "was still there." The moment inspired Key to write "The Star-Spangled Banner," but more important, it convinced Cochrane and Cockburn that they could not batter their way into Baltimore. The British troops disembarked from North Point, and on 19 September the vessels of the Royal Navy set sail for their bases in Bermuda and Halifax.

Welcome though the victories at Plattsburg and Baltimore were, they did not ease the administration's dealings with Congress. The legislators were in a sulky mood in the unpleasant conditions that prevailed in Washington – they were forced to meet in the Patent Office and the Post Office – and the House of Representatives elected as Speaker Langdon Cheves of South Carolina, a Republican who was a known critic of the administration. Worse was the decision of the House in late September to consider a petition from the Common Council of Philadelphia to remove the federal government to greater safety in that city. Undoubtedly, Madison would have vetoed the measure had it passed, but the debate lasted for more than six weeks before it failed. The president also scrambled to hold together a cabinet. Within a two-week period in September, both Jones and Campbell submitted their resignations, the former to take effect by 1 December and the latter immediately. This left Madison entirely dependent on the support of Monroe, who still believed he could manage both the State and the War Departments. Madison would agree only to nominate Monroe as a replacement for Armstrong, and to fill the State Department, he turned to Governor Daniel Tompkins of New York. Much to the president's irritation, Tompkins declined to exchange Albany for Washington, thus leaving Monroe in the State Department until the end of the war. As Campbell's successor, Madison chose Alexander James Dallas, a somewhat controversial Republican politician from Philadelphia who had served as U.S. attorney for Pennsylvania.

Only after these personnel problems had been addressed could the administration return to the problem of how to continue the war. As Campbell left office on 26 September, he reported that the nation faced a financial crisis – more than $23 million was still required to meet the estimates for the remainder of 1814, and the ability of the Treasury to conduct its financial transactions had been imperiled by the failure of many banks to meet the demands for specie payments that had been imposed on them by Federalist-controlled banks in New England. Furthermore, Campbell offered no solution for these difficulties, beyond hinting, somewhat ambiguously, that Congress might "exert" its powers to recharter a national bank. Upon taking office, Dallas unambiguously called for a national bank, but in doing so, he earned the undying enmity of Chairman Eppes of the House Ways and Means Committee. Eppes's father-in-law, Thomas Jefferson, was also opposed to the restoration of a Hamiltonian system of finance, and to counter that possibility, the third president immediately sent Monroe an elaborate paper-money scheme in the form of a proposal that Congress should issue treasury notes to the extent of the government's needs, make them legal tender, and pledge all duties and taxes for their redemption. Eppes reported a bill to that effect to the House, much to the horror of Dallas, who believed that bankers and the existing holders of the government debt would never support measures that threatened a return to paper money and the financial chaos of the Revolutionary War.

Madison prevailed upon Eppes to withdraw his bill, but the episode shaped the outcome of all future debates on war finance. Dallas, with the backing of the president, persisted in his demands for a national bank and for loans and new taxes as well, pointing out that such measures were necessary to fund the war in 1815, as there was as yet no evidence that Great Britain would make peace. Congress, in response on two occasions before the end of year, debated at interminable length bills that either approximated to the wishes of the Treasury or embodied efforts to reach compromises between Dallas and the antibank Republicans. These compromises were framed as schemes to issue treasury notes as paper money through the medium of a bank, but they all went down to defeat because of divisions in the Republican ranks that were exploited by the Federalists, who cast their votes in ways that favored amendments designed to thwart the administration. By the end of the year, the War Department had run out of money, and Dallas had become so frustrated with rage that he could no longer work with the House Ways and Means Committee. Madison then diverted him away from these disputes by having him draft a pamphlet justifying American policy against Great Britain that was intended for release in 1815.[17] In a last desperate attempt to raise revenue for the coming year, Congress passed a bank bill in January 1815, but the bank's capital ($30 million) was set too low for the administration's needs (which were then estimated at $56 million); its directors were not required to make loans to the United States; and it could still issue half its capital in treasury notes. Madison vetoed it on 30 January 1815. After four months of debate the upshot was that Congress failed to provide funding for an American war effort in 1815.

Monroe fared little better in matters relating to the army. Within four days of the meeting of Congress, the Senate military affairs committee requested from the new secretary a statement of his policies. The request went unanswered for more than three weeks as Monroe concentrated on dealing with the British presence in the Chesapeake while at the same time trying to acquire basic information about the state of the army. In the interval, Madison asked Jones for his thoughts, and these surprised both the president and the secretary of war. Rather than providing a plan for the United States to win control of Lake Ontario, Jones suggested giving up altogether on the Great Lakes. The problem was not that the Navy Department could not build vessels, but that it still could not find the trained seamen to man them – landsmen and makeshift sailors drafted from the army being unsuited to the task – and Jones did not think it wise to strip the coastal cities of seamen and guns while the British might still attack anywhere along the Atlantic. Moreover, Jones warned that the United States had just about reached the limits of its war-making capacities, and he gently chided the president by remarking, "We seem to forget that we are at War with the most potent Naval power in the

---

[17] The pamphlet was published in April 1815 under the title *An Exposition on the Causes and Character of the Late War between the United States and Great Britain* (Philadelphia, 1815). It would go through multiple printings in many cities, including London, over the following two years.

world," whose resources and abilities to employ them far exceeded those available to the administration. Seeing no point in trying to outmatch the Royal Navy, Jones concluded it would be better for the army to shift its future operations against Canada eastward, by taking a strong position at St. Regis on Lake St. Francis, which could cut enemy communications on the St. Lawrence, and then prepare to launch a major blow against Montreal.[18]

Monroe did not challenge these arguments, agreeing that the United States needed not only to make a "firm and vigorous" resistance to future British aggression but also to try to end the war once and for all. Further to that goal he began conversations with Scott, who was convalescing in Washington in October, about taking some fifty thousand or sixty thousand men "to carry the war to the walls of Quebec by the first of November 1815 and perhaps [dictating] a peace within that fortress."[19] The plan he finally delivered to the Senate therefore called for the existing ranks to be filled – these were believed to be some twenty-eight thousand men short of their authorized strength – while also recommending the enlistment of another forty thousand men for defensive duties. To obtain nearly seventy thousand new recruits, Monroe proposed four different plans, asking that Congress choose among them. The least favored of them was to continue with voluntary enlistments; and the other three all involved various ways in which the militia might be classified to furnish a guaranteed number of men. That barely ten months previously Monroe had recoiled in horror from similar suggestions coming from Armstrong did not seem to trouble him.

The Senate refused to take any of this seriously. Its military committee ignored most of Monroe's suggestions and would consider classifying the militia only in ways to ensure that the men raised would serve in local defense corps. The House was even less receptive, ruling out both classification and local defense forces in favor of yet another attempt to recruit twelve-month volunteers. Thwarted, Monroe retired briefly to Virginia and left Congress to its own devices. Senators then came forward with plans to improve the incentives for voluntary enlistment – the land bounty was raised to 320 acres – and to require militia quotas totaling one hundred thousand men to be held for two years' service. The House reduced the quota to eighty thousand men and the two-year service to one

[18] See Jones to Madison, 26 October 1814, James Madison Papers, Library of Congress.
[19] See Winfield Scott to Martin Van Buren, 22 October 1814, Martin Van Buren Papers, Library of Congress.

while also passing a bill to fill the existing ranks of the army. But none of these proposals could be merged into bills that might pass both houses, and in December the Senate Federalists even managed to have further discussion of these measures postponed until the end of the session.

The resulting stalemate threatened to kill any prospects for carrying the war to Canada in 1815, so Monroe was compelled to try again. Seizing on a plan that had earlier originated in the Senate to the effect that state governments might organize volunteer forces that could be used in federal service, he asked both the House and the Senate whether this would be acceptable. Indeed, some eight states by the end of 1814 were already considering creating such forces, and Monroe hoped that he might be able to use them to realize his goals. The idea was not without its risks. Its success presumed that the state and federal governments would be able to agree on how the forces might be used, and the newly elected governor of Virginia, Wilson Cary Nicholas, noted that the scheme could well bring the republic "back to the disjointed state from which it was fondly hoped that the federal constitution had rescued us."[20] Nevertheless, there seemed to be no other alternative, and in the last week of January 1815 Congress passed a bill permitting the president to call on forty thousand state troops for twelve months' service – with the proviso that none of them could be employed outside their home state or an adjoining state without the consent of the governor of the state that had raised them. Such restrictive terms reflected a deeply held suspicion that was only occasionally articulated in public – that the War Department in its present difficulties should not be given powers enabling it to "derange" the militias for its own purposes. More seriously, though, the measure was an implicit rejection of the idea that another Canadian campaign was the best way to carry on the war.

Even so, immediately after the passage of the law, Monroe sent copies to the state governors and began to strategize within its limitations. As far as an invasion of Canada was concerned, Monroe realized that his best prospects for success lay in New York and Vermont, and he wrote letters to local Republican leaders, urging them to make "patriotic exertions" on behalf of the war. Even "honest Federalists" who were willing to serve their country would be acceptable candidates for officers' commissions. To lead the forces thus raised, Monroe turned to Brown, who was in Washington in January 1815, and he held several meetings with the

---

[20] Wilson Cary Nicholas to Monroe, 24 December 1814, Letters Received by the Secretary of War, Records of the Office of the Secretary of War, RG 107, National Archives.

New York general. Both men agreed that it was time to direct the war toward Lower Canada and to break out of the "lingering," "fish-pond" war on the lakes of the past two years. No point of entry into Canada was chosen, but the secretary thought it should be either at the head of Lake Champlain or somewhere between Kingston and Montreal. Ultimately, he envisaged that some fifty thousand regulars and volunteers would enter Lower Canada and break "British power there to the utmost practicable extent."[21] What Monroe probably meant by this was that the British army could be defeated in the field near Montreal and its remnants then driven back into Quebec.

Plans were also made to distribute troops elsewhere near the Canadian border to deceive the British, and efforts were made to organize privately raised volunteer companies to supplement the American forces. None of this was ever put into effect. A peace treaty ending the war arrived in February 1815, and Monroe directed all district commanders to cease hostilities on 16 February. That Monroe's plans could have succeeded in the manner he had devised, however, is unlikely. By 1815, the idea of a Canadian war to vindicate the nation's maritime rights had become deeply unpopular. Congress had failed to provide for its funding, and it is by no means clear that the War Department could have surmounted all of the logistical and organizational difficulties that had hobbled its prosecution between 1812 and 1814. Nor is it clear how Americans would have responded to continuing attacks by British forces, especially along the Atlantic coast or even across the western frontier of New York. And the success of the plans for 1815 depended as much on the capabilities and cooperation of the states than they did on the might of the War Department. Thirty months of conflict had weakened the capacities of the federal government more than it had strengthened them.

[21] See Monroe to John Holmes, 3 April 1815, James Monroe Papers, New York Public Library; Monroe to Brown, 10 February 1815, Confidential and Unofficial Letters Sent by the Secretary of War, Records of the Office of the Secretary of War, RS 107 National Archives; and the discussion in C. P. Stacey, "An American Plan for a Canadian Campaign," *American Historical Review* 46 (1941): 348–56.

5

Peace

Attempts to end the War of 1812 began at its outset and continued intermittently throughout its duration. The first occurred between June and September 1812. Within a week of the declaration, Monroe had communicated to the American chargé d'affaires in London, Jonathan Russell, the terms for peace, principally that Great Britain repeal the Orders in Council and cease the practice of impressment. The first goal would be achieved when Great Britain undertook by treaty to adopt more limited methods of blockade, and the second could be accomplished through a mutual understanding, to be written into American and British law, that the two nations forgo the employment of each other's seamen in their merchant marines. If Great Britain agreed, the United States would enter into an armistice pending the negotiation of a treaty that would return it to the status of a neutral. When it proposed these terms, the United States did not know that the British ministry, now headed by Lord Liverpool after the assassination of Spencer Perceval, had already lifted the Orders in Council. Consequently, in early September the ministry rejected the offer, not because it wished to fight the United States but because it assumed that Madison would not persist with his war, once he learned the Orders in Council had gone. Impressment was another matter. The British had no intention of renouncing the practice, but they had never supposed it would be a sufficient cause for war. From London's perspective, therefore, there was no need for the conflict to continue.

Madison thought otherwise. Having brought the nation to the point of war, he saw no reason to cease hostilities before all of America's grievances had been settled by treaty. The first opportunity for peace thus went by, a victim of the sorts of misunderstandings and accidents of bad timing that had characterized much of the diplomacy of the prewar years. That development troubled Alexander I of Russia, who did not want to see Great Britain divert resources to North America at the height of Napoleon's invasion of his empire and who also wished to preserve a significant Russian-American trade that, despite French efforts to end it, had been flourishing in the Baltic. The emperor tendered his services as a mediator. Madison lost little time in March 1813 in accepting, assigning a trio of negotiators to St. Petersburg as he did so. Shortly after their arrival in the Russian capital in July 1813, the American commissioners learned that Great Britain would reject the mediation, although many more months were to elapse before they were officially informed of this. In the interim, Adams, Bayard, and Gallatin struggled to accommodate themselves to the demands of the social scene at the imperial court and to endure the rigors of a Russian winter, to say nothing of the discomfort they inflicted on themselves by virtue of their personality conflicts and their differences over what sort of diplomatic strategies might end the war.

For its part, the British government had decided by July 1813 to decline the mediation, with the foreign secretary, Lord Castlereagh, directing the British ambassador in St. Petersburg to explain that Great Britain could not risk seeing disputes over maritime rights and naval power becoming entangled with the problems of waging and settling the war in Europe. In part, this attitude reflected British suspicions about the impartiality of Alexander I as a mediator – as Lord Liverpool was later to remark, the emperor was "half an American" anyway – but Napoleon had also mud-died the waters here.[1] Following inconclusive and costly battles at Bautzen and Lützen in the spring of 1813, the French emperor had accepted Aus-trian proposals for an armistice as a preliminary to a congress of the European nations to be held in Prague. That Napoleon hinted that rep-resentatives of the United States be invited to this congress indicated that any peace proposals he might put forward would be shaped to deny Great Britain the flexibility to use its naval power in ways that had often antag-onized European nations as much they did the United States. Indeed, this idea was not a new one for Napoleon. As long ago as 1800 he had planned a league of maritime neutrals to counter British naval supremacy

[1] See Lord Liverpool to the Duke of Wellington and Lord Castlereagh, 27 September 1814, *Supplementary Despatches, Correspondence, and Memoranda of Field Marshall Arthur Duke of Wellington* (13 vols., Arthur R. Wellesley, ed.; London, 1858–1871), 9:291.

and Russia itself, during the American Revolution, had also joined an anti-British league of armed neutrality. The congress held at Prague in August 1813 produced no results, however. Napoleon's behavior suggested that he was still so far from making a generally acceptable peace that his enemies concluded they had no choice but to press on and invade France.

To minimize offense to Alexander I, the British ministry offered direct peace talks to the United States in November 1813. The offer reached Washington by the end of the year and Madison accepted it a week later. There was, however, no reason to suppose that diplomacy at this stage could produce peace. Lord Castlereagh had stipulated that the negotiations should establish a "perfect reciprocity not inconsistent with the established maxims of public law, and with the maritime rights of the British empire," which meant that neither impressment nor blockades would be up for discussion. Madison had responded by stating that the talks should be based on a reciprocal acceptance of the rights of both parties as "sovereign and independent nations," but this formula was bound to produce a stalemate.[2] Even so, the president had little choice but to accept the British offer. Ever since June 1812 he had consistently justified the war, especially to its Federalist opponents, by demonstrating that the United States had always been willing to seek peace, while casting the odium for not achieving it on British obstructionism. Consequently, in preparing for the negotiations, the administration did little more than nominate the commissioners it had already sent to Russia while adding to them the names of Speaker Henry Clay, as a spokesman for the Republican majority in Congress, and Jonathan Russell, by then reappointed as minister-designate to Sweden, where the talks would take place. The instructions for the negotiations were essentially the same as those that had been issued in 1813, with Monroe supplementing them from time to time with other concerns, as he did in April 1814 by directing his diplomats to recover Astoria, a fur-trading post on the Columbia River that had been seized by the British in late 1813. That instruction suggested that the United States was looking ahead to postwar rivalry with Great Britain in the Pacific Northwest as Spain lost control of its American possessions in that region.

Of more immediate importance was the question of what sort of peace Great Britain had in mind when it had offered to negotiate. The problem

---

[2] The correspondence of Lord Castlereagh and Monroe between 4 November 1813 and 5 January 1814 is published in *American State Papers: Foreign Relations*, 3:621–23.

was not merely that the ministry would not make concessions on impressment and maritime rights but that it regarded Madison's concern with these issues as little more than specious pretexts to destroy the British Empire by annexing Canada and weakening the Royal Navy. Nevertheless, Lord Liverpool's cabinet had decided in December 1813 that the best outcome for Great Britain would be a peace based on "the *status quo ante bellum* without involving in such Treaty any decision on the points in dispute at the commencement of hostilities."[3] The considerations governing that conclusion reflected continuing unease and uncertainty about future developments in Europe, an unwillingness to restrict British maritime policy by treaty, and a growing awareness that, although a war with the United States had its uses in justifying Great Britain's desire to control all trade with Europe, it could not serve that purpose once peace returned to the continent. Indeed, increased sympathy for the American cause in Europe promised only to reduce the diplomatic options available to the ministry.

The time at which Great Britain might sign a peace treaty was left to depend on circumstances, but circumstances changed so radically in the first six months of 1814 that the ministry fell into the trap of believing that procrastination and calculated opportunism would best serve British interests. In response to the unexpectedly rapid fall of Napoleon, the ministry insisted that the location of the peace talks be moved from Gothenburg in Sweden to the Flemish city of Ghent. Thereafter it flirted with, without definitively adopting, a whole range of proposals for a peace that were being advocated in the press and thrust on it by a very disparate group of lobbyists, including Canadian merchants, West Indian traders, army officers, old Loyalists seeking revenge for the past, and Indian agents of one sort or another. Each of these groups had an agenda, and when these were considered collectively, they coalesced into a formidable set of proposals designed to restructure the prewar patterns of Anglo-American relations as well as to punish the United States for going to war at a time when Napoleon might have accomplished his goal of total domination in Europe. And taken as a whole, it should be noted, the proposals went far beyond the contents of the instructions the ministry would actually send to its armed forces in North America over the summer of 1814.

There was, nevertheless, a good deal of talk in London over the summer of 1814 about the need to readjust the Canadian-American boundary,

---

[3] See *British Diplomacy: Select Documents Dealing with the Reconstruction of Europe* (Charles K. Webster, ed.; London, 1921), 126.

both to compensate for what was seen as excessive British generosity in the 1783 peace treaty and to protect the interests of Indians who had fought with Great Britain. Here the goal was to push the northwestern boundary line southward into the Mississippi Valley and to create an Indian buffer state between Canada and the United States, from which Americans would be excluded. This was an old idea that hearkened back to the days of the Quebec Act of 1774 and the events that had preceded the signing of the Jay Treaty in 1794. The Canadian boundary also required rectification to ensure British access to the Mississippi River, a right that had been confirmed in 1783 but subsequently rendered problematic by the Louisiana Purchase and the discovery that the source of that river was not to be found in Canada's Lake of the Woods. In the northeast, the boundary was to be moved further south to improve overland communications between the Maritimes and Lower Canada and, in particular, the District of Maine might be reshaped to give Great Britain control over that territory to the Penobscot River as well as some of its offshore islands. The boundaries running through the Great Lakes and the Niagara Peninsula might also be redrawn – to prevent the United States from constructing naval vessels on the lakes and possibly even to deny Americans commercial access to them altogether. The rights and privileges to fish in the Maritimes, granted in 1783, were to be revoked, on the grounds that the American declaration of war in 1812 had invalidated the 1783 peace treaty. And the British, it was said, should also redress the grievances of their Spanish ally against the United States, certainly to oppose American attempts to encroach on East and West Florida and even to get the 1803 Louisiana Purchase restored to Madrid.

At the end of July, Lord Castlereagh, as he was making one of his many journeys between London and Paris during the negotiations that would lead to the Congress of Vienna, organized these proposals into a loosely cast set of points that were designed to probe how much the United States might concede under pressure. As he did so, he and his cabinet colleagues, principally Lord Liverpool and Earl Bathurst, the secretary of state for war and the colonies, still had no clear idea about which proposals stood the best chance for success, either on the battlefield or at the bargaining table. Outcomes on the former would depend on the performance of British forces over the summer, whereas the latter were to be entrusted to three fairly undistinguished diplomats: William Adams, a doctor of civil law; Rear Admiral Lord James Gambier, a naval bureaucrat whose only combat claim to fame (or notoriety) was the destruction of the Danish fleet at Copenhagen in 1807; and Henry Goulburn, a member of

Parliament and rising undersecretary of state for war and the colonies. There were, nonetheless, two overriding concerns that were to shape British diplomacy at Ghent – namely that whatever concessions might be won had to be achieved within the budgetary and temporal limits of the 1814 campaigns and that their central purpose should be to improve Canada's position to resist future American aggression.

In the first week of August 1814 the British negotiators traveled to Ghent, where they met their American counterparts, who had been waiting for them since the end of June. There then ensued some four months of intense, and sometimes bitter, confrontations, coupled with the exchange of lengthy notes and protocols, the latter business being prolonged by the constant need for the British negotiators to refer back to their superiors for directions. This process took about ten days to complete on each occasion. The British opened the talks on 8 August by stating that they would require major adjustments in the Canadian-American boundary, protection for the Indians, and a reconsideration of American fishing rights and privileges. They also made it clear they would not discuss impressment. At the next meeting three days later, the British stipulated that protection for the Indians was a sine qua non for a treaty, or at the very least the Americans should be willing to accept a provisional article to that effect. By taking so inflexible a position at the outset, the British envoys had gone further than Lord Castlereagh had intended, an error that would come back to embarrass them.

The Americans protested they were not instructed to discuss these matters. Indeed, by August 1814 the United States had nothing to discuss at all, the administration having finally decided that it would not even contend for an end to impressment and that it would settle, as the British had been prepared to do in December 1813, for the *status quo ante bellum*. At Ghent, however, the Americans concealed the weakness of their position. By the first week in September, the talks were on the point of rupture over the Indian article, an outcome that neither Lord Castlereagh nor Lord Liverpool desired. They accordingly scaled back their demands concerning the Indian buffer state, replacing it with a proposal to restore the Indians to their rights and territories as these had existed in 1811, a decision that was taken without much awareness that the Indian nations on both the northwestern and southwestern frontiers in America had recently signed away substantial amounts of territory in their peace treaties with the United States. The American commissioners, nevertheless, accepted the new British position, in part because they had no wish to be held responsible for rupturing the talks and in part because they suspected it could not be enforced anyway. This agreement eventually emerged as article 9 in the peace treaty.

Rebuked by their superiors, the British envoys tried another tack. This consisted of the demand that the basis for a peace should be the uti possidetis. In practical terms, this meant that the war would end with Great Britain in possession of about one-half of the District of Maine and its offshore islands as well as Forts Michilimackinac and Niagara. The United States would gain Forts Malden and Erie (even though the U.S. Army, after driving the British away from the latter post, was on the point of destroying it altogether). This tactic also permitted the British to continue discussions about boundaries, this time under the pretense that given the propensity of the United States to expand its territory in all directions, the British and their allies required protection against future American aggression. Here much was made of the disputes between Spain and the United States over the Louisiana Purchase and American encroachments on Spanish Florida, as well as the unfortunate proclamations issued by generals Hull and Smyth in 1812 to the effect that Upper Canada would be annexed to the United States.

The British were confident of success. They assumed the United States could have no objection to the uti possidetis, and by October 1814 news of the fall of Washington had reached Ghent. On that basis future British victories could only strengthen the hand of Adams, Gambier, and Goulburn. The Americans, however, rejected this proposal for essentially the same reasons as they had rejected earlier ones relating to boundaries and Indians: they were not instructed on such matters; and it had never occurred to any American that the uti possidetis could settle the issues that had given rise to the war. As for the expansionist tendencies of the United States, the American commissioners pointed out that the Louisiana Purchase was no concern of the British, who had not objected to the transaction at the time it had been made; a similar argument was put forward in response to British protests about American activities in Spanish Florida. The proclamations of Hull and Smyth were simply disavowed. The only basis for a peace, the Americans hinted, could be the *status quo ante bellum*.

By the time the Americans had formulated this response, news of the British checks at Baltimore and Plattsburg had reached Ghent. While these developments cheered the Americans, they did not immediately lead the British to reconsider their position. Lord Liverpool merely shifted tactics again by suggesting that the Duke of Wellington be sent to North America to take charge of the British war effort. The impact of such a move could have been considerable, although the ministry also wished to remove the duke from Paris for other reasons: political instability in France was seen as threatening his life, and the emergence of serious differences in Vienna between Russia and its allies over the future of Poland was beginning to hamper Great Britain's diplomatic flexibility. Sending Wellington to North America offered partial solutions for these problems. The duke, however, was less than enthusiastic about the idea. If he did not absolutely rule it out, he did not think it was immediately necessary for him to depart for Canada, and not at all if his military services might still be required in Europe. In the intervening period, he bluntly informed the ministry that there was no point in continuing the American war: the British did not have adequate naval control on the lakes, and their territorial gains in 1814 were not sufficient to justify a peace of the uti possidetis. In effect, Wellington told his superiors to settle for the *status quo ante bellum*.

The ministry was in no position to argue. In the last two months of 1814, it became clear that little of substance had been accomplished in America, and the mounting costs of the campaigns there were creating difficulties for the ministry in Parliament. Even so the British still hesitated, and bereft of a better alternative, their envoys at Ghent had requested their American counterparts to draft the project of a treaty. They were more than willing to do so, offering the restoration of the *status quo ante bellum*, to which they added proposals for the establishment of binational commissions to settle boundary disputes, such as those over the northern limits of Maine and the ownership of its offshore islands and the redrawing of a line relating to British access to the Mississippi River. The only other dispute of real substance was the retention of American rights and privileges to catch and to dry fish in the Canadian Maritimes, and because these rights and privileges had been established under the 1783 peace treaty, as had the British right of access to the Mississippi, it was clear that the two issues would stand or fall together. The problem occasioned a sharp quarrel on the American side between Adams and Clay, with the former refusing to surrender the gains his father had won in 1783 while the latter declined to trade away the American right to control the Mississippi to satisfy Adams's constituents. The matter was eventually resolved by the Americans saying nothing about either matter in their draft project.

The British were uneasy. They had overplayed their hand and had been compelled to retract or to modify their initial demands until little or nothing remained of them. Moreover, the problems confronting the ministry in Vienna and Parliament were intensifying rather than abating.

After reworking the wording of many of the American proposals – and adding to them an article that would commit the United States to make greater efforts to suppress the Atlantic slave trade – the British ministry and their envoys reached their final positions during the first three weeks of December. There were further fruitless exchanges with the Americans over the fisheries and Mississippi problem, and by 23 December, both sides were ready to settle. The negotiators met for the last time on Christmas Eve to sign the Treaty of Ghent, a document that was silent on all the issues that had led to the war and was largely concerned with procedural matters for the termination of hostilities and the tying up of loose ends over boundaries thereafter. The prince regent ratified the treaty for Great Britain on 28 December. It was then sent across the Atlantic to see what reception it would meet in an America that was still at war.

II

As the peace negotiations wound down, the administration was still trying to coax supplies of men and money from Congress. Madison even sent copies of the dispatches from Ghent to Congress to demonstrate how far Great Britain was from ending the war, but this news had no effect on the legislative proceedings. The president's difficulties were compounded by a recurrence of one of the most difficult obstacles he had faced in taking the nation to war: Federalist opposition to the conflict, centered in the states of New England. The intensity of this opposition had fluctuated according to circumstances – brief but sharp criticism upon the declaration of war in 1812, followed by further angry protests against the embargo imposed between December 1813 and April 1814 – but after the Royal Navy had blockaded the New England coastline and began the occupation of portions of the District of Maine and its islands, it reached hitherto unprecedented heights of seriousness. On 18 October 1814 the Massachusetts General Court called for a convention of New England states to meet in Hartford, Connecticut. Ostensibly, this convention was to deal with problems of local defense and control of the tax revenues to pay for it, but it would also address longer-standing Federalist grievances against Republican rule in Washington: discriminatory economic policies, such as the embargo; the undue advantages conferred on southern states by slave representation; and the rapid admission of new states from the South and the West that was undermining New England's influence in national politics.

Republicans throughout the nation regarded the call for the convention as an ominous development. They saw it as the first in a series of disloyal steps that would lead to the Federalists seeking a separate peace with the enemy, to be followed by secession and possibly the reunion of New England with the British Crown. Even Madison was not entirely immune to these fears, and one observer described him as being "miserably shattered and woe-begone" at the prospect.[4] In the past the administration had refused to be diverted by problems of dissent on the home front. There had been no return to the policies embodied in the Alien and Sedition Acts of 1798 – Madison's disgust at the repressive behavior of John Adams during the Quasi-War with France had seen to that[5] – and the president had never believed the Federalists would attempt secession, if for no other reason that the numbers and strength of the Republicans throughout New England were sufficient to ensure that extreme actions could not be taken without risking a regional civil war. But now it seemed that stronger measures might be necessary. In mid-November, Madison decided to attempt the expulsion of the enemy from Maine, starting with the recapture of Castine. The effort had to be abandoned as a result of difficulties in raising men and money as well as those of selecting a suitable commander. Worse, the governor of Massachusetts, Caleb Strong, was decidedly cool about the proposal, and he was probably responsible for leaking some of its details to the newspapers, where all, including the British, could read them.

As the date for the assembling of the convention in Hartford approached – 15 December 1814 – the administration turned its attention to the local scene. To strengthen federal power on the local level Monroe ordered the Twenty-Third and Twenty-Fifth Infantry regiments into Hartford – to prevent the city government from obstructing army recruiting over the winter months and to overawe the convention more generally. In the event of its activities coinciding with any British attempts to strike at the United States, either at Buffalo or at New York City, high

---

4 See William Wirt to Elizabeth Gamble Wirt, 14 October 1814, William Wirt Papers, Maryland Historical Society.

5 This is not to say there were no infringements of civil liberties during the war. Pro-war, or Republican, mobs had attacked Federalist newspapers in Norristown, Savannah, and Baltimore in the days immediately after the declaration of war. The most serious of these assaults was made on the Baltimore *Federal Republican*, during the course of which one person was killed and two others badly injured, but it is not at all clear how far the Madison administration might be held responsible (see Frank Cassell, "The Great Baltimore Riot of 1812," *Maryland Historical Magazine* 70 [1975]: 241–59).

army officers, including Jacob Jennings Brown and Governor Tompkins of New York, received the authority to use force. In short, the administration was prepared to coerce obedience to its writ. But there is also evidence to suggest that some more positive inducements were offered to retain the loyalty of New England. Through the commander of the Twenty-Fifth Infantry, Colonel Thomas Sidney Jesup, Monroe seems to have held out to the convention the prospect of the conquest and annexation of New Brunswick and Nova Scotia during the 1815 campaigns. And according to Jesup, the mayor of Hartford, Chauncey Goodrich, who also sat in the convention, seems to have been at least moved, if not wholly persuaded, by the offer.[6]

Jesup was unimpressed by what he observed in Hartford. As he pointed out, New Englanders were hardly united behind the convention – Vermont and New Hampshire were not officially represented there – and Connecticut itself, with substantial land investments in New York and Ohio, had stated that its participation would be consistent with its obligations as a member "of the national union." On 5 January 1815 the convention adjourned and one week later issued its report. After all the anxious speculation that had preceded it, the contents were distinctly anticlimactic. The men at Hartford condemned the administration for failing to defend New England, but they did little more than recommend that the states negotiate with Washington to earmark their share of the nation's taxes for their own defense as well as raise local forces for the same purpose. They were more critical of recent Republican attempts to conscript the militias, even going so far as to advocate nullification as an appropriate response. Otherwise the delegates contented themselves with another timeworn recitation of Federalist grievances against Republicanism – embargoes, slave representation, expansionism, and the admission of new states – for which they recommended seven constitutional amendments by way of remedy. Republicans were generally relieved. If there were extremists and potential traitors in New England, and few Republicans doubted that there were, it would seem that they had not controlled the proceedings in Hartford. Or, as Charles Jared Ingersoll was to put it more graphically at a later date, the report of the convention was "the abortion of an enigma."[7]

---

[6] For this story, see Ingersoll, *Historical Sketch of the Second War*, 2:237. No contemporary written evidence for it can be found, but Ingersoll, by virtue of his close relationship with Madison, was certainly in a position to learn of it.

[7] Ibid., 2:216.

Regardless of the developments at Ghent and Hartford, the administration still had to deal with the problem of the British expeditionary force that had recently burned Washington. The Royal Navy retained the capacity to move at will around the nation's coasts, and as the summer gave way to fall and winter, it seemed likely that the British would strike again, probably somewhere in the South. The decisions of their commander, Vice Admiral Cochrane – who harbored an intense and visceral dislike of all things American – did nothing to belie this assumption. By September 1814 he had received reinforcements totaling ten thousand men whom he intended to employ against New Orleans. But his approach to the city was to be an indirect one rather than a frontal assault. The plan was first to seize Mobile, which would provide access to the rivers of inland Georgia and the Mississippi Territory as well as permit the British to recruit what allies they could from the local populations of discontented Indians and potentially rebellious slaves. The advance on New Orleans would be either through Lake Pontchartrain or overland, after isolating the city by the capture of Baton Rouge. This main strategy could be supplemented by auxiliary raids in the interior from the Apalachicola River and coordinated with attacks on the Atlantic coast, directed by Rear Admiral Cockburn.

Cochrane was attracted to New Orleans for a variety of reasons: its strategic location on the Gulf Coast, its significance for the American control of the Mississippi Valley, and as a source of prize money. Its capture, moreover, would enhance the British negotiating position at Ghent, although there is no evidence to suggest that Cochrane's plans formed part of any larger scheme to extend British rule into the lower Mississippi Valley or to connect such conquests with the revised Canadian boundary and Indian buffer-state proposals that were being put forward at Ghent. (British strategic planning was by no means as well coordinated and integrated as such a plan would require.)[8] And New Orleans was very vulnerable. The state of Louisiana had only recently been admitted to the Union (in 1812), and its internal politics, which were governed by ethnic and cultural tensions between its polyglot population of old French settlers, recent French refugees from the Caribbean, Spanish settlers, American migrants, urban free blacks, and slaves, were widely regarded as a source

---

[8] One of the hardiest myths about the War of 1812 is the view that the British, had they won the Battle of New Orleans, intended to disavow the Treaty of Ghent to detach Louisiana from the Union. For a refutation, see James A. Carr, "The Battle of New Orleans and the Treaty of Ghent," *Diplomatic History* 3 (1979): 273–82.

of weakness. As the state's governor, William C. C. Claiborne, wrote as he pleaded for outside aid: "I have a difficult people to manage."[9]

The administration was aware of the danger to New Orleans, but its defense would have to be entrusted to Major General Andrew Jackson, fresh from his victory over the Creek Indians, and to whatever resources could be mustered in Georgia, Kentucky, Tennessee, and the Mississippi Territory. And at first Jackson was much more concerned with the larger American strategic position on the Gulf Coast than he was with the fate of New Orleans alone. His personal goal, which was not endorsed by the administration, was to expel the Spanish from Pensacola in West Florida to prevent them from giving aid to the British and the Indians, especially after the British had tried to capture Fort Bowyer at the entrance to Mobile Bay in September. Local forces drove the enemy away from the fort, but in the first week in November Jackson stormed Pensacola anyway. On that occasion he encountered no British troops or vessels – they withdrew from the area as Jackson approached – but by seizing the Spanish post and holding Mobile, Jackson had effectively thwarted Cochrane's first move in his southern campaign.

Cochrane realized as much and readjusted his preparations to make a direct approach to New Orleans by sea and through the region's lakes and bayous. Jackson responded by going to New Orleans in the first week of December to organize the defenses of the city. This was no simple matter. The British might be able to approach by one or more of six routes, including two southern routes, one up the Mississippi River from its mouth and the other overland after entering Lake Barataria; two eastern approaches in the area between Bayou Terre aux Boeufs and the Plains of Gentilly; a western approach through the Bayou La Fourche; and a descent from the north through Lake Pontchartrain and the Bayou St. John. No one could be sure which the British would chose, so Jackson decided to block off as many as he could, by positioning guns and men in all six places and obstructing the water routes. To enforce the cooperation of the local residents, Jackson exerted his overbearing and authoritarian personality to the fullest, eventually declaring martial law in the city on December 16.[10] But the real difficulty was whether Jackson would have the men and resources to support so comprehensive

---

[9] See William C. C. Claiborne to Andrew Jackson, 24 August 1814, Andrew Jackson Papers, Library of Congress.

[10] In so acting, Jackson was the first U.S. general to extend military rule over a civilian population (see Matthew Warshauer, *Andrew Jackson and the Politics of Martial Law* [Knoxville, TN, 2006], 19–45.

a defense. To ensure that he did, Jackson took two additional measures that went against his personal inclinations: he called for volunteers from the free black population of New Orleans, and he made an alliance with the smugglers and pirates in the Bay of Barataria headed by the notorious Jean Lafitte.

Thereafter, the defense of New Orleans became largely a matter of waiting for the British. In mid-December, the Royal Navy defeated the small American gunboat fleet on Lake Borgne, thus permitting Cochrane to transfer troops to the Isle aux Pois as a preliminary to crossing to the mainland. Jackson received substantial reinforcements from Tennessee and the Mississippi Territory a week later, but he was caught by surprise when the British advanced to within nine miles of New Orleans through the Villeré Canal, a waterway that had not been blocked off sufficiently rapidly in response to his earlier orders. The enemy was now positioned to make a direct assault, which Jackson tried to preempt on 23 December by making a night attack on the forces at the Villeré plantation. Although he failed to dislodge the British, Jackson demonstrated that he could manage troops under difficult conditions and inflict serious casualties. British losses in killed, wounded, and missing amounted to nearly three hundred men.

On the face of it the invaders still seemed to have the upper hand, although their new army commander – Lieutenant General Sir Edward Packenham, another veteran of the Peninsula War and the brother-in-law of the Duke of Wellington, who arrived on Christmas Day to take charge of some six thousand troops on land – had misgivings about the options available to him: either to make a frontal assault against the enemy or to find an alternative route to the city. Encouraged by Cochrane, he chose to continue the advance, if for no other reason that the British army might as well try to defeat the Americans where they were. And by then Jackson had decided to make a main stand on the east bank of the Mississippi River at the Rodriguez Canal, where he built lines of mud fortifications to protect his artillery and riflemen. Packenham tested these defenses in a reconnaissance in force on 28 December, but if he had been hoping that the Americans would retreat at the sight of a British army, as they had at Bladensburg, he was to be disappointed. A sustained British artillery attack on 1 January 1815 was no more successful. Finally, Packenham decided to risk everything and directly assaulted Jackson's main line of defense on 8 January. The result was a short and shocking slaughter of the British army. These veteran troops sustained more than two thousand casualties, including the loss of Packenham and two of his generals. American casualties, by contrast, amounted to seventy-one, only thirteen of which were deaths.

There could be no denying the magnitude of the American victory, even if it was as much the result of rash tactics on the part of the British as it was a tribute to Jackson's skills on the defense. Indeed, the Battle of New Orleans revealed that Jackson's measures had not been adequate for every contingency – a smaller American force on the west bank of the Mississippi River had, in fact, been overwhelmed – but the employment of his artillery on the east bank was more than sufficient to stop the enemy. And the heavy British casualties were not, as has been so often supposed, inflicted by sharpshooting Kentucky riflemen. Most of the enemy's losses were caused by musket balls, packed into canisters and fired from cannon. Nor were these losses, for all their severity, enough to end the British campaign. Under the command of Major General John Lambert, the British army retired to its transport vessels on Lake Borgne, from where they revived Cochrane's earlier strategy of attacking Mobile. This time they succeeded in capturing Fort Bowyer at Mobile Point on 11 February, three days before they received news of the Treaty of Ghent. The final action in the South, though, belonged to Cockburn, who sent six barges up the St. Marys River on the border between Georgia and Spanish East Florida on 24 February, destroying local vessels and military stores while incurring moderate losses as he did so.

For his part, Jackson did not regard the engagement on 8 January as the end of the war either. Not only did he not know about the peace treaty, but he was also reluctant to relax his control over New Orleans. That cost him much of the goodwill he had earned in the city, especially among the French-speaking community, many of whose members sought legal discharges from the militia on the grounds that they were really French rather than American nationals. Jackson refused to honor these requests, for which he was eventually fined $1,000 for contempt of court. News of the peace did not reach New Orleans until 13 March, but it had arrived in Washington on 14 February. Madison had forwarded it to the Senate, which gave its advice and consent within twenty-four hours. There was no opposition to the terms of the treaty, although Rufus King of New York, speaking for the Federalists, pointed to its omissions in a speech of "biting satire scarcely ever equaled."[11] But speaking for the Republicans, Jonathan Roberts of Pennsylvania remarked that the general sense of

---

[11] See *The Life and Correspondence of Rufus King*, 5:470.

relief was almost "childish" in its exuberance.[12] Two days later, on 17 February, the president issued a proclamation. Describing the treaty as "highly honorable to the United States," he declared the war at an end.[13]

III

The reception of the Treaty of Ghent was governed more by the circumstances surrounding its arrival than by the contents of its articles. Here the timing of the peace was more fortunate for the Americans than it was for the British. For the latter the restoration of the *status quo ante bellum* came after a prolonged period of heightened expectations for an important British victory. These were deflated by the release of parliamentary papers that disclosed the retreat of the British diplomats at Ghent, coupled with the considerable costs of a campaign that had brought no significant gains. For the former the news of peace came after the trials in the summer of 1814, the failure of the third session of the Thirteenth Congress to provide adequate means for an offensive in 1815, the prospect of disunion as presented by the Hartford Convention, and finally the victory at New Orleans. If the Americans were exultant in a moment of cathartic relief, the British were despondent, although their depression was dispelled shortly afterward by the final campaign in the European war when the Duke of Wellington vanquished Napoleon once and for all, after his brief return to France in March 1815, at the Battle of Waterloo in June.

At the war's end few Americans or Britons bothered to calculate its gains and losses with any precision. If many Britons more or less forgot about the war after Waterloo, the same was not true for Americans. As early as 1816 British visitors to the United States were complaining that they had to endure such boastful claims that Andrew Jackson was a greater general than the Duke of Wellington and that Stephen Decatur was a better sailor than Lord Nelson. In reality, the business of assessing the outcomes of the war is far more complicated. Many historians, including some Americans as well as most Britons and Canadians, have asserted that, as the United States accomplished none of its declared war aims, the result was an American defeat. But those who argue on that basis for a British victory overlook the circuitous path the British took to achieve it.

---

[12] See Philip S. Klein, ed., "Memoirs of a Senator from Pennsylvania: Jonathan Roberts, 1771–1854," *Pennsylvania Magazine of History and Biography* 62 (1938): 377–78.
[13] For the proclamation, see the *Daily National Intelligencer*, 18 February 1815.

Even if the British demands at Ghent were never intended as ultimatums to be forced on the United States at all costs, the ministry did hope to make the Canadian colonies more secure against future American aggression. In that matter, the British failed – and it can be argued they could never have succeeded, even if their diplomacy at Ghent had prevailed. Lord Liverpool himself realized as much within days of the signing of the peace. Admitting that it would have been "impractical" to have continued fighting "for a better frontier for Canada," he underscored the fundamental weaknesses of Canada and Great Britain in any conflict with the United States, namely that "the United States possess 7,500,000 people; the two Canadas not more than 300,000"; that "the government of the United States have access to Canada at all times of the year, whereas Great Britain is excluded from such access for nearly six months"; and that the American-Canadian boundary was "of such prodigious extent that it could never be made, as frontier, defensible against the means which the Americans might bring against it."[14] To put it another way, even if the British had won the war, they could never have won any sort of peace.

More complex considerations come into play when the results are measured from the perspectives of the Canadians and the Indians. For the former, the war can be regarded as a victory inasmuch as they survived a serious threat to their existence as members of the empire, albeit with considerable assistance from British regular troops and the Royal Navy. Without that survival there could have been no Canadian confederation of the sort that was formed in 1867, and the successes of the war in repulsing the American invader provided many mythical stories that contributed to the formation of a Canadian national identity, at least for the English-speaking, if not necessarily for the Francophone, population. For the Indians, the results were devastating, especially for those who resided within the boundaries of the United States. Regardless of whether they had fought on the side of the Americans or the British, these American Indians were deprived of significant amounts of land in the peace settlements, and the hopes of many of them for a united front against American expansion were dashed. After 1815 they were also unable to play any role as a makeweight in the international balance of power in North America in the ways they had done throughout the eighteenth century. The Indians in Canada were somewhat more fortunate. They were spared the fate of being conquered by Americans and their contribution to the successful

[14] Lord Liverpool to George Canning, 28 December 1814, *Supplementary Despatches, Correspondence, and Memoranda of Field Marshall Arthur Duke of Wellington*, 9:513.

British defense of Upper Canada had been a vital one. Only later in the
nineteenth century were they to suffer the same pressures on their culture
and their land that had driven their American counterparts to war in
1812.

The human and material costs of these outcomes have always been
regarded as slight, at least in comparison with the losses sustained by
Europeans during the Napoleonic Wars. The number of American combat deaths is usually given as 2,260, although that figure leaves a misleading impression for an age in which soldiers were always more likely to die
from sickness and primitive medical care than they were from the actions
of an enemy. At least 5,200 American regulars were lost to the former
causes between 1812 and 1815, and one historian has estimated that
somewhere in the region of 15,000 Americans of all descriptions, including regulars, militia, naval personnel, and civilians, might have died from
causes that were directly related to the conflict. British and Canadian
losses have never been calculated with any comparable precision, but it is
possible that some 2,700 regulars and provincial troops died from combat and sickness, and as many as 10,000 Britons and Canadians from
all backgrounds, including men serving on privateers and naval vessels,
might have perished as a result of the war. As percentages of the relatively small European populations of North America, these figures are
less trivial than might at first be imagined; and for the American and
British forces in the 1814 Niagara campaigns, the battlefield casualties,
as a percentage of the forces engaged, were comparable to those incurred
in European battles at the same time.[15]

For the Indians inside the United States, the picture was far worse.
The events of 1811–1814 proved that neither accommodation to nor
resistance against American encroachments would suffice to preserve their
cultural and political autonomy. After the United States dictated harsh
peace treaties that took land from all groups within the Indian nations in
question, advocates of the former approach to dealing with the Americans
suffered almost as severely as those who had supported the British. In all,
as many as 3,500 warriors may have been killed on the northwestern and
southwestern frontiers of the United States and possibly another 10,000
Indian men, women, and children could have died as a result of the war-
related diseases and starvation that were always more regular features
of Indian life than they were for Americans or Canadians. Many of the

---

[15] To the extent that historians have data on these matters, they have been conveniently
gathered in Hickey, *Don't Give Up the Ship!*, 296–97.

smaller Indian nations, such as the Shawnee, lacked the demographic depth to absorb such losses, and if the total population of all the Indian peoples involved in the war was in the region of seventy-five thousand, their casualties can be described only as disastrous.[16]

The economic and financial consequences of the war are difficult to calculate. Although the war strained American finances to the breaking point and increased the national debt from $57 million in 1812 to $127 million in 1815, it cannot be argued that the conflict itself had any profound impact on the larger contours of American economic development. The United States would still have emerged as a liberal capitalist society even if the war had never been fought. Domestic manufacturing, certainly, received a boost as a result of the policies of commercial restriction and war between 1807 and 1815, but many of the gains here were lost in the postwar period, partly as result of the resumption of trade with Great Britain and partly because of business failures during the Panic of 1819. But in most other respects, the American economy and government revenues rebounded quickly after 1815 and were further stimulated by rising immigration from Europe. As a result, the enlarged national debt was entirely eliminated by 1836.

The situation with respect to Canada is less certain, it being difficult to separate the costs of the war in North America from the larger expenses incurred by Great Britain as a result of the wars in Europe and the Caribbean. But it is clear that the economies of Lower and Upper Canada did not revive so quickly. Both provinces were hard hit by the cessation of British military expenditures, as were the Maritimes, and these were not greatly offset by advantages that might otherwise have arisen from any increase in postwar immigration. In fact, immigration into Upper Canada from the United States was effectively terminated after 1816, and postwar politics in the province were dominated by disputes about how to pay for the widespread damages that had been inflicted by both American and British forces between 1812 and 1815. Compensation claims paid by governments hardly covered the losses here and economic growth in Upper Canada thereafter was modest, and often uneven, until more significant transformations occurred in the mid-nineteenth century.

These matters notwithstanding, it is more important to stress that the significance of the war, particularly for the United States, cannot be meaningfully assessed by the calculation of gains and losses. Nor do these matters greatly impinge on what has always been the central question

[16] Ibid., 298–99.

posed by the war: why did the United States, which in 1812 demon-
strably enjoyed great advantages over Canada in terms of population
and resources, fail to mount a more effective military effort than it did
and in ways that would have permitted the Madison administration to
hold enough Canadian territory to force concessions from Great Britain.
Admittedly, this is a peculiarly American question – it is of little interest
to Britons and Canadians – and it assumes that the United States should
have been able to win the war without much difficulty. It is possible to
object that even if the United States had occupied all of Upper Canada
and Lower Canada as far eastward as Montreal that this might not have
sufficed to carry the day. As long as the British retained Quebec and the
Maritimes, they would remain a significant presence in North America,
and it is not clear that the Americans could have easily removed them
from these outposts of imperial power. Indeed, it is quite possible to imagine that, even if the Americans had commenced a siege of Quebec – a very
difficult enterprise – the British could have utilized their naval superiority
in the Gulf of St. Lawrence and on the lower St. Lawrence River to drive
away any invading forces.

But questions remain about the poor American military performance,
or as John Quincy Adams asked: why was it "a burlesque upon war?"[17]
In addressing this issue, historians have traditionally pointed to a range
of factors that are assumed to have interacted in ways that produced
unsatisfactory outcomes in all aspects of war making. These include a
weak and divided administration that made bad strategic decisions, most
notably because of its preoccupation with Upper Canada to the exclusion
of understanding the importance of securing control on the Great Lakes; a
more widespread incompetence in all aspects of the art of war, especially
among the generals of the U.S. Army; an overreliance on untrained militia forces; severe logistical and organizational difficulties that crippled the
implementation of strategy; and a superior British military performance
in the defense of Canada. It might be observed that the superiority of the
British military effort owed as much to the impact of the other aforemen-
tioned factors on the Americans as it did to the virtues the British forces
themselves possessed. But for as long as the British remained on the defensive, their performance was adequate for Canada's needs, even under the
leadership of Prevost, who has often been condemned for fussy behavior
and excessively cautious tactics. And once they took the offensive, as they

---

[17] See John Quincy Adams to Abigail Adams, 5 June 1813, Worthington C. Ford, ed., *The
Writings of John Quincy Adams* (7 vols; New York, 1914–1923), 4:488.

did in the summer of 1814, the British were no more successful than the Americans. They failed for some of the same reasons, too, including poor strategic and tactical decisions, combined with an overweening sense of superiority over the Americans, especially at New Orleans, that bordered on a species of incompetence in its own right.

With respect to the other factors said to have precluded an American victory, it can be maintained that they are not so much incorrect as they have been overemphasized or misunderstood. In the matter of presidential leadership, for example, Madison has always been subjected to severe criticism, especially for allowing himself to be pushed into a war he did not really want and then for failing to provide sufficient energy and direction as commander in chief. Indeed, so great has been the emphasis on Madison's personal limitations – his "unmilitary" bearing, his shy and retiring nature, his dislike of public speaking, and his toleration of too many conflicts in his cabinet – that these characteristics have been seen as contributing directly to the failure of the war. But Madison was not pushed into war against his will; he chose to resort to war after he had concluded in the summer of 1811 that he had no better alternative. And although it may be true that he did not provide the style of executive leadership that has been associated with later war presidents, most notably Abraham Lincoln and Franklin Roosevelt, it should be remembered that he and his contemporaries had deeply ingrained concerns about the misuse of executive power in times of war, so much so that they had hardly developed the expectation that a president should be seen as a publicly active commander in chief. Madison's revulsion at the spectacle of John Adams personally whipping up hysteria for war with France in 1798 goes a long way toward explaining why he was so restrained as a war president after 1812. Even so, Madison usually made his policy preferences plain enough to his fellow politicians and he was persistent, if not always successful, in seeking their implementation. And although he tolerated for too long too many ineffective and disputatious colleagues, it was not always clear that he had better options available to him at the time.

As for the matter of war strategy, it is said that the United States expended too much effort in attacking the wrong places – that is, that instead of concentrating on Montreal and Quebec, they frittered away their resources on targets to the west, such as Fort Malden and the Niagara Peninsula. And in the latter places, they would have succeeded better if they had first secured the command of both Lakes Erie and Ontario. This is true enough, but the problem was not that the administration failed to grasp the significance of either Montreal or the Great Lakes. In every year of the war Montreal was consistently identified as the ultimate and most important target for the American armies, and after its capture it was assumed that the focus would shift to Quebec and the Maritimes. The difficulties arose when the administration, as a result of unanticipated military and political pressures, or, in some cases, as a preliminary to advances on places of greater strategic importance, allowed itself to be diverted from its original goals. The failure of these diversionary efforts then created problems that required additional attention and resources. The result was that the United States became bogged down in a series of small conflicts that did not develop according to its larger conception of how the war should be won.

Regarding the control of the Great Lakes, its importance was always understood, in general terms. In 1812, though, the administration hoped that quick successes on land would obviate the need to construct inland naval forces. That mistake was not repeated in either 1813 or 1814, and the naval buildup of those years succeeded on Lake Erie while never being quite enough to overmatch the efforts undertaken by the British on Lake Ontario. In the case of the latter lake, it might be argued that Chauncey should have taken more risks than he did, as his overly prudent approach served the goals of the British defense better than they did the American need to take the offensive. More puzzling was the failure to seize Kingston. Its capture could well have gained many of the objectives that were promised by the fall of Montreal – undermining Canada's economic contribution to the British Empire and depriving the British army of access to the Indian nations that were essential for its defense of Upper Canada. Armstrong clearly understood this, but in 1813 he allowed himself to be diverted to other targets, and he lacked either the force of personality or the diplomatic skills to compel Wilkinson to do the job. And in 1814, although Kingston was to be the ultimate goal of a successful campaign, too many intermediate objectives and difficulties were interposed to make its attainment possible.

That being the case, the problem with the American war effort was not so much defective strategy as it was the inability to develop sufficient military power to surmount the other obstacles to success. Here the logistic and organizational obstacles to victory seem to loom large. Undeniably, the problems of waging an offensive war along a frontier nearly one thousand miles in length and having to supply invading forces from towns and cities well to the rear of the front were enormous. On many parts of the northern frontier the population density was too low and the terrain too difficult to permit armies to forage off the country as they

advanced. The problems of supply were also compounded by administrative and structural defects in the supply agencies themselves, especially
their lack of centralization and their inability to obtain efficiencies in the
purchase and delivery of food and matériel to the troops. Yet too much
can be made of these matters. The few victories the United States did
achieve in the war – at the Battle of the Thames, in the Creek War, and
at New Orleans – were all accomplished on the farthermost extremities
of the nation, where logistic and organizational difficulties were most
acutely felt. The critical offensive failures occurred on the Niagara and in
northern New York and Vermont, all areas with larger populations and
better communications than many other places on the military frontier.
Logistical problems, in themselves, do not explain the failed campaigns
there.

Nor will it do to single out other factors, such as an overreliance on
untrained militia and the incompetence of the generals, as the essential
keys to American military weakness. In fairness to the militias, it can
be said that they fought both badly and well during the war. They dis-
graced themselves on some occasions, such as in the fall of Detroit and
on the Niagara Peninsula in 1812 and again at Bladensburg in 1814.
But they also fought well in the Northwest in 1813, on the Niagara
Peninsula in 1814, and at New Orleans in 1815. Their performance,
in short, depended very much on the circumstances of time and place.
That might seem to leave only the element of military incompetence to
consider, and most historians of the war have usually been content to
stress the inadequacies of the American generals as a complete and sufficient explanation for the misfortunes of the war and to leave matters
there. And the evidence of incompetence in the American armed forces
between 1812 and 1815 is oppressively abundant. Indeed, it is unlikely
that any American president has ever been afflicted with so wretched a
crop of generals as was Madison when he commissioned the likes of Hull,
Van Rensselaer, Smyth, Dearborn, Winchester, and Wilkinson. Their personal and professional shortcomings have always made good copy for
historians bent on telling a tale of woe (or a comedy of errors), but seldom have historians probed beneath the surface to get some sense of
why incompetence and ineptitude were so pervasive throughout the U.S.
Army.

That concern should direct our attention to the army as a whole, for
it would seem logical to conclude that had the United States had a better
army than it did, its performance in the war would have been better than
it was. And there were a number of underlying factors that prevented

the army, especially the infantry, from functioning as an effective instrument of American policy. One of them has always been assumed to be its size. The army of the early republic was not a single establishment but a composite of several establishments, each with its own history, strengths, and weaknesses. Collectively, these establishments by 1814 could have provided the nation with an armed force totaling some sixty-two thousand officers and men, but at no time during the war was the army at full strength. How large it actually was is uncertain. By the end of 1814, it was generally believed that there were somewhere between thirty-five thousand and thirty-eight thousand men in the ranks. This number is too low, and the real figure may have been closer to forty-eight thousand (even without recourse to a classification of the militia). Or, to put it differently, the recruiting and record-keeping systems of the War Department were so cumbersome that it did not know how many men it had at its disposal. And generals and politicians who are uncertain about their own resources are likely to overestimate the resources of their enemy – and erroneous estimates about manpower constantly misinformed American strategic and tactical decisions throughout the war.

Recruiting as such was not at the root of the army's problems during the war. With a total strength of more than forty thousand men in the summer of 1814, the United States should have been able to field a force that could have defeated the far smaller number of British regulars in Canada – but only if that force was properly organized and adequately trained. Yet at no stage in the war did the army master these prerequisites for success, and there were three main reasons why this was so. One was that the officer corps lacked stability and cohesion – it was always afflicted with high rates of turnover resulting from resignations and dismissals – and it was not properly trained in basic skills and maneuvers. Few, if any, officers had much military experience, and even fewer had received any military education. West Point had produced only eighty-nine graduates by 1812, and to the extent that officers appointed after 1812 had any skills at all, they were self-taught or acquired through militia service. It was by no means uncommon for regimental adjutants to have to arrange for special training sessions for officers, especially those newly commissioned, before essential skills could be imparted to large numbers of raw recruits. And too many officers were guilty of neglecting their own duties in managing the units under their command, to say nothing of the fact that they often appeared before their men in too casual a manner, failed to issue commands in a clear and distinct voice, and turned the business of training over to noncommissioned officers rather than directing it themselves. Mastery of basic routines is essential for the functioning of any military force, but the U.S. Army failed to demonstrate this between 1812 and 1815. The resulting "slovenliness" was frequently deplored by the commanding generals, but it was a regular and recurring feature of wartime army life.[18]

The second reason was that the War Department never clarified which methods of training the officers should adopt, with the result being that the army followed three incompatible systems of drill throughout the war. One was a reworking of the discipline that had been prescribed by Baron von Steuben during the Revolutionary War; the second was an infantry handbook compiled by the Philadelphia newspaper editor and military enthusiast William Duane, which was heartily disliked for being too "theoretical" and "innovative" by most officers who attempted to use it; and the third was a manual, drawn up in 1812 by Alexander Smyth, which was a distillation of the tactics followed by the French army at the end of the eighteenth century. All too often officers would experiment with combinations of any two of these systems, such as those of Smyth and Steuben, even as they were aware that, although this might have been suitable for introducing raw recruits to elementary drill, it was far from an adequate preparation for encountering British regulars on the field of battle. It was not until November 1814 that the War Department finally convened a board of officers to prescribe a uniform method of training, and it was only in January 1815 that the board decreed that training should follow an adaptation – made by Winfield Scott – of the drill of the French army.

And the third reason why the problem of training was never surmounted was that the army could never assemble large enough bodies of men for sufficiently lengthy periods of time to permit the troops to acquire the proficiency necessary to prevail on the battlefield. The making of a regular soldier in both America and Europe in the Napoleonic era was a slow and laborious business, as indeed it had been throughout the eighteenth century. Raw recruits had to be taught how to march and how to load and fire cumbersome and heavy smoothbore muskets. They

---

[18] Complaints of this nature pervade the very sizable collection of company and orderly books, most of them dating from the War of 1812, preserved in Records of United States Army Commands, 1784–1821, RG 98, National Archives. The general court martial case files of army officers during the war, held in the Records of the Judge Advocate General's Office (RG 153, National Archives) also furnish abundant evidence of the inability of large numbers of them to master the most basic duties associated with the responsibilities of their rank.

also had to be drilled in small squads, then in companies, and finally in regiments and divisions to practice battlefield maneuvers – the evolutions of the line that would permit them to change from columns into lines and back and to wheel in various directions – that would ultimately permit them to discharge a massive weight of shot at the enemy.[19] What happened, instead, particularly in 1812 and 1813, was a very different story. The War Department, needing to dispatch whatever troops were at hand to wherever they might be required for hastily improvised offensives, detached companies from their regiments before they had been fully equipped and prepared for combat. These patchwork forces then disintegrated under the impact of defeat, desertion, and sickness. In short, the United States between 1812 and 1815 created the skeleton of an army, but it could never put flesh and muscle on that skeleton. As a consequence, the army, as a national institution, had few opportunities to consolidate, mature, and evolve into disciplined and cohesive units that could meet an opposing force on equal terms.

The only partial exception to this state of affairs was the case of the well-trained left division of the Northern Army under Brown and Scott on the Niagara Peninsula in the summer of 1814. Yet Brown and Scott could take little more than four thousand regular troops into Upper Canada while at the same time the army, as a whole, had more than forty thousand enlisted men on its rolls. The difference between the figures of four thousand and forty thousand speaks volumes about the difficulties the United States encountered in translating its manpower advantage over Canada into an effective fighting force. (It also confirms another truth about the realities of army life – that it is often the case that large numbers of troops seldom see active service in the course of a war; and that was certainly true for most of the men of the U.S. Army between 1812 and 1815.) The result was a largely untrained and haphazardly organized army, led by too many manifestly inadequate generals, that was in no condition to fulfill the strategic requirements of the Madison administration, namely that it seize enough Canadian territory to compel Great Britain to respect American neutral rights in a peace treaty intended to insulate the United States from the maritime depredations of the European belligerents.

[19] It should be recalled here that the smoothbore, muzzle-loading musket – the basic weapon used in all infantry forces of the period – was notoriously inaccurate beyond a range of about thirty yards. These weapons were not equipped with gunsights and their effectiveness depended on the impact of a massed volley on an opposing force, not on the accuracy of any particular shot.

IV

After 1815, the Madison administration and its successor, headed by James Monroe, made serious efforts to deal with the weaknesses that had been exposed by the difficulties of mobilization after 1812. Most notable in this regard were the army reforms implemented by John C. Calhoun during his tenure in the War Department between 1817 and 1825. Among them was the creation of an army that was nearly four times larger than the Peace Establishment that had been reformed by Jefferson in 1802. There was also an insistence on the importance of professional training for its officers, and in consequence an education at West Point became an essential requirement for most men who sought a military career. Nor did Calhoun neglect the army's staff organizations. These, too, were enlarged and reformed, with particular attention being given to the Corps of Engineers, which had the vital task of improving the nation's coastal defenses against future attacks by the Royal Navy. Even the U.S. Navy itself, despite its successes in the war, was not spared from reform. The fleet was expanded, plans were drawn up for the standardization of shipbuilding, and the secretary of the navy was to be advised by a Board of Naval Commissioners consisting of at least three senior naval officers. And the financial problems encountered during the war were finally addressed in 1816 by the adoption of higher tariffs and the establishment of a second Bank of the United States, conceived along the lines that had been so bitterly disputed in 1814.

The impetus for these changes diminished somewhat in the 1820s, largely because of government cost cutting that followed the onset of the Panic of 1819. The army, for example, was reduced to six thousand officers and men, scarcely larger than it had been on the eve of war in 1812. Great Britain also experienced difficulties in maintaining adequate land and naval forces in Canada, and after 1817 it began to reduce expenditures in these areas as well. A more important factor underlying these developments, however, was a growing awareness that after 1820 the world was becoming a safer place than it had been between 1789 and 1815, for both the nations of Europe and for North America. With the final defeat of Napoleon, coupled with the settlements worked out at the Congress of Vienna, Europe was at peace for the following four decades. Exactly how the statesmen at Vienna accomplished this has been a matter of dispute. If they did not do it by consciously restoring an older style of balance of power politics – which could just as easily give rise to a war as it could preserve peace – they seem to have succeeded nonetheless in creating an equilibrium among the competing interests and spheres of influence in Europe, one in which no single nation, not even Russia after its defeat of France, could dominate the continent, and Great Britain's naval power and its pursuit of trade and markets remained unchallenged.[20] When war broke out again in Europe, it was in the Crimea, on the farthermost extremities of Eastern Europe, in an area where the United States had few tangible interests. Moreover, France and Great Britain were allies, not enemies, in that conflict and North America in general, and the United States in particular, was thus spared a repetition of a war for trade and empire of the sort that had characterized transatlantic international relations between 1689 and 1815.

The settlements at Vienna contributed in other ways to a more peaceful world, most notably by excluding colonial and maritime disputes from their agendas. There is no doubt that some Americans, Madison especially, were disappointed by that decision. Despite the failure of the Russian mediation in 1813, American hopes lingered that Russia and the Baltic nations might still be able to impose treaty restraints on British maritime power. Great Britain would have none of it, with the result being that commercial and colonial disputes among the nations at Vienna were fenced off from their disagreements over European affairs. By the same token, disagreements between the United States and the nations of Europe were unlikely to assume the degrees of seriousness that they had before 1815, when they added fuel to the life and death struggles of the Napoleonic Wars. Nowhere was this situation more helpful to the United States than in the matter of the collapse of the Spanish-American Empire. Its disintegration had begun in 1808 and continued apace after 1815; by 1822 it was essentially complete, with only Cuba and Puerto Rico still under the rule of Madrid. Throughout those years the United States was in near conflict with Spain, a British ally, over the possession of East and West Florida, and British forces had attacked the republic through Spain's Gulf Coast territories. After 1815, Great Britain no longer had any need for such Spanish assistance, nor was it much disposed to rescue Spain in its disputes with the United States. The full benefit of that state of affairs accrued to Washington in 1819, when Spain finally abandoned not only its Florida colonies but also a sizable portion of its claims in the Pacific Northwest, thereby making the United States a truly continental power in its own right.

[20] For a discussion of this point, see Paul W. Schroeder, "Did the Vienna Settlement Rest on a Balance of Power," *American Historical Review* 97 (1992): 683–706.

It was in this context of a largely peaceful Europe that the United States, Canada, and Great Britain were able to resolve most of the differences that had led to war in 1812. Commercial relations were restored in a convention of July 1815, which provided for reciprocity in the transatlantic trade between Great Britain and the United States but without making any arrangements for trade between the latter nation and the Canadian and West Indian colonies of the former. Other matters, including impressment, boundary disputes, fishing rights, and naval armaments on the Great Lakes, were taken up in negotiations that culminated in a more comprehensive convention in October 1818. A potential naval armaments race on the Great Lakes was averted by the Rush-Bagot agreement of April 1817, so named after acting Secretary of State Richard Rush and British minister Charles Bagot. Neither the lakes nor the boundary line between Canada and the United States was ever completely disarmed, but the two nations agreed to maintain no more than one naval vessel on each of the lakes, including Lake Champlain, to be limited in its armaments and its burden. Otherwise, all vessels built during the war were laid up and dismantled. This agreement did not at all reflect any increase in trust between the two signatories so much as it did a pragmatic awareness, on the part of Great Britain particularly, that it could not outstrip its rival in ship construction on the inland lakes and that in those regions only American future goodwill could guarantee the security of Canada.

Similarly, with respect to fishing rights in the Maritimes, Great Britain could never enforce a complete exclusion there, regardless of its hopes at Ghent – unless it could maintain a far larger naval force to patrol those waters in the fishing season than it wished to. The dispute was hardly worth a war, so there was no alternative but to negotiate a fresh agreement. This consumed the better part of two years, but by 1818 jurisdictions were established in which Americans could fish and dry their catches in Newfoundland and Labrador. The problem of impressment was also much discussed, with the British coming close to accepting the American idea of a mutual exclusion of each nation's citizens from their merchant marines. No final settlement was reached, however, because of differences over how to establish lists that would include, or at least not exclude, mariners who had been previously naturalized by the United States. On boundary matters, most of the disputed islands off the coast of Maine were given the United States, although Grand Manan went to Great Britain. The border between Canada and the United States was readjusted in ways that denied the British access to the source of the Mississippi River and then extended along the forty-ninth parallel to the Rocky Mountains. Because there was no agreement on whether the line should extend through the mountains to the Pacific Ocean, a joint occupation of the Oregon Country was established instead. But the British did accept the American reoccupation of Astoria on the Columbia River in 1818, a concession that strengthened the position of the United States in the negotiations with Spain that led to the establishment of an American coastline on the Pacific Ocean.

The matter of American trade with the British colonies in Canada and the West Indies proved more complicated and more protracted. There were substantial interests on both sides, especially in trade with the West Indies, and it had been the British wish to exclude Americans from this trade that had underlain much of the tension in Anglo-American relations before 1812. After the war, Americans, as they had in 1783, sought unrestricted access to the islands, but Great Britain refused to grant it. Congress retaliated, in 1817 and 1818, with two navigation acts, the first excluding British colonial imports into the United States unless they were carried in American bottoms, and the second prohibiting both exports to and imports from all British colonial possessions closed to American shipping. There then ensued twelve years of commercial warfare, even though by the mid-1820s it was apparent to all concerned that the West Indies were becoming of less value to the British Empire than they had been previously and that the mother country was, at the same time, moving toward a general liberalization of its trade policy and the abolition of slavery in all its colonial territories. By 1822 the British were ready to settle the dispute, provided that the United States would accept a degree of preference for British goods and ships in the event of the West Indies being opened to American trade, but John Quincy Adams, in his capacity as secretary of state before 1825 and as president thereafter, refused to accept any compromise. The quarrel lasted until 1830, when Andrew Jackson ended it – and on terms that favored Americans more than they did Britons or Canadians. As these developments played out, the armistice of Ghent was gradually transformed into a permanent peace.

By the 1830s, moreover, the rapid growth of the American republic, territorially, demographically, and economically, was such that it was almost impossible for Great Britain, even with its naval supremacy on the Atlantic Ocean, to contemplate the costs of a war with the United States, a conclusion that was reinforced by the ever-increasing value and volume of trade between the two nations. Even so cautious a person as Abraham Lincoln, in his celebrated 1838 address to the Young Men's Lyceum of Springfield, Illinois, realized as much when he boasted that "all the armies of Europe, Asia and Africa combined, with all the treasure of the earth (our own excepted) in their military chest; with a Buonaparte for a commander, could not by force, take a drink from the Ohio, or make a track on the Blue Ridge, in a trial of a thousand years."[21] The Canadians, who were the third and weakest members of this transatlantic triangle, knew full well that they benefited less from this expanding consortium of Anglo-American interests than did the two greater powers that continued to dominate almost every aspect of their existence. Many of them envied the progress of their larger and more dynamic neighbor to the south, although others came to resent what they saw as a British failure to adopt policies that might foster a greater degree of Canadian development. And for every Canadian who feared that one day Canada might be overwhelmed by the United States, there were as many who worried that Great Britain would abandon them to that fate. Indeed, it was not always clear who and what was Canadian at all, an uncertainty that contributed to the reluctance of many nineteenth-century Canadian conservatives to see much good in anything emanating from the United States.

It would be tempting to conclude that Americans had fewer anxieties. After all, by the 1830s the United States was about to enter the age of Manifest Destiny, but appearances were deceptive. Well into the nineteenth century, Americans fretted about threats to their interests from British commercial and naval power. Many feared, too, the apparent superiority of British cultural influence, although by the time Great Britain and the United States celebrated the centennial of the Treaty of Ghent in 1914, both nations could agree to congratulate themselves for having displayed enough good sense to have avoided another war. Yet echoes of the older tensions in the triangulated relationships among Canada, Great Britain, and the United States persist in ways that still hit raw nerves. The filmmaker Michael Moore manipulated them to satirical advantage in his 1995 movie *Canadian Bacon*, the story of how a weakened U.S. president – albeit not one who bore much resemblance to James Madison – attempted to shore up his declining popularity by mismanaging a war against Canada; and as recently as 2010 American diplomats reported concerns about the high levels of anti-Americanism in Canadian television shows depicting "nefarious American officials" carrying out "nefarious deeds in Canada, from planning to bomb Quebec to stealing Canadian

[21] See *The Collected Works of Abraham Lincoln* (9 vols., Roy P. Basler, ed.; New Brunswick, NJ, 1953–1955), 1:109.

water supplies."[22] And what should anyone make of the popularity of the sketch by the comedy group Three Dead Trolls in a Baggie, in which Canadians entertain the fantasy that it was they, and not the British, who burned Washington in 1814?[23] Perhaps the War of 1812 has not been forgotten at all. Its ghosts linger with us still?

---

[22] See *The New York Times*, 1 December 2010. The contents of the American diplomatic cables were released from the Wikileaks Archive.

[23] The sketch can be accessed at http://www.youtube.com/watch?v=o7jlFZhprU4.

An Essay on Sources

The literature on the War of 1812 is a vast one that cannot possibly be fully listed in a short study of this nature. In addition to the works mentioned in the footnotes to the chapters – which are not discussed here – the titles cited in this essay represent only some of the most important materials I have drawn on. If my omissions here offend anyone, it is not my intention to give offense, and it goes without saying that I am enormously indebted to several generations of scholars who have contributed to a historiography that extends across two centuries. I have, however, concentrated on listing titles that appeared after the turn of the twentieth century, to the exclusion of the very large number of works on the war published in the nineteenth century. These latter writings are not always easily available to today's readers.

The most valuable listings of the sources, primary and secondary, that relate to the War of 1812 have been made by John C. Fredriksen, notably his *Free Trade and Sailors' Rights: A Bibliography of the War of 1812* (Westport, CT, 1985), *War of 1812 Resource Guide* (Los Angeles, 1989), and *War of 1812 Eyewitness Accounts: An Annotated Bibliography* (Westport, CT, 1997). Fredriksen has also published several other important reference works and sources, including *Officers of the War of 1812 with Anecdotes and Portraits* (Lewiston, NY, 1989), *The United States Army in the War of 1812: Concise Biographies of Commanders and of Regiments, with Bibliographies of Published and Primary Sources* (Jefferson, NC, 2009), and *The War of 1812 in Person: Fifteen Accounts of the United States Army Regulars, Volunteers and Militiamen* (Jefferson, NC, 2010). Another useful guide is Dwight L. Smith, *The War of 1812: An Annotated Bibliography* (New York, 1985); and a valuable early compilation of American sources is John Brannan, ed., *Official Letters of the Military and Naval Officers of the United States, during the War with Great Britain in the Years 1812, 13, 14 & 15* (Washington, D.C., 1823). Some individual studies of the war also contain particularly comprehensive bibliographies of primary and secondary sources. See especially the revision by Donald E. Graves of J. Mackay Hitsman's *The Incredible War of 1812: A Military History* (Toronto, 1999) and Jon Latimer's *1812: War with America* (Cambridge, MA, 2007).

On the British and Canadian aspects of the war, the most valuable collections have been compiled by Earnest A. Cruikshank, *Documentary History of the Campaigns upon the Niagara Frontier in 1812–1814* (9 vols.; Welland, ON, 1896–1908), *Documents Relating to the Invasion of Canada and the Surrender of Detroit* (Ottawa, 1913), and *Documents Relating to the Invasion of the Niagara Peninsula by the United States Army, Commanded by General Jacob Brown* (Niagara-on-the-Lake, ON, 1920). These compilations contain a very wide range of sources, but they are not always easy to use because of their rather haphazard organization. A more easily accessible collection of sources is William Woods, ed., *Select British Documents of the Canadian War of 1812* (4 vols.; Toronto, 1920–1928). Also useful is Stuart Sutherland, *His Majesty's Gentlemen: A Directory of Regular British Army Officers in the War of 1812* (Toronto, 2000).

The war has been the subject of many one-volume studies, both academic and popular, most of which focus on its military and naval dimensions. The leading titles here are Francis Beirne, *The War of 1812* (New York, 1949); Pierre Berton, *The Invasion of Canada, 1812–1813* (Toronto, 1980) and *Flames across the Border: The Canadian-American Tragedy, 1813–1814* (Boston, 1989); Jeremy Black, *The War of 1812 in the Age of Napoleon* (Norman, OK, 2009); Walter Borneman, *1812: The War That Forged a Nation* (New York, 2004); Harry Coles, *The War of 1812* (Chicago, 1965); John Elting, *Amateurs to Arms! A Military History of the War of 1812* (Chapel Hill, NC, 1991); James Hannay, *History of the War of 1812 between Great Britain and the United States of America* (Toronto, 1905); Donald Hickey, *The War of 1812: A Forgotten Conflict* (Chicago, 1990); J. Mackay Hitsman, *The Incredible War of 1812: A Military History* (Toronto, 1965); Reginald Horsman, *The War of 1812* (New York, 1969); A. J. Langguth, *Union 1812: The Americans Who Fought the Second War of Independence* (New York, 2006); Charles P. Lucas, *The Canadian War of 1812* (Oxford, U.K., 1906); John K. Mahon, *The War of 1812* (Gainesville, FL, 1972); J. C. A. Stagg, *Mr.*

Madison's War: Politics, Diplomacy and Warfare in the Early American Republic, 1783–1830 (Princeton, NJ, 1983); George F. Stanley, *The War of 1812: Land Operations* (Toronto, 1983); Victor Suthren, *The War of 1812* (Toronto, 1999); Glenn Tucker, *Poltroons and Patriots: A Popular Account of the War of 1812* (2 vols.; Indianapolis, 1964); Wesley B. Turner, *The War of 1812: The War That Both Sides Won* (Toronto, 1990); Patrick T. C. White, *A Nation on Trial: America and the War of 1812* (New York, 1965); and Mark Zuehlke, *For Honor's Sake: The War of 1812 and the Brokering of an Uneasy Peace* (New York, 2006).

There are also two journals devoted to the war: see *The War of 1812 Magazine*, published by the Napoleon Series and available at http://www.napoleon-series.org/; and the *Journal of the War of 1812: An International Journal Dedicated to the Last Anglo-American War, 1812–1815.*

Accounts of the events leading to war are a staple item in almost all histories of the conflict, as well as in most studies of early American foreign policy and the biographies of the most prominent American political leaders of the first two decades of the nineteenth century. Most diplomatic histories of the subject set the war in the context of Anglo-American relations, where the most important work is the trilogy by Bradford Perkins, *The First Rapprochement: England and the United States, 1795–1805* (Berkeley, CA, 1955), *Prologue to War: England and the United States, 1805–1812* (Berkeley, CA, 1961), and *Castlereagh and Adams: England and the United States, 1812–1823* (Berkeley, CA, 1964). Also useful is Albert H. Carr, *The Coming of War: An Account of the Remarkable Events Leading to the War of 1812* (New York, 1960); Ronald Hatzenbuehler, "Party Unity and the Decision for War in the House of Representatives, 1812," *William and Mary Quarterly*, 3d ser., 29 (1972): 367–90; Hatzenbuehler and Robert Ivie, *Congress Declares War: Rhetoric, Leadership and Partisanship in the Early Republic* (Kent, OH, 1983); Reginald Horsman, *The Causes of the War of 1812* (Philadelphia, 1962); and Leland Johnson, "The Suspense Was Hell: The Senate Vote for War in 1812," *Indiana Magazine of History* 65 (1969): 247–67. There are three relevant articles by J. C. A. Stagg, "James Madison and the 'Malcontents': The Political Origins of the War of 1812," *William and Mary Quarterly*, 3d ser., 33 (1976): 557–85; "The Coming of the War of 1812: The View from the Presidency," *Quarterly Journal of the Library of Congress* 37 (1980): 223–41; and "James Madison and the Coercion of Great Britain: Canada, the West Indies, and the War of 1812," *William and Mary Quarterly*, 3d ser., 38 (1981): 3–34. Also pertinent in this

context is the debate over the role of the so-called War Hawks in precipi-
tating the conflict – see Roger Brown, "The War Hawks of 1812: An Historical Myth," *Indiana Magazine of History* 60 (1964): 137–51; Reginald
Horsman, "Who Were the War Hawks," ibid., 121–36; Ronald Hatzenbuehler, "The War Hawks and the Question of Congressional Leadership
in 1812," *Pacific Historical Review* 45 (1976): 1–22; Harry Fritz, "The
War Hawks of 1812: Party Leadership in the Twelfth Congress," *Capitol
Studies* 5 (1977): 19–30; Rudolph Bell, "Mr. Madison's War and Long-
Term Congressional Voting Behavior," *William and Mary Quarterly*, 3d
ser., 36 (1979): 373–95; and also J. C. A. Stagg, "Between Black Rock
and a Hard Place: Peter B. Porter's Plan for an American Invasion of
Canada in 1812," *Journal of the Early Republic* 19 (1999): 385–422.
These political studies should be read in the context of the economic
history provided by George R. Taylor, "Agrarian Discontent in the Mississippi Valley Preceding the War of 1812," *Journal of Political Economy*
39 (1931): 471–505, and Margaret K. Latimer, "South Carolina – A Pro-
tagonist of the War of 1812," *American Historical Review* 61 (1956):
914–29.

Almost as important as Anglo-American relations is the context of
Franco-American relations, although the subject has been much less stud-
ied. The most important monographs are Frank Melvin, *Napoleon's Nav-
igation System: A Study of Trade Control during the Continental Block-
ade* (New York, 1919); Ulaine Bonnel, *La France, Les États-Unis et la
Guerre de la course (1797–1815)* (Paris, 1961); Clifford Eagan, *Neither
Peace nor War: Franco-American Relations, 1803–1812* (Baton Rouge,
LA, 1983); and Peter Hill, *Napoleon's Troublesome Americans: Franco-
American Relations, 1804–1815* (Washington, D.C., 2005). See also the
two articles by Lawrence Kaplan, "France and Madison's Decision for
War, 1812," *Mississippi Valley Historical Review* 50 (1964): 652–71,
and "France and the War of 1812," *Journal of American History* 57
(1970): 36–47.

Essential for any understanding of the War of 1812 is the background
literature on European international relations during the Napoleonic
Wars, which is far too vast to enumerate. The most useful studies for
those interested in the War of 1812 are Alfred Crosby, *America, Russia, Hemp, and Napoleon* (Columbus, OH, 1965); François Crouzet,
L'Economie britannique et le blocus continental (1803–1813) (2 vols.;
Paris, 1958); Derek McKay and H. M. Scott, *The Rise of the Great
Powers 1648–1815* (London, 1983); Rory Muir, *Britain and the Defeat
of Napoleon, 1807–1815* (New Haven, CT, 1996); Paul Schroeder, *The*

Transformation of European Politics 1763–1848 (Oxford, U.K., 1994); Charles Esdaile, *Napoleon's Wars: An International History, 1803–1815* (New York, 2007); and David Bell, *The First Total War: Napoleon's Europe and the Birth of Warfare as We Know It* (Boston, 2007). Biographies of the leading British statesmen seldom contain very much information of direct relevance to American historians, but see Denis Gray, *Spencer Perceval: The Evangelical Prime Minister* (Manchester, U.K., 1962); Norman Gash, *Lord Liverpool: The Life and Political Career of Robert Banks Jenkinson, Second Earl of Liverpool, 1779–1828* (Cambridge, U.K., 1984); Neville Thompson, *Earl Bathurst and the British Empire* (Barnsley, U.K., 1999); and Charles Webster, *The Foreign Policy of Castlereagh* (2 vols.; London, 1925).

For the diplomacy of the Russian offer of mediation in the war, a most valuable collection of documents is Nina Bashkina et al., eds., *The United States and Russia: The Beginning of Relations, 1765–1815* (Washington, D.C., 1980). See also N. Bolkhovitinov, *The Beginnings of Russian-American Relations, 1775–1815* (Elena Levin, trans.; Cambridge, MA, 1975), and Frank Golder, "The Russian Offer of Mediation in the War of 1812," *Political Science Quarterly* 31 (1916): 380–91.

Most of the leading American political leaders have their biographers. For Madison, the most comprehensive (and sympathetic) study is that by Irving Brant, *James Madison* (6 vols.; Indianapolis, 1941–1961). Shorter studies are Ralph Ketcham, *James Madison: A Biography* (New York, 1971), and Robert Rutland, *James Madison: The Founding Father* (New York, 1987), as well as his *The Presidency of James Madison* (Lawrence, KS, 1990). The best study of Monroe is Harry Ammon, *James Monroe: The Quest for National Identity* (New York, 1971). For Gallatin, see Henry Adams, *The Life of Albert Gallatin* (Philadelphia, 1880) and Raymond Walters Jr., *Albert Gallatin: Jeffersonian Financier and Diplomat* (New York, 1957). The only biography of Armstrong is C. Edward Skeen, *John Armstrong, Jr., 1758–1843* (Syracuse, NY, 1981). There is no biography of William Jones, but see Edward Eckert, "William Jones: Mr. Madison's Secretary of the Navy," *Pennsylvania Magazine of History and Biography* 96 (1972): 167–82. For George Washington Campbell and Alexander James Dallas, see Weymouth T. Jordan, *George Washington Campbell of Tennessee: Western Statesman* (Tallahassee, FL, 1955), and Raymond Walters Jr., *Alexander James Dallas: Lawyer, Politician, Financier, 1759–1817* (Philadelphia, 1943), respectively. There is no biography of William Eustis.

On the Canadian side, much of the relevant biographical material is incorporated into studies of the British generals and other military figures; see, for example, Ferdinand B. Tupper, ed., *The Life and Correspondence of Major-General Sir Isaac Brock, K.B.* (London, 1847); Reginald Horsman, *Matthew Elliott, British Indian Agent* (Detroit, 1964); William Dunlop, *Tiger Dunlop's Upper Canada* (Toronto, 1967); George Raudzens, "'Red George' Macdonell, Military Saviour of Upper Canada?" *Ontario History* 62 (1970): 199–212; Enid Mallory, *The Green Tiger: James Fitzgibbon, a Hero of the War of 1812* (Toronto, 1976); Patrick Wohler, *Charles Michel de Salaberry, Soldier of the Empire, Defender of Quebec* (Toronto, 1984); and Sandy Antal, *A Wampum Denied: Proctor's War of 1812* (Ottawa, 1997). For a collective portrait, see Wesley B. Turner, *British Generals in the War of 1812: High Command in the Canadas* (Montreal, 1999). Two new biographies of Isaac Brock – Jonathan Riley, *A Matter of Honour: The Life, Campaigns and Generalship of Isaac Brock* (Toronto, 2011) and Wesley B. Turner, *The Astonishing General: The Life and Legacy of Sir Isaac Brock* (Toronto, 2011) – came to hand too late to be consulted for this study. For insights into the considerable literature on Laura Secord and her famous walk to Beaver Dams, see Colin Coates and Cecilia Morgan, *Heroines and History: Representations of Madeleine de Verchères and Laura Secord* (Toronto, 2000).

American military leaders have been reasonably well served by biographers. The leading titles include Freeman Cleaves, *Old Tippecanoe: William Henry Harrison and His Time* (New York, 1939), which should be supplemented by Robert Owens, *Mr. Jefferson's Hammer: William Henry Harrison and the Origins of American Indian Policy* (Norman, OK, 2007), and by David Skaggs, "The Making of a Major General: William Henry Harrison and the Politics of Command, 1812–1813," *Ohio Valley History: The Journal of the Cincinnati Historical Society* 10 (2010): 32–52. See also Walter Durham, *James Winchester, Tennessee Pioneer* (Gallatin, TN, 1979); Charles W. Elliot, *Winfield Scott: The Soldier and the Man* (New York, 1937); Richard Erney, *The Public Life of Henry Dearborn* (New York, 1979); Allan Everest, *The Military Career of Alexander Macomb and Alexander Macomb at Plattsburgh* (Plattsburgh, NY, 1989); Eugene Hollon, *The Lost Pathfinder: Zebulon Montgomery Pike* (Norman, OK, 1949); James Jacobs, *Tarnished Warrior: Major-General James Wilkinson* (New York, 1938), which is probably the best of the three extant biographies on its subject for the period between 1812 and 1815; Chester Kiefer, *Maligned General: The Biography of Thomas Sydney Jesup* (San Rafael, CA, 1979); Frank Latham,

Jacob Brown and the War of 1812 (New York, 1971); Leyland Meyer, *The Life and Times of Colonel Richard M. Johnson of Kentucky* (New York, 1932); John Morris, *Sword of the Border: Major General Jacob Jennings Brown* (Kent, OH, 2000). Robert Remini, *Andrew Jackson and the Course of American Empire, 1767–1821* (New York, 1977), is the best study of Jackson's early career, although it should be read in conjunction with a more speculative psychobiography by Michael Rogin, *Fathers and Children: Andrew Jackson and the Subjugation of the American Indian* (New York, 1975); and James Silver, *Edmund Pendleton Gaines: Frontier General* (Baton Rouge, 1949). There is no scholarly biography of William Hull. There is also no modern biography of George Izard, but readers can consult his *Official Correspondence with the Department of War, Relative to the Military Operations of the American Army under the Command of Major-General George Izard on the Northern Frontier of the United States, in the Years 1814 and 1815* (Philadelphia, 1816). They should also read John Fredriksen, "The War of 1812 in Northern New York: General George Izard's Journal of the Chateauguay Campaign," *New York History* 76 (1995): 173–200.

Although almost all studies of the War of 1812 consist largely of operational histories of its campaigns, there has been remarkably little published on the U.S. Army, the War Department, and the state militias. Robert Quimby's *The U.S. Army in the War of 1812: An Operational and Command Study* (2 vols.; East Lansing, MI, 1997) is hardly an exception to this generalization, although it has considerable value as an extended narrative of the campaigns of the war. For institutional studies, see Edward Coffman, *The Old Army: A Portrait of the American Army in Peacetime, 1784–1898* (New York, 1986); Theodore Crackel, *Mr. Jefferson's Army: Political and Social Reform of the Military Establishment, 1801–1809* (New York, 1987); James Jacobs, *The Beginnings of the U.S. Army, 1783–1812* (Princeton, NJ, 1947); Russell Weigley, *History of the U.S. Army* (New York, 1967); and William Skelton, *An American Profession of Arms: The Army Officer Corps, 1784–1861* (Lawrence, KS, 1992). On the problems of training the army, see Donald Graves, "Dry Books of Tactics: U.S. Infantry Manuals of the War of 1812 and After, Part 1," *Military Collector and Historian* 38 (1986): 51–61. The only general history of the militias (in federal service) is C. Edward Skeen, *Citizen Soldiers in the War of 1812* (Lexington, KY, 1999), which should be read in conjunction with Robert Kirby, "The Militia System and the State Militias in the War of 1812," *Indiana Magazine of History* 73 (1977): 102–24, and John Mahon, "The Principal Causes for the Failure of the

United States Militia System during the War of 1812," *Indiana Military History Journal* 4 (1979): 15–21. For some discussion of staff and logistical issues, see Erna Risch, *Quartermaster Support of the Army: A History of the Corps, 1775–1939* (Washington, D.C., 1962); Marguerite McKee, "Service of Supply in the War of 1812," *Quartermaster Review* 6 (1927): 53–76; Brereton Greenhous, "A Note on Western Logistics in the War of 1812," *Military Affairs* 34 (1970): 41–44; and Jeffrey Kimball, "The Fog and Friction of Frontier War: The Role of Logistics in American Offensive Failures during the War of 1812," *Old Northwest* 5 (1979): 323–43. On the medical department, the most valuable work remains that of James Mann, *Medical Sketches of the Campaigns of 1812, 13, 14* (Dedham, MA, 1816), which can be supplemented by Mary Gillett, *The Army Medical Department, 1775–1818* (Washington, D.C., 1981).

As is the case with the army, there are comparatively few studies of the institutional development of the U.S. Navy, even as there is an enormous literature on ships, commanders, and naval battles. The foundational work on naval administration was produced in the early twentieth century by Charles O. Paullin (see *Paullin's History of Naval Administration, 1775–1911: A Collection of Articles from the U.S. Naval Institute Proceedings* [Annapolis, MD, 1968]). Later work that bears on the War of 1812 is by Edward Eckert (see his "Early Reform in the Navy Department," *American Neptune* 33 [1973]: 23–45, and *The Navy Department in the War of 1812* [Gainesville, FL, 1973]). For a discussion of the lengthy controversy over the role of a navy in early American defense policy, see Craig Symonds, *Navalists and Anti-Navalists: The Naval Policy Debate in the United States, 1775–1827* (Newark, DE, 1980); for the debate over whether to employ the navy in 1812, see Peter Kastor, "Toward 'the Maritime War Only': The Question of Naval Mobilization, 1811–1812," *Journal of Military History* 61 (1997): 455–80. On the subject of the officer corps, the study by Christopher McKee, *A Gentlemanly and Honorable Profession: The Creation of the U.S. Naval Officer Corps, 1794–1815* (Annapolis, MD, 1991), is an invaluable contribution, although it remains unclear to what extent the combat performances of individual officers were determined by the structural and administrative factors that shaped the corps as a whole. On the vessels, see Howard Chapelle, *The History of the American Sailing Navy: Their Ships and Their Development* (New York, 1949) and Donald Canney, *Sailing Warships of the U.S. Navy* (Annapolis, MD, 2002). For the gunboat navy, see Spencer Tucker, *The Jeffersonian Gunboat Navy* (Columbia, SC, 1993), and Gene Smith, *"For the Purposes of Defense": The Politics of the Jeffersonian Gunboat Program* (Newark, DE, 1995). Of the popular histories of the naval war, the best known is that by C. S. Forester, *The Naval War of 1812* (London, 1957); the most recent example of the genre is Stephen Budiansky, *Perilous Fight: America's Intrepid War with Britain on the High Seas, 1812–1815* (New York, 2010).

Otherwise, much of the information about the navy has been incorporated into the biographies of its leading commanders. For the most important of these, see Robert Allison, *Stephen Decatur: American Naval Hero, 1779–1820* (Amherst, MA, 2005); Claude Berube and John Rodguard, *A Call to the Sea: Captain Charles Stewart of the USS* Constitution (Dulles, VA, 2005); James Bradford, ed., *Command Under Sail: Makers of the American Naval Tradition, 1775–1850* (Annapolis, MD, 1985); Virginia Burdick, *Captain Thomas Macdonagh: Delaware Hero of the Battle of Lake Champlain* (Wilmington, DE, 1991); James De Kay, *A Rage for Glory: The Life of Commodore Stephen Decatur, USN* (New York, 2004); Charles Dutton, *Oliver Hazard Perry* (New York, 1935); Ira Dye, *The Fatal Cruise of the* Argus: *Two Captains in the War of 1812* (Annapolis, MD, 1994); Alfred Fenton, *Oliver Hazard Perry* (New York, 1944); Bruce Grant, *Isaac Hull, Captain of Old Ironsides* (Chicago, 1947); Edwin Hoyt, *The Tragic Commodore: The Story of Oliver Hazard Perry* (London, 1966); David Long, *Nothing Too Daring: A Biography of Commodore David Porter, 1780–1843* (Annapolis, MD, 1970); David Long, *Ready to Hazard: A Biography of Commodore William Bainbridge, 1794–1843* (Hanover, NH, 1981); Linda Maloney, *The Captain from Connecticut: The Life and Times of Isaac Hull* (Boston, 1986); Charles Paullin, *Commodore John Rodgers, 1773–1838* (Annapolis, MD, 1967); and David Skaggs, *Thomas Macdonagh: Master of Command in the Early U.S. Navy* (Annapolis, MD, 2003). There is no biography of Commodore Isaac Chauncey.

It would be pointless here to list works on the history of the Royal Navy during the age of Napoleon, but a small number of studies do have particular relevance for the War of 1812. Among them are Myron Brightfield, *John Wilson Croker* (Berkeley, CA, 1940), a key figure in the British Admiralty; Peter Padfield, *Broke and the Shannon* (London, 1968), for the 1813 encounter between the USS *Chesapeake* and HMS *Shannon*; and Wade Dudley, *Splintering the Wooden Wall: The British Blockade of the United States, 1812–1815* (Annapolis, MD, 2003). The practice of impressment has been much studied by British historians – see, for example, the works cited in Kevin McKranie, "The Recruitment of Seamen for the British Navy, 1793–1815: Why Don't You Raise More Men," in Donald Stoker et al., eds., *Conscription in the Napoleonic Era: A Revolution in Military Affairs?* (New York, 2009), 84–101 – but surprisingly it has not received all that much attention from American scholars. James Zimmerman's *Impressment of American Seaman* (New York, 1925) remains the only published monograph, which should be supplemented by the unpublished doctoral dissertation by Scott Jackson, "Impressment and Anglo-American Discord, 1787–1818 (University of Michigan, 1976). For a cultural study of impressment, see Paul A. Gilje, "Free Trade and Sailors' Rights: The Rhetoric of the War of 1812," *Journal of the Early Republic* 30 (2010): 1–24. Privateering, however, has been studied much more, by both Canadians and Americans. The leading recent works on the Canadian side are Faye Kert, *Prize and Prejudice: Privateering and Naval Prizes in Atlantic Canada in the War of 1812* (St. John's, NL, 1997) and Kert, *Trimming Yankees Sails: Pirates and Privateers of New Brunswick* (Fredericton, NB, 2005). For the United States, Jerome Garitee's *The Republic's Private Navy: The American Privateering Business as Practiced by Baltimore during the War of 1812* (Mystic Seaport, CT, 1977) is a model study.

As befits the importance of the Indian nations residing within and on the borders of the United States, there is a very substantial literature. For two general studies of the Indian resistance to American expansion, see Alfred Cave, *Prophets of the Great Spirit: Native American Revitalization Movements in Eastern North America* (Lincoln, NE, 2006), and Gregory Dowd, *A Spirited Resistance: The North American Indian Struggle for Unity, 1745–1815* (Baltimore, 1992). For studies of the American and Canadian Northwest, see Robert Allen, *His Majesty's Indian Allies: British Indian Policy in the Defense of Canada, 1774–1815* (Toronto, 1992); Bert Anson, *The Miami Indians* (Norman, OK, 1970); Carl Benn, *The Iroquois in the War of 1812* (Toronto, 1998); Colin Calloway, *Crown and Calumet: British Indian Relations, 1783–1815* (Norman, OK, 1987); and Colin Calloway, *The Shawnees and the War for America* (New York, 2007); Harvey Carter, *The Life and Times of Little Turtle: First Sagamore of the Wabash* (Urbana, IL, 1987); Benjamin Drake, *The Life of Tecumseh, and of His Brother the Prophet: With a Historical Sketch of the Shawanoe Indians* (Cincinnati, OH, 1841), an older study with marked biases but one that, nonetheless, contains useful information and insights; David Edmunds, *The Pottawatomies, Keepers of the Fire* (Norman, OK, 1978); Edmunds, *The Shawnee Prophet* (Lincoln, NE, 1985); and Edmunds, *Tecumseh and the Quest for Indian*

Unity (Boston, 1984); Arrell Gibson, *The Kickapoos: Lords of the Middle Border* (Norman, OK, 1963); William Hagan, *The Sac and Fox Indians* (Norman, OK, 1958); Reginald Horsman, *Expansion and American Indian Policy, 1783–1812* (Norman, OK, 1992); John Norton, *The Journal of Major John Norton, 1816* (C. Clinck and J. Talman, eds.; Toronto, 1970); John Sugden, *Tecumseh: A Life* (New York, 1997), which is by far the best-researched and most informed study; John Sugden, *Tecumseh's Last Stand* (Norman, OK, 1985); John Sugden, *Blue Jacket: Warrior of the Shawnees* (Lincoln, NE, 2008); and Timothy Willig, *Restoring the Chain of Friendship: British Policy and the Indians of the Great Lakes, 1783–1815* (Lincoln, NE, 2008).

The leading studies of Indians on the southwestern frontier include Robert Cotterill, *The Southern Indians: The Story of the Five Civilized Tribes before Removal* (Norman, OK, 1954); Angie Debo, *The Road to Disappearance: A History of the Creek Indians* (Norman, OK, 1979); James Doster, *The Creek Indians and their Florida Lands, 1740–1823* (2 vols.; New York, 1974); Robbie Ethridge, *Creek Country: The Creek Indians and their World* (Chapel Hill, NC, 2003); Benjamin Griffith, *McIntosh and Weatherford, Creek Indian Leaders* (Tuscaloosa, AL, 1988); Henry Halbert and Timothy Ball, *The Creek War of 1813 and 1814* (Chicago, 1895); James Holland, *Andrew Jackson and the Creek War: Victory at Horseshoe Bend* (Tuscaloosa, AL, 1968); William McLoughlin, *Cherokee Renascence in the New Republic* (Princeton, NJ, 1986); Joel Martin, *Sacred Revolt: The Muskogees' Struggle for a New World* (Boston, 1991); Sean O'Brien, *In Bitterness and Tears: Andrew Jackson's Destruction of the Creeks and Seminoles* (Westport, CT, 2003); Frank Owsley Jr., *Struggle for the Gulf Borderlands: The Creek War and the Battle of New Orleans, 1812–1815* (Gainesville, FL, 1981); Claudio Saunt, *A New Order of Things: Property, Power, and the Transformation of the Creek Indians, 1773–1816* (New York, 1999); John Swanton, *Social Organization and Social Usages of the Indians of the Creek Confederacy* (Washington, D.C., 1928); Gregory Wasikov, *A Conquering Spirit: Fort Mims and the Red Stick War of 1813–1814* (Tuscaloosa, AL, 2006); and J. Leitch Wright Jr., *Creeks and Seminoles: The Destruction and Regeneration of the Musculgee People* (Lincoln, NE, 1986).

Military operations in the American Northwest have been the subject of a large number of collections and studies (not including those that focus more exclusively on the Indian peoples of the region). A major collection of documents is Richard Knopf, ed., *Document Transcriptions of the War of 1812 in the Northwest* (10 vols.; Columbus, OH, 1961–1962).

The more important studies include Robert Allen, *The Battle of Moraviantown, October 15, 1813* (Ottawa, 1994); Gerard Altoff, *Among My
Best Men: African Americans and the War of 1812* (Put-in-Bay, OH,
1996); Gerard Altoff, *Deep Water Sailors, Shallow Water Soldiers* (Put-
in-Bay, OH, 1993); Harrison Bird, *War for the West, 1790–1813* (New
York, 1971); Glen Clift, *Remember the Raisin! Kentucky and Kentuckians in the Battles and Massacres at Frenchtown, Michigan Territory, in
the War of 1812* (Frankfort, KY, 1961); Richard Dillon, *We Have Met
the Enemy: Oliver Hazard Perry, Wilderness Commodore* (New York,
1978); Alec Gilpin, *The War of 1812 in the Old Northwest* (East Lansing,
MI, 1958); Fred Hamil, *Michigan in the War of 1812* (East Lansing, MI,
1969); James Hammack, *Kentucky in the Second American Revolution:
The War of 1812* (Lexington, KY, 1976); Robert Ilisevich, *Daniel Dobbins: Frontier Mariner* (Erie, PA, 1993); Denys Knoll, *Battle of Lake Erie:
Building the Fleet in the Wilderness* (Washington, D.C., 1979); Richard
Knopf, *Return Jonathan Meigs and the War of 1812* (Columbus, OH,
1957); Perry LeRoy, *The Weakness of Discipline and Its Consequent
Results in the Northwest during the War of 1812* (Columbus, OH, 1958);
David Skaggs and Gerard Altoff, *A Signal Victory: The Lake Erie Cam-
paign* (Annapolis, MD, 1997); William Welch and David Skaggs, eds.,
*War on the Great Lakes: Essays Commemorating the 175th Anniversary
of the Battle of Lake Erie* (Kent, OH, 1991); and David Skaggs, "River
Raisin Redeemed: William Henry Harrison, Oliver Hazard Perry, and
the Mid-Western Campaign, 1813," *Northwest Ohio History* 77 (2010):
67–84.

For the literature on New York, New England, and the Canadian
Maritimes, see Martin Auger, "French Canadian Participation in the
War of 1812: A Social Study of the *Voltigeurs Canadiens*," *Canadian
Military History* 10 (2001): 23–41; Louis Babcock, *The War of 1812
on the Niagara Frontier* (Buffalo, NY, 1927); James M. Banner Jr., *To
the Hartford Convention: The Federalists and the Origins of Party Politics in Massachusetts, 1789–1815* (New York, 1970); Richard Barbuto,
Niagara 1814: America Invades Canada (Lawrence, KS, 2000); John
Bilow, *Châteauguay, New York, and the War of 1812* (St. Lambert, QC,
1984); John Boileau, *Half-Hearted Enemies: Nova Scotia, New England
and the War of 1812* (Halifax, NS, 2005); Karen Campbell, "Propa-
ganda, Pestilence, and Prosperity: Burlington's Camptown Days during
the War of 1812," *Vermont History* 64 (1996): 133–58; Christopher
Densmore, *Red Jacket: Iroquois Diplomat and Orator* (Syracuse, NY,
1999); James Elliott, *Strange Fatality: The Battle of Stoney Creek, 1813*

(Cap-Saint-Ignace, QC, 2009); Allan Everest, *The War of 1812 in the Champlain Valley* (Syracuse, NY, 1981); Donald Graves, *Field of Glory: The Battle of Crysler's Farm, 1813* (Toronto, 1999); Donald Graves, *Red Coats and Grey Jackets: The Battle of Chippawa, 5 July 1814* (Toronto, 1994); Donald Graves, *"Where Right and Glory Lead!" The Battle of Lundy's Lane, 1814* (Toronto, 1997); Michelle Guitard, *The Militia at the Battle of Chateauguay* (Ottawa, 1983); Alison LaCroix, "A Singular and Awkward War: The Transatlantic Context of the Hartford Convention," *American Nineteenth Century History* 6 (2005): 3–32; Harry Landon, *Bugles on the Border: The Story of the War of 1812 in Northern New York* (Watertown, NY, 1954); Barry Lohnes, "A New Look at the Invasion of Eastern Maine, 1814," *Maine Historical Society Quarterly* 15 (1975): 5–29; Robert Malcomson, *Lords of the Lake: The Naval War on Lake Ontario, 1812–1814* (Toronto, 1998); Robert Malcomson, *A Very Brilliant Affair: The Battle of Queenston Heights* (Annapolis, MD, 2003); Robert Malcomson, *Capital in Flames: The American Attack on York, 1813* (Annapolis, MD, 2008); Joshua Smith, *Borderland Smuggling: Patriots, Loyalists, and Illicit Trade in the Northeast, 1783–1820* (Gainesville, FL, 2006); John Stahl, *The Battle of Plattsburg: A Study in and of the War of 1812* (Argos, IN, 1918); George Stanley, *Battle in the Dark: Stoney Creek, 6 June 1813* (Toronto, 1991); Joseph Whitehorn, *While Washington Burned: The Battle of Fort Erie, 1814* (Baltimore, 1992); and Patrick Wilder, *The Battle of Sackett's Harbor: 1813* (Baltimore, 1994).

The Chesapeake theater of the war has always been of great interest to both scholars and popular historians, largely because of the circumstances that led to the burning of Washington and the composition of the national anthem. See the following: Gilbert Byron, *The War of 1812 on the Chesapeake Bay* (Baltimore, 1964); Frank Cassell, "Slaves of the Chesapeake Bay Area and the War of 1812," *Journal of Negro History* 57 (1972): 144–55; Hulbert Footner, *Sailor of Fortune: The Life and Adventures of Commodore Barney* (New York, 1940); Christopher George, *Terror on the Chesapeake: The War of 1812 on the Bay* (Shippensburg, PA, 2000); David Healey, *1812: Rediscovering Chesapeake Bay's Forgotten War* (Bella Rosa, SC, 2005); E. D. Ingraham, *A Sketch of the Events Which Preceded the Capture of Washington by the British* (Philadelphia, 1849); Steven Kroll, *By the Dawn's Early Light: The Story of the Star-Spangled Banner* (New York, 1994); Alan Lloyd, *The Scorching of Washington: The War of 1812* (Newton Abbott, U.K., 1974); Walter Lord, *The Dawn's Early Light* (New York, 1972); William Marine,

The British Invasion of Maryland, 1812–1815 (Baltimore, 1913); Roger Morris, *Cockburn and the British Navy in Transition: Admiral Sir George Cockburn 1772–1853* (Exeter, U.K., 1997); Charles Miller, *The Darkest Day: 1814; The Washington-Baltimore Campaign* (Philadelphia, 1963); Louis Norton, *Joshua Barney: Hero of the Revolution and 1812* (Annapolis, MD, 2002); A. J. Pack, *The Man Who Burned the White House: Admiral Sir George Cockburn* (Emsworth, U.K., 1987); Anthony Pitch, *The Burning of Washington: The British Invasion of 1814* (Annapolis, MD, 1998); Scott Sheads, *Guardian of the Star-Spangled Banner: Lt. Colonel George Armistead and the Fort McHenry Flag* (Baltimore, 1999); Scott Sheads, *The Rockets' Red Glare: The Maritime Defense of Baltimore in 1814* (Centreville, MD, 1986); Scott Sheads and Merle Cole, *Fort McHenry and Baltimore's Harbor Defenses* (Charleston, SC, 2001); Donald Shomette, *Flotilla: Battle for the Patuxent* (Calvert, MD, 1981); Joseph Whitehorn, *The Battle for Baltimore, 1814* (Baltimore, 1997); and J. S. Williams, *History of the Invasion and Capture of Washington and of the Events Which Preceded and Followed* (New York, 1857). Also of great interest and value as a reference source is Ralph Eshelman et al., *The War of 1812 in the Chesapeake* (Baltimore, 2010).

Because of the long-standing interest in the early career of Andrew Jackson and the Battle of New Orleans, those subjects have generated their own historiography, which should, however, be read in conjunction with the literature on the southern Indians. The most important titles are Harry Albright, *New Orleans – The Battle of the Bayous* (New York, 1990); Charles Brooks, *The Siege of New Orleans* (Seattle, WA, 1961); Wilbur Brown, *The Amphibious Campaign for West Florida and Louisiana, 1814–1815: A Critical Review of Strategy and Tactics at New Orleans* (Tuscaloosa, AL, 1969); Samuel Carter, *Blaze of Glory: The Fight for New Orleans, 1814–15* (New York, 1971); Powell Casey, *Louisiana in the War of 1812* (Baton Rouge, LA, 1963); Donald Chidsey, *The Battle of New Orleans: An Informal History of the War That Nobody Wanted* (New York, 1961); William Davis, *The Pirates Lafitte: The Treacherous World of the Corsairs of the Gulf* (New York, 2005), which is the best treatment of this colorful subject; Jane deGrummond, *The Baratarians at the Battle of New Orleans* (Baton Rouge, LA, 1961); Ernest Eller et al., *Sea Power and the Battle of New Orleans* (New Orleans, 1965); Winston Groom, *Patriotic Fire: Andrew Jackson and Jean Lafitte at the Battle of New Orleans* (New York, 2006); David Heidler and Jean Heidler, *Old Hickory's War: Andrew Jackson and the Quest for Empire* (Baton Rouge, LA, 2003); Leonard Huber, *New*

Orleans as It Was in 1814–15 (New Orleans, 1989); Arsène Latour, *Historical Memoir of the War in West Florida and Louisiana in 1814–15* (Philadelphia, 1817); John Mahon, "British Strategy and Southern Indians, War of 1812," *Florida Historical Quarterly* 44 (1966): 287–302; Frank Owsley Jr., "The Role of the South in British Grand Strategy in the War of 1812," *Tennessee Historical Quarterly* 31 (1972): 22–35; Charles Patton, *Chalmette: The Battle for New Orleans and How the British Nearly Stole the Louisiana Territory* (Athens, GA, 2001); Robin Reilly, *The British at the Gates: The New Orleans Campaign in the War of 1812* (New York, 1974); Robert Remini, *The Battle of New Orleans: Andrew Jackson and America's First Military Victory* (New York, 1999); and Matthew Warshauer, *Andrew Jackson and the Politics of Martial Law: Nationalism, Civil Liberties, and Partisanship* (Knoxville, TN, 2006). Of great value also is Ted Birkedal, ed., *The Search for the Lost Riverfront: Historical and Archeological Investigations at the Chalmette Battlefield, Jean Lafitte National Historical Park and Preserve* (3 vols.; U.S. National Park Service, 2009). This publication can be accessed online at the Web site of the National Park Service (http://www.nps.gov/history/online_books/jela/lost_riverfront/index.htm).

Accounts of the southern theater and of the southern Indians should also be read in the context of American disputes with Spain over the boundaries of the Louisiana Purchase and the American claim to East and West Florida. See Isaac Cox, *The West Florida Controversy, 1798–1813: A Study in American Diplomacy* (Baltimore, 1918); James Cusick, *The Other War of 1812: The Patriot War and the American Invasion of Spanish East Florida* (Gainesville, FL, 2003); Rembert Patrick, *Florida Fiasco: Rampant Rebels on the Georgia-Florida Border, 1810–1815* (Athens, GA, 1954); and J. C. A. Stagg, *Borderlines and Borderlands: James Madison and the Spanish-American Frontier, 1776–1821* (New Haven, CT, 2009).

For a war that has provoked so much controversy over its causes, there is remarkably little literature on its ending. Aside from the writings on the Russian mediation, see Frank Updyke, *The Diplomacy of the War of 1812* (Baltimore, 1915); and Fred Engelman, *The Peace of Christmas Eve* (New York, 1962). See also Matthew Moten, ed., *Between War and Peace: How America Ends Its Wars* (New York, 2011); Paul Pillar, *Negotiating Peace: War Termination as a Bargaining Process* (Princeton, NJ, 1983); and J. C. A. Stagg, "The Politics of Ending the War of 1812," in Arthur Bowler, ed., *War along the Niagara: Essays on the War of 1812 and Its Legacy* (Youngstown, NY, 1991), 93–104. For the British perspective, see Brian Jenkins, *Henry Goulburn, 1784–1856: A Political Biography* (Liverpool, U.K., 1996), and Wilbur Jones, ed., "A British View of the War of 1812 and the Peace Negotiations," *Mississippi Valley Historical Review* 45 (1958): 481–87.

For the aftermath of the war, the following titles are useful: F. Lee Benns, *The American Struggle for the British West Indian Carrying Trade, 1815–1830* (Bloomington, IN, 1923); Kenneth Bourne, *Britain and the Balance of Power in North America, 1815–1908* (London, 1967); Francis Carroll, *A Good and Wise Measure: The Search for the Canadian-American Boundary, 1783–1842* (Toronto, 2001); Sam Haynes, *Unfinished Revolution: The Early American Republic in a British World* (Charlottesville, VA, 2010); John Murrin, "The Jeffersonian Triumph and American Exceptionalism," *Journal of the Early Republic* 20 (2000): 1–25; Robert Schuyler, *The Fall of the Old Colonial System: A Study in British Free Trade, 1770–1870* (New York, 1945); C. Edward Skeen, *1816: America Rising* (Lexington, KY, 2003); Charles Stacey, "The Myth of the Unguarded Frontier, 1815–1871," *American Historical Review* 56 (1950): 2–12; Reginald Stuart, *United States Expansionism and British North America, 1775–1871* (Chapel Hill, NC, 1988); Sidney Wise and Robert Brown, *Canada Views the United States; Nineteenth-Century Political Attitudes* (Seattle, 1967); and Wise, *God's Peculiar Peoples: Essays on Political Culture in Nineteenth Century Canada* (Ottawa, 1993).

Index